Intelligence,
Instruction,
and Assessment

Theory Into Practice

The Educational Psychology Series

Robert J. Sternberg and Wendy M. Williams, Series Editors

Marton/Booth • *Learning and Awareness*

Hacker/Dunlosky/Graesser • *Metacognition in Educational Theory and Practice*

Smith/Pourchot • *Adult Learning and Development: Perspectives From Educational Psychology*

Sternberg/Williams • *Intelligence, Instruction, and Assessment: Theory into Practice*

Intelligence, Instruction, and Assessment

Theory Into Practice

Edited by

Robert J. Sternberg
Yale University

and

Wendy M. Williams
Cornell University

LAWRENCE ERLBAUM ASSOCIATES, PUBLISHERS
1998   Mahwah, New Jersey   London

Lawrence Erlbaum Associates, Inc., Publishers
10 Industrial Avenue
Mahwah, New Jersey 07430

Cover design by Kathryn Houghtaling Lacey

Library of Congress Cataloging-in-Publication Data

Intelligence, instruction, and assessment / edited by Robert
J. Sternberg and Wendy M. Williams
        p.   cm. — (Educational psychology series)
    Includes bibliographical references and indexes.
    ISBN 0-8058-2510-X (c.). — ISBN 0-8058-2511-8 (p.)   1.
Teaching—Psychological aspects. 2. Intellect. 3. Learning,
Psychology of. 4. Cognitive Styles. 5. Educational tests and
measurements. I. Sternberg, Robert J. II. Williams, Wendy
M. (Wendy Melissa), 1960-   . III. Series.
    LB1027.I6655   1998
    370.15—dc21   98-9401
                                                CIP

Books published by Lawrence Erlbaum Associates are printed on
acid-free paper, and their bindings are chosen for strength and
durability.

Printed in the United States of America
10 9 8 7 6 5 4 3 2

Contents

Preface   vii

1 Applying the Triarchic Theory of Human Intelligence in the Classroom   1
Robert J. Sternberg

2 Minds at Work: Applying Multiple Intelligences in the Classroom   17
Mara Krechevsky and Steve Seidel

3 Intelligent Schooling   43
Roger C. Schank and Diana M. Joseph

4 Learnable Intelligence and Intelligent Learning   67
Heidi L. Goodrich Andrade and David N. Perkins

5 The Practical Use of Skill Theory in Classrooms   95
Jim Parziale and Kurt W. Fischer

6 The g Factor and the Design of Education   111
Arthur R. Jensen

7 Intelligent Thinking and the Reflective Essay   133
Jonathan Baron

8 A Three-level Theory of the Developing Mind: Basic Principles and Implications for Instruction and Assessment   149
Andreas Demetriou and Nicos Valanides

9 Mastering Tools of the Mind in School (Trying Out Vygotsky's Ideas in Classrooms)   201
Elena L. Grigorenko

Author Index   233

Subject Index   239

Contributors   245

Preface

The goal of this book is to show how modern theories of intelligence can be directly applied in classrooms to the education of children. The book is for anyone who is interested in knowing how modern theories of intelligence can be applied to education. The book will be especially helpful to teachers who want to take recent work on intelligence and put it to use in their classrooms.

The goal of users of this book will typically be not to increase intelligence, per se, but to increase disciplinary knowledge and understanding. Hence, the chapters of the book deal with how teachers can teach more effectively what they are already teaching. The book takes an international perspective, including chapters reflecting both American and European perspectives.

In Chapter 1, Robert J. Sternberg shows how his triarchic theory of human intelligence can be applied across grade levels and subject-matter areas to classroom practice. In Chapter 2, Mara Krechevsky and Steve Seidel demonstrate the application of Howard Gardner's theory of multiple intelligences to classroom settings. In Chapter 3, Roger Schank and Diana Joseph discuss the use of Schank's ideas about human and artificial intelligence in classrooms. In Chapter 4, Heidi Goodrich Andrade and David Perkins describe the application of Perkins's theory of learnable intelligence to the classroom. In Chapter 5, Jim Parziale and Kurt Fischer show how Fischer's skill theory can be applied in classroom settings. In Chapter 6, Arthur Jensen shows how the traditional theory of general intelligence can be applied to education. In Chapter 7, Jonathan Baron shows how his theory of rationality and intelligence can be applied to the classroom, in general, and to the formulation and grading of reflective essays, in particular. In Chapter 8, Andreas Demetriou and Nicos Valanides discuss the application of a three-level theory to the developing mind.

In Chapter 9, Elena L. Grigorenko describes how Lev Vygotsky's theory of the zone of proximal development has been applied in Russian schooling.

This book is unique in showing how a variety of theories of intelligence have been applied and can be applied immediately to classroom settings. The book therefore has the goal of linking theory and practice, and of showing that the two-far from being separate-are wholly compatible and intermeshed.

—*Robert J. Sternberg*
—*Wendy M. Williams*

CHAPTER 1

Applying the Triarchic Theory of Human Intelligence In the Classroom

Robert J. Sternberg
Yale University

A CASE STUDY

When Bob was taught French in high school, his main job was to memorize lists of French vocabulary words, learn grammatical rules, and mimic and memorize phrases and their variants. The key to success in his courses was memorization, but he was not a good memorizer, in French or in any other kinds of courses. He was a decent student in French, but definitely nothing special.

When Bob went to France, his reward for 3 years of study was minimal: He could hardly speak at all, and his understanding of what people were saying to him was virtually nonexistent. His teachers were generally unimpressed with his performance in French, and one even commented to him that it was obvious, based on the mistakes he was making, that he did not have much ability to learn foreign languages. He took the comment seriously, and never again studied foreign language in school.

Bob would have been content never again to learn a foreign language, but circumstances dictated otherwise. As an adult, he was asked to develop a program to be used with schoolchildren in Venezuela. Because the program was to be taught in Spanish by Spanish-speaking teachers to Spanish-speaking children, Bob realized, with displeasure, that he would need to learn some Spanish.

He started learning Spanish, but the way he was taught Spanish was entirely different from the way he had been taught French. All of the instruction was in Spanish, and he was totally immersed in the language. He was discouraged from memorizing anything. Rather, he was to learn Spanish by using it. The instruction emphasized practical rather than memory learning. To his surprise, Bob learned Spanish quickly and well, and within a couple of years was able to go to various Latino countries and communicate effectively with people from them. Today, he speaks Spanish fluently and continues to travel to such countries. His French continues to be halting.

Bob's French performance was so middling that both Bob and his teachers concluded that Bob did not have much ability to learn foreign languages. In contrast, Bob's Spanish performance was so strong, that Bob was able to reassess his foreign-language abilities totally, and to realize that what he lacked was not the ability to learn foreign languages, but the ability to learn them via memorization.

HOW WE MAKE FALSE INFERENCES
ABOUT INTELLIGENCE

Millions of students in all disciplines and at all levels are confronting today exactly the same problem that Bob confronted earlier in his life. They are being taught by methods that fit poorly with their pattern of abilities. As a result, they are not learning or they learn at minimal levels. At the same time, they and their teachers are concluding that they lack vital learning abilities. In fact, many of them have impressive learning abilities but not the kind that are used in the methods of teaching to which they are exposed. As a result, they never reach the high levels of learning that are possible for them.

This claim is not based on only a single case (Bob's—my own!), nor is its validity confined to case-study research. Probably, many individuals could give their own examples of how, under one method of instruction, they succeeded, whereas under another method of instruction, they failed. Is there scientific evidence supporting these observations? There is.

We did a 5-year study in which we developed a high school psychology course. We recruited students from all across the United States and some from abroad on the basis of their patterns of abilities as specified by what I call the triarchic theory of human intelligence, according to which intelligence is composed of three main kinds of abilities (Sternberg, 1985, 1988, 1996).

1. *Analytical abilities*, the abilities used to analyze, judge, evaluate, compare or contrast
2. *Creative abilities*, the abilities used to create, invent, discover, imagine, or suppose
3. *Practical abilities*, the abilities used to apply, put into practice, implement, or use.

Some students were high in analytical abilities, others in creative abilities, and still others in practical abilities. We found that students who were taught more of the time in a manner that fit their pattern of abilities outperformed students who were taught only minimally or not at all in a manner that fit their pattern of abilities (Sternberg, 1997; Sternberg, Ferrari, Clinkenbeard, & Grigorenko, 1996). In other words, students can improve their performance if taught in a way that is appropriate for them. Much of the teaching done in classrooms reaches only students whose strength is in learning by memory. Students with other kinds of strengths—analytical, creative, or practical, for example—may be taught in a way that almost never matches their pattern of abilities. They should be taught in a way that matches all of these patterns of abilities, however (Sternberg & Spear-Swerling, 1996).

STRENGTHS AND WEAKNESSES

Should we teach to strengths rather than weaknesses? No. We should teach both to strengths and weaknesses. Students need to learn what their strengths and weaknesses are and then to learn to make the most of their strengths at the same time that they learn to correct their weaknesses. Eventually, they will not only learn to correct weaknesses but also to compensate for them.

In practical terms, the implication of this view is that instruction need not be individualized across ability patterns, but rather it can be more or less uniform across these patterns. All students should be taught in a way that enables them to use memory abilities as well as analytical, creative, and practical abilities, so they can both capitalize on their strengths and correct their weaknesses.

INTEGRATION OF MODES OF LEARNING
AND THINKING

Good teaching enables students to capitalize on strengths and to correct weaknesses, but it does not typically do so through activities that isolate these strengths and weaknesses from each other. In everyday life, we rarely encounter activities that are purely analytical, creative, or practical. And for certain, we do not encounter many activities that require us to memorize. How many times does someone graduate from school sit down to memorize anything? Good teaching involves activities that may draw more or less on any particular kind of skill, but ultimately, that involve the same kinds of complex integration that we need to learn in order to survive.

It is useful for teachers to choose activities that particularly emphasize certain skills over others, because it is easy to fall into the trap of just assuming that any one activity involves some of each of analytical, creative, and practical thinking. In fact, many activities require little or none of these kinds of thinking. What are examples of such activities?

TEACHING FOR MEMORY, AND FOR ANALYTICAL, CREATIVE, AND PRACTICAL THINKING

The following are examples of activities at both the primary and secondary levels that emphasize memory as well as analytical, creative, and practical thinking. The activities are organized by subject matter areas, because most teachers either teach a single subject matter area or multiple subject matter areas in separate portions of the school day.

Language Arts

Memory
1. What was the name of Jay Gatsby's wife?
2. Who said "To be or not to be, that is the question"?
3. Who wrote Ethan Frome?

Analytical
1. How were Daisy Miller (from *Daisy Miller*) and Catherine Earnshaw (from *Wuthering Heights*) similar and different?
2. Analyze the relationship Ivan had with his brothers in *The Brothers Karamazov*.
3. Why did Javert commit suicide in *Les Miserables*?

Creative
1. Write an alternative ending to *Don Quixote*.
2. Write a poem about the cruelty of people to each other.
3. Write a skit (in German) about a teenager's first day in Munich.

Practical

1. Write an advertisement that could be placed in the newspaper to convince people to go to see Ibsen's *Ghosts*.
2. If you were trying to persuade a friend to do something for you, how might you use the techniques Tom Sawyer used to convince his friends to whitewash Aunt Polly's fence?
3. What can we learn about ambition from *Macbeth*?

Mathematics

Memory

1. State the Pythagorean theorem.
2. How much is 9 x 6?
3. How are distance, time, and rate related?

Analytical

1. If one receives $4.52 in change from a $20 bill, how much was the cost of the purchase (not including the 5% sales tax)?
2. If $3x + 9 = 30$, what is x?
3. Express the number 46 in base 3.

Creative

1. Write a test problem measuring understanding of factoring.
2. Invent a new mathematical operator (in addition to the four usual ones: +, -, x, â), and show how it can be used.
3. Design a manipulative material that will help children learn their numbers and show how it might be used.

Practical

1. How might trigonometry be used in the construction of a bridge?
2. Route 87 goes straight north for 30 miles and connects to Route 48, which goes straight west for 45 miles. How much time will someone who drives at a constant 60 miles per hour save when the new Route 94 is opened, which will go diagonally from the beginning of Route 87 to the end of Route 48?

Social Studies

Memory

1. In what year was the Magna Carta signed?

2. Which king of France was referred to as the "Sun King"?
3. Who won the Battle of the Bulge?

Analytical
1. In what ways were the American and French Revolutions similar and different?
2. How did the events in Germany after World War I lead to World War II?
3. To what extent did the governmental policies of Lenin follow the tenets of Karl Marx?

Creative
1. If you were Harry Truman and wanted to put an end to World War II without dropping any bombs, what might you have done?
2. Write a hypothetical future history of Mexico in the second half of the 21st century?
3. Write a skit including a discussion between Robert E. Lee and his comrades on the night before Lee's final surrender.

Practical
1. Design and draw an illustration for a poster intended to encourage people to join the Army to fight in an upcoming war.
2. Cut out a product advertisement in a magazine, and discuss the persuasive techniques used to encourage people to buy the product.
3. What lessons do the rise and fall of Nazism hold for us in the contemporary world?

Art and Music

Memory
1. Who composed the music for the opera *Aida*?
2. What is the school of painting with which Edvard Munch is associated?
3. What is *chiaroscuro*?

Analytical
1. Compare and contrast the artistic styles of Monet and Manet.
2. What factors cause a cello and a trombone to sound differently?
3. What message was Hieronymous Bosch trying to convey in *The Garden of Earthly Delights*?

Creative

1. Draw the Earth from an insect's point of view.
2. Compose the music for a love song.
3. Design a new musical instrument, and describe how it will sound.

Practical

1. How did Rembrandt achieve his remarkable effects with regard to the lighting in the rooms he drew?
2. What are typical characteristics of patriotic music, which is intended to encourage people's loyalty to their country?
3. Draw an advertisement for a new kind of soup that is designed to encourage people to buy the soup.

Science

Memory

1. Which of these rocks is bauxite?
2. What is the relation of force to mass?
3. Of what genus are human beings?

Analytical

1. Why have many types of bacteria become resistant to antibiotics?
2. Why is the sky blue?
3. How can you determine whether orange juice or grapefruit juice is more acidic?

Creative

1. How might you design an experiment to determine which of two medications that fight high blood pressure is more effective?
2. Do a science project on a topic of your choice in the field of physics.
3. If you were to design a space suit that would be suitable for use on Mars, what factors would you take into account in designing it?

Practical

1. How can we reduce or possibly even eliminate red tide?
2. What nutritional and other information should consumers be given about the foods they buy?
3. If an unscrupulous politician accused an opponent of being an extraterrestrial alien, how might we figure out whether the opponent really was an alien?

Physical Education

Memory
1. Who was the "home run king"?
2. How many points are needed to win a tennis game?
3. Who is the only player allowed to touch the ball with his or her hands in a soccer match?

Analytical
1. Watch a tennis match between two professionals. Analyze how each player sought to capitalize on the weaknesses of the other player.
2. Why might a pitcher purposely walk a batter in baseball?
3. What are the characteristics of a successful team player in basketball?

Creative
1. Invent a competitive sport involving two people, and describe the rules. Now play it with a classmate.
2. How would baseball be affected if the distance between bases were doubled?
3. Watch a game of football, and suggest how the losing team might have altered their play in order to win.

Practical
1. Make three concrete suggestions on the playing field (for whatever team sport in which you are involved) for how to improve your team's play.
2. Suggest a strategy that will improve your play in any sports activity in which you engage, and explain how you might implement that strategy.
3. How does playing in team sports improve our citizenship?

THE PROBLEM-SOLVING CYCLE

Regardless of whether one is solving an analytical, creative, or practical problem, one needs to go through certain steps of problem solving. These steps can be referred to as a *problem-solving cycle*.

The exact steps depend upon the particular problem. Moreover, there is no absolutely fixed order for these steps. The order in which they are executed can vary across problems and situations. They may also be executed more than once until the given problem is solved.

In general, the steps, illustrated by the problem of writing an essay, are these:

1. *Recognizing the problem.* The individual needs to recognize that there is a problem—in this case, that he or she needs to write an essay. Problem recognition is important to children in school. They need to recognize when they are not performing well, when they are not getting along with others, or when they do not understand material that has been presented. Often students do not solve problems because they do not recognize that they have them.

2. *Defining the problem.* The individual needs to define exactly what the problem is. For example, he or she needs to choose a topic for the essay. In other instances, the student might need to recognize why he or she is not performing well, or getting along with others, or not understanding material that has just been presented.

3. *Devising a strategy for solving the problem.* Devising a strategy for solving the problem. The individual needs to devise a strategy to solve the problem. For example, the student needs to decide on the types of references to consult, where to find the references, how to evaluate their value, and so on. The student might also want to devise a strategy to improve his or her performance, ability to get along with others, or understanding of presented material.

4. *Representing information about the problem.* The individual needs to represent information, both externally and internally. External representations would include note cards, computer files, dictated tapes, and so on. Internal representations are organizations of information in long-term memory. The student might also collect from various teachers information about why he or she is not performing up to his or her level of ability or about why he or she is not getting along with others, and represent it as seems appropriate.

5. *Allocating resources.* The individual needs to decide what kinds of resources to allocate to a problem and to decide how many resources to devote to the problem. Few problems are worth all of one's attention, but allocation of no resources results in never solving the problem. For example, the student might decide that preparing to write an essay is worth up to a week of his or her time but no more. On the other hand, the student might decide that he or she needs to launch a long-term effort to improve school performance or relations with other people.

6. *Monitoring problem solving. Monitoring* refers to keeping track of how well problem solving is going. Is the essay getting closer to being written? Is general school work, or relations with other students improving? If not, what can be done to get the problem-solving process back on target?

7. *Evaluating problem solving. Evaluation* refers to checking after the problem solving is completed. Has the process led to a solution, and is the

solution plausible? If not, what can be done? For example, is the essay one in which the student has confidence? Has school work, or relations with other people improved?

The steps in problem solving are referred to as a cycle because, typically, the solution to one problem leads to a new problem. For example, finishing one assignment, such as an essay, means one is ready for the next assignment. Improving school work allows one to take on new challenges that earlier might have seemed out of reach. In other words, the solution to one problem typically initiates recognition and definition of the next problem.

ASSESSING ANALYTICAL, CREATIVE, AND PRACTICAL ACHIEVEMENTS

The Relation Between Assessment and Instruction

An important feature of the triarchic approach described here is that instruction and assessment become unified. Instead of largely wasting instructional time, tests become instructional. Students learn from taking the test, because they have to think rather than merely retrieve information. Moreover, the kinds of activities a teacher prepares for an assessment are largely the same as the activities the teacher prepares for instruction. Thus, instruction and assessment are practically indistinguishable from each other.

In our summer psychology course, for example, we taught a unit about depression. We used as a homework assignment an activity in which students were asked to engage in three activities: (a) to compare and contrast two theories of depression; (b) to propose their own theory of depression, combining aspects of previous theories but adding their own thoughts as well; and (c) to suggest how they might use what they learned about depression to help a depressed friend. Although the particular set of activities formed a homework assignment, it might equally well have been used as either a class discussion problem or as an essay test problem.

It is essential that instruction and assessment match each other. What happens too often in classrooms is that students are taught in one way and assessed in another. I observed a social studies classroom, for example, in which class discussions were wide-ranging in their inclusion of analytical, creative, and practical thinking, but in which the assessments were multiple-choice, factual-recall tests. The assessments were obviously poorly matched to what had been taught. It would be equally inappropriate to teach for memory, and then to assess students for their analytical, creative, and practical achievements.

The Need for Balance

It should be emphasized here that analytical, creative, and practical assessments should complement, not replace, conventional memory-based assessments. Having information about which to think, analytically, creatively, or practically is as important as the thinking process itself. In other words, thinking requires information to analyze, creative thinking, to go beyond the given, requires knowledge of the given, and practical thinking must make use of knowledge of the situation.

In the 1960s, educators made the mistake of introducing curricular programs that were intended to encourage thinking in the absence of much content information. The programs all failed. Today most educators realize that good teaching and assessment involve a balance.

In education, we have a tendency to let the pendulum swing from one extreme to the other. At one point we use exclusively conventional and largely memory-based assessments, and then we use almost exclusively performance-based assessments. In effect, we move the spotlight from one group to another, instead of shining it on all students. Good assessment samples many kinds of information and skills rather than a narrow range. It combines more conventional objective assessments with the newer performance-based assessments.

Scoring Analytical, Creative, and Practical Assessments

Some teachers would like to use analytical, creative, and practical performance assessments, but they are scared off by what they perceive as subjectivity in evaluation. They find themselves unsure of what and how to evaluate. Yet, evaluations can be done in a way that is appropriate for the assessments being used.

It is important to note that evaluation for analytical, creative, and practical strength does not replace but rather supplements conventional evaluation of knowledge base as well as of good writing (grammar, spelling, punctuation, capitalization, and so on). The mechanics of good writing continue to be important, regardless of how evaluation is done.

Most teachers have evaluated essays or other products for analytical strength at some point, and often at many points, in their assessments. Such essays should be scored on the strength of analysis. Are the student's arguments (a) internally consistent, (b) logical, (c) relevant with respect to the given information, (d) correct with respect to the information, and (e) complete?

Products need to be evaluated by a different set of standards when they are evaluated for creativity. The main criteria for evaluating such products are whether the products are (a) original or novel, (b) high in quality, and (c) appropriate to the task at hand. Note that originality is not enough: The ideas must also be good. Although quality is somewhat subjective, our research (Sternberg & Lubart, 1995) shows that quite high consistency can be achieved across evaluators of creativity if the evaluators look for more or less the same elements. This research also shows, however, that the evaluations are only as good as are the evaluators. If the evaluators do not appreciate creativity, they can be consistent in punishing truly creative work. Evaluating products for practical strength means simply assessing them on the extent to which they are practical—useful in everyday settings.

Students often do not spontaneously produce work that is creative, or practical, or even analytical if the teacher does not make it clear that such work is desired and valued. Teachers should not assume that students know that they should produce work that is analytically, creatively, and practically strong. Teachers need to make it clear that they wish to receive such work.

OBSTACLES TO TRIARCHIC TEACHING AND ASSESSMENT

Teachers sometimes find they like the idea of triarchic teaching and assessment, but at the same time they fear that the obstacles to such teaching and assessment are insurmountable. What are some of the main obstacles they encounter? I have found that teachers most often voice the following seven obstacles:

1. *I can't do it.* Really, any teacher can. Many teachers are already teaching in these various ways, or have at some point in their career. No teacher is going to be exactly equally strong in analytical, creative, and practical thinking. Teachers are likely to find one or another kind of teaching harder to do. But such unevenness is to be expected. Moreover, teachers can actually turn this difficulty into an advantage by pointing out to their students that just as they, the students, are not equally strong in all three kinds of thinking, neither is any teacher. Teachers are more effective when they role-model the difficulties of diverse kinds of thinking than when they pretend to be perfect.

2. *The administration and other teachers won't support me.* It is quite possible that support will not be forthcoming. To an extent, each teacher has to use his or her own practical skills to try to convince administrators and other teachers of the worth of what he or she is doing. Ultimately, however, creative individuals, whether teachers or anyone else, rarely achieve full support for anything they do (Sternberg & Lubart, 1995;

Sternberg & Williams, 1996). Often, the best way to convince others is to show results of the effort, both in terms of student performance and student enthusiasm.

3. *Parents are extremely conservative and won't stand for it.* Parents often are the most conservative element in the educational system. They may be deeply suspicious of innovations, especially ones they do not understand. For this reason, it may make sense for teachers to explain what they are doing to parents and even to enlist their support. Their goals are probably the same as the teachers', and thus teachers typically need only to convince them that these are the right means to be used.

4. *My students need to be prepared for conventional tests, and so this kind of instruction is noble but irrelevant to me.* On its face, it might seem as though teaching triarchically might actually hurt students' performance on conventional tests. In fact, the opposite is true. We did a study investigating the effects of triarchic teaching on performance both on conventional memory-based tests and on performance assessments of analytical, creative, and practical achievements (Sternberg, Torff, & Grigorenko, in press). Third graders were taught a set of social studies lessons on communities and eighth graders were taught a set of psychology lessons in one of three ways. Roughly one third of the students were in a conventional instruction group. Another third were in a group that was taught primarily for critical (analytical) thinking. And the last third were in a group that was taught triarchically. We found that the triarchic group generally performed better than the other two groups not only in analytical, creative, and practical performance assessments, but in memory-based multiple-choice assessments as well.

Why would students taught triarchically perform better than conventionally taught students when achievement was assessed conventionally? It seems that such assessment benefits conventionally taught students. There are at least two reasons for this result. First, students generally learn more if they are taught material in multiple ways, rather than only in one way. Teaching the material in three different ways (as well as for memory) gives the students multiple ways of encoding information, and thus of learning it better. Second, students who are taught triarchically are able to capitalize on strengths and correct or compensate for weaknesses in a way that conventionally students taught are not.

5. *The students are used to conventional teaching, so they are silent when I teach for thinking.* When teachers first start teaching for triarchic thinking, students may react with stunned silence, or even punish them for diverging from the kinds of teaching with which they are familiar. In the face of being ignored or punished, teachers often revert to their old

patterns of behavior. For triarchic teaching to work, the teacher must be prepared for a transition period with the students, one that may not be altogether pleasant.

6. *I don't have time to teach all these three different ways because of the amount of material I need to cover.* The decision to teach triarchically means teachers must be more selective about material taught than before. Teaching is always selective: It is virtually impossible to cover in the classroom every little bit that appears in the textbook. The teacher must be prepared to make hard decisions as to what is worth covering. But such selectivity of coverage benefits rather than harms students. It is an illusion that presenting every little thing will improve students' learning. For the most part, the students quickly forget the little bits. The students learn better when teachers are more selective and make clear to them what is really worth learning.

7. *The evaluation of the assessments is too subjective.* Often, in assessment situations, there is a trade-off between the meaningfulness of the assessment and the objectivity with which it is done. Straight multiple-choice tests may be quite objective and reliable, but they typically measure only surface-level understanding of what is being taught. Performance assessments can measure deeper levels of understanding, but they are typically more subjective. Ideally, the teacher will combine the more objective but more surface-structural assessments with the more subjective but more deep-structural assessments so that all of the different bases of assessment are covered.

CONCLUSIONS

Any teacher can teach triarchically. The main obstacle is not really external—it is internal, in the individual teacher. The main obstacle is the set of objections the teacher raises to convince himself or herself that such teaching is not possible. If a teacher decides it is not the right kind of teaching for himself or herself, then by all means, another way of teaching should be found. But if a teacher believes that triarchic teaching has something important to offer to students, then the main obstacle to starting is with the teacher. The best predictor of whether teachers will do it, and of how well they will do it, is their own determination to do it and to succeed.

Ultimately, teaching triarchically will improve student attention, learning, thinking, and satisfaction. What more could a teacher ask of any method for teaching?

ACKNOWLEDGMENT

Preparation of this chapter was supported under the Javits Act Program(grant number R206R50001), as administered by the Office of Educational Research and Improvement, U.S. Department of Education. Grantees undertaking such projects are encouraged to express their professional judgment freely. This book, therefore, does not necessarily represent the positions or policies of the government, and no official endorsement should be inferred.

REFERENCES

Sternberg, R. J. (1985). *Beyond IQ: A triarchic theory of human intelligence.* New York: Cambridge University Press.

Sternberg, R. J. (1988). *The triarchic mind: A new theory of human intelligence.* New York: Viking-Penguin.

Sternberg, R. J. (1996). *Successful intelligence.* New York: Simon & Schuster.

Sternberg, R. J. (1997). What does it mean to be smart? *Educational Leadership, 54,* 20–24.

Sternberg, R. J., Ferrari, M., Clinkenbeard, P., & Grigorenko, E. L. (1996). Identification, instruction, and assessment of gifted children: A construct validation of a triarchic model. *Gifted Child Quarterly, 40,* 129–137.

Sternberg, R. J., & Lubart, T. I. (1995). *Defying the crowd: Cultivating creativity in a culture of conformity.* New York: Free Press.

Sternberg, R. J., & Spear-Swerling, L. (1996). *Teaching for thinking.* Washington, DC: American Psychological Association.

Sternberg, R. J., Torff, B., & Grigorenko, E. L. (in press). *Teaching triarchically improves school achievement.* Journal of Educational Psychology.

Sternberg, R. J., & Williams, W. M. (1996). *How to develop student creativity.* Alexandria, VA: Association for Supervision and Curriculum Development.

CHAPTER 2

Minds at Work: Applying Multiple Intelligences in the Classroom

Mara Krechevsky

Steve Seidel
Harvard Graduate School of Education

A BRIEF INTRODUCTION TO THE THEORY OF MULTIPLE INTELLIGENCES

All teachers have had at least one student who surprised them with the way the student solved a particular problem or demonstrated that he or she understood something. It may have been a child who solved a math problem correctly but differently from the way it was taught. It could have been an adolescent who played Romeo's first scene with the Friar with surprising insight into Romeo's character. Or perhaps it was a shy seventh grader who shocked her classmates by becoming the most articulate voice in leading the group through a web of moral and social dilemmas and resolving a crisis over a case of cheating in the classroom. Why were these students surprising?

Perhaps there are two reasons. First, there were things about these children their teachers did not know, things about the ways their minds worked. (The students may not have known these things about themselves,

17

either.) So their teachers did not anticipate that the students would solve a problem or express their ideas in a particular way. But a second reason may be that the teachers themselves may not have ever thought about the problem in that way.

Our sensitivity to the diverse ways in which children think, solve problems, and express themselves is often limited both by our notions of intelligence (for example, that it is something finite one is born with) and our own intellectual preferences. Intentionally or not, teachers design their classrooms (curriculum, instruction, and assessment) to reflect their ideas about intelligence and how learning happens as well as their own ways of making sense of the world. Almost all of us can fall into believing that if we can only make clear the way we have come to understand something, others will understand, too.

Based on long and careful observation, especially of children who do not seem to understand easily what may seem obvious to others, many teachers recognize that there are, indeed, many different ways of perceiving the world and multiple ways of making sense of one's experiences. Certainly, in any group, each person notices and attends to different aspects of an experience. It often seems there are as many ways of knowing as there are people. But a closer look at theories of intelligence can provide a middle ground between the idea that there is a single way in which minds work and the notion that every mind is unique. Theories, of course, are only theories; but in attempting to understand the mind and, particularly, the minds in a teacher's classroom, a good theory can help educators make sense of the surprising moves and strategies that students reveal.

Virtually every aspect of classroom life is, in some way, constructed around what teachers want children to learn, and how they think they are most likely to learn it. In some classrooms, desks are in rows and children sit quietly much of the day. In other rooms, there are stations or work areas, each designated for distinct kinds of activity. From the physical design of the room, to the structure of assignments, to the resources provided, to the questions posed in class discussions, each choice a teacher makes reflects, to some degree, an idea about intelligence and learning.

In this chapter, we discuss the theory of multiple intelligences (MI) posed by Gardner in his book, *Frames of Mind* (1983/1993). We describe the ways teachers have considered the implications of a notion of intelligence that takes for granted that students bring a broad range of capacities, each in a distinctive balance, to their work as learners. In particular, we discuss how teachers in various grade levels have applied MI theory to their teaching and assessment practices. Acknowledging and working with diversity of almost any kind in the classroom often seems overwhelming initially. In time, however, this diversity becomes an opening into the creation of much more vibrant learning environments in which all kinds of minds can be encouraged to do their best work. Multiple intelligences theory can provide support for creating such environments.

What Is MI Theory and Where Does It Come From?

For most of this century, psychologists' ideas about intelligence were derived from statistical analyses of short-answer tests. Using these instruments and analyses, psychologists articulated arguments isolating between 1 and 150 factors of intelligence (Carroll, 1993; Guilford, 1967; Horn & Cattell, 1966; Spearman, 1904; Vernon, 1950). However, "g" or general intelligence often emerged as a factor common to various kinds of problem solving (Carroll, 1993; Spearman, 1904/1961).

In *Frames of Mind*, Gardner argued that using these instruments and methods does not adequately capture human problem-solving capabilities. Instead of defining intelligence in terms of performances on mental tests, Gardner (1983/1993) defines an *intelligence* as the ability to solve problems or fashion products that are valued in at least one culture. Gardner identified eight criteria to determine whether or not a capacity qualifies as an intelligence. For example, he looked at the potential isolation of an ability by brain damage; distinctive and recognizable developmental paths; the existence of special populations like savants and prodigies who exhibit unusually jagged intellectual profiles; and an identifiable set of core operations (see Figure 2.1).

Based on his survey of these types of data, Gardner suggested that all human beings possess at least seven relatively independent faculties. In addition to thinking of intelligence as involving linguistic and logical-mathematical abilities, Gardner said that we should consider musical, spatial, bodily-kinesthetic, interpersonal, and intrapersonal abilities intelligences as well (see Figure 2.2.) All human beings possess all of the intelligences, but we differ in our relative strengths and weaknesses.

What Is the Relation Between MI Theory and Traditional Ideas About Intelligence?

Aside from its unorthodox origins, Gardner's theory diverges from some traditional conceptions in several ways. Gardner, like other past and current theorists (see e.g., Ceci, 1990; Guilford, 1967; Sternberg, 1985, 1988; Thurstone, 1938), argued for a more pluralistic notion of intelligence. Rather than fixing intelligence at birth, as some traditional ideas of intelligence imply (Eysenck & Kamin, 1981; Herrnstein & Murray, 1994; Jensen, 1969, 1980), MI theory suggests that intelligences change and grow

1. Potential of isolation by brain damage.

2. A distinctive developmental history with a definable set of expert "end-state" performances.

3. The existence of savants, prodigies, and other exceptional individuals.

4. An identifiable set of core operations or information-processing mechanisms.

5. Support from experimental psychological tasks.

6. Support from psychometric findings.

7. Evolutionary history and evolutionary plausibility.

8. Susceptibility to encoding in a symbol system.

FIG. 2.1: Criteria for considering the intelligences.

Linguistic intelligence allows individuals to communicate and make sense of the world through language. Typical professions include journalists, novelists, and lawyers.

Logical-mathematical intelligence enables individuals to use and appreciate abstract relations. Typical professions include scientists, accountants, and philosophers.

Musical intelligence allows people to create, communicate, and understand meanings made out of sound. Typical professions include composers, conductors, and singers.

Spatial intelligence makes it possible for people to perceive visual or spatial information, to transform this information, and to recreate visual images from memory. Typical professions include architects, sculptors, and mechanics.

Bodily-kinesthetic intelligence allows individuals to use all or part of the body to create products or solve problems. Typical professions include athletes, dancers, and actors.

Intrapersonal intelligence helps individuals to distinguish among their own feelings, to build accurate mental models of themselves, and to draw on these models to make decisions about their lives. Typical professions include therapists and certain kinds of artists and religious leaders.

Interpersonal intelligence enables individuals to recognize and make distinctions about others' feelings and intentions. Typical professions include teachers, politicians, and salespeople.

Naturalist intelligence allows people to distinguish among, classify, and use features of the environment. Typical professions include farmers, gardeners, and geologists.

FIG. 2.2: The multiple intelligences.

in response to a person's experiences. Like a number of other scholars (e.g., Bronfenbrenner, 1979; Ceci, 1990; Feuerstein, 1980; Perkins, 1995), Gardner viewed the intelligences as educable. They are the result of a constant interaction among biological and environmental factors.

Moreover, traditional conceptions of intelligence hold that intelligence remains the same in all situations (Herrnstein & Murray, 1994; Spearman, 1904, 1961, 1925). That is to say, one's intelligence does not change, whether one is solving a math problem, learning how to ski, or finding one's way around a new city. Modern conceptions point out that the thinking and learning required outside of school are often situated and contextualized (Brown, Collins, & Duguid, 1989; Ceci, 1990; Resnick, 1987, 1991). Most intellectual work does not occur in isolation: When people work in different kinds of settings, their abilities to problem solve differ (Resnick, Levine, & Teasley, 1991; Rogoff & Lave, 1984). Apart from traditional test settings, problem solving is usually tied to certain tasks or goals and often aided by other people and an assortment of tools and resources (Brown, Collins, & Duguid, 1989; Lave, 1988; Pea, 1990; Perkins, 1993; Salomon, 1993; Vygotsky, 1978).

In keeping with the theories of the thinkers just mentioned, Gardner's definition of *intelligence* is likewise highly contextualized. Further, an intelligence never exists in isolation from other intelligences: All tasks, roles, and products in our society call on a combination of intelligences, even if one or more may be highlighted. For instance, concert pianists do not draw solely on musical intelligence to become accomplished in their field. They also must rely on interpersonal skills to connect to an audience or work with a manager, bodily-kinesthetic skills to develop manual dexterity, and intrapersonal ability to understand and express the meaning and feeling of a piece of music.

Recent Developments in MI Theory

The theory of MI is constantly evolving. Recently, Gardner (in press) has suggested that another faculty should be added to the list—the naturalist intelligence. (The core ability of the naturalist intelligence is the ability to recognize and classify the species in one's environment.) Although some critics claim there is no empirical evidence to support MI, Gardner examined hundreds of empirical studies in identifying the original seven intelligences and he continues to review new data as they emerge. Indeed, Gardner added the naturalist intelligence to his list based on his examination of newly published studies. Several recent investigations provide evidence for the relative independence of interpersonal intelligence (e.g., Astington, 1993; Damasio, 1994) but refute the independence of musical and spatial intelligences (Rauscher, Shaw, & Ky, 1993).

Even though to our knowledge, there have been no large-scale studies of schools using MI or the effectiveness of MI-based practices on student learning, some educators have reported educational benefits for their students (see, e.g., Campbell, 1992; Hecker, 1997; Mann, 1996). Clearly, more research on the impact of MI on schools needs to be conducted. Several researchers at Project Zero at Harvard are beginning to undertake such studies to look systematically at practices associated with effective use of the theory (Kornhaber & Hatch, 1996). They hope to convert these practices into practical resources and products that can support educators in their efforts to apply MI.

Some Common Misconceptions about MI Theory

It may be helpful to clear up two common confusions with regard to MI. The first is the confusion between an intelligence and a domain of knowledge or discipline (Gardner, 1995). In Gardner's scheme, an intelligence is a biological and psychological potential—a capacity that resides in each person. A domain or discipline is the arena or body of knowledge that gives people the opportunity to use their intelligences in different ways and in which varying degrees of expertise can be developed (see Csikszentmihalyi, 1988; Kornhaber & Gardner, 1993). Examples of disciplines or domains in our culture are mathematics, medicine, and gardening. Carrying out work in a domain or discipline requires that a person use several different intelligences, as we saw in the example of the concert pianist. Similarly, each intelligence can be used in a variety of domains—for example, bodily-kinesthetic ability contributes to proficiency in surgery, theater, and athletics.

Another source of confusion is the equation of multiple intelligences with learning styles. *Learning styles* refer to the different approaches that individuals take when trying to make sense of diverse kinds of content (see, e.g., Dunn & Dunn, 1978, 1992; Gregorc, 1985; McCarthy, 1982; Myers, 1980). Typically, a learning style is thought to cut across all content areas. So, if a person is a tactile learner, she will learn best when learning new material—whether history or cooking—by using her hands or sense of touch. In contrast, the intelligences represent potentials or capacities that are linked to neurological functions and structures and that respond to particular content in the world. We cannot assume that because one has demonstrated a good memory or ability to focus in music that he or she will behave similarly when presented with linguistic or spatial information.

Moreover, unlike learning styles, intelligences have distinct developmental paths that are tied to the achievement of valued roles in our society. If we want children to become skilled artists, mathematicians, or solid citizens, then we need to nurture particular intelligences. Learning styles do not share this connection to meaningful societal roles. One can be a tactile or auditory learner and still become an accountant or a botanist. However, if one has not developed strong logical-mathematical or naturalist intelligences, success in those professions will be limited.

IMPLICATIONS OF MULTIPLE INTELLIGENCES THEORY FOR INSTRUCTION

MI theory raises many questions for classroom practice. Should teachers try to nurture all of the intelligences equally or should they focus on identifying and developing children's strengths? Should schools offer a wider selection of courses or should they maintain a traditional curriculum and provide more varied ways of engaging students in the standard subject matter? It is important to remember that MI is not an end in itself. If a colleague proclaims, "I have an MI classroom," or "I teach at an MI school," one's next question should be, "What does that mean?" or "What are your educational goals for your students and school and how does using MI theory help you get there?"

At first glance, MI appears to be compatible with many other educational philosophies and approaches, such as educating the "whole child," "project-based learning," an "interdisciplinary curriculum," "whole language," and so on. But this leads to the question of whether adopting the theory simply becomes a new label to describe existing practices and beliefs. Although MI may sometimes serve this purpose, it also can provide a theoretical foundation and validation for teachers' beliefs and practices, deepening and/or extending them to new domains (Kornhaber, 1994). The theory can become a framework for thinking about the students we teach and how to teach them, helping teachers become more reflective and explicit about the pedagogical choices they make. As with any theory, people may initially use MI in superficial ways, and some may continue to do so for years. But if educational goals and criteria for reaching those goals can be articulated, then MI can become an ally to rigorous learning.

There is never a single, direct route from scientific theory to daily practice and there are many different ways that MI can be applied in the classroom. As we noted above, applications vary depending on the educational goals and values for the class and the school (see also Gardner, 1993b). Although some people may believe it is important for students to be introduced to and develop competence in all areas, others think certain content (e.g., language or social skills) deserves more attention than others and spend a lot of time nurturing students' linguistic or interpersonal intelligences. Some teachers prefer to teach to children's strengths; others prefer to focus on deficits. Even though there is no one right way to apply the theory, we believe there are at least four important implications for classroom instruction.

Individualizing Students' Education

One implication of MI theory for instruction is that teachers need to get to know their students well enough to become familiar with each student's interests, strengths, and weaknesses, and shape their instructional practices accordingly. Of course, Gardner is not alone in suggesting that education needs to be individualized. Sizer (1984, 1982), the founder of the Coalition of Essential Schools at Brown University, also wrote about the critical importance of teachers' knowing their students well. At the elementary level, Comer (1988) talked about the value of understanding the six developmental pathways (physical, psycho-emotional, social-interactive, cognitive-intellectual, speech and language, and moral) along which all children progress. The theory of multiple intelligences adds a theory about intelligence and the way the mind works that supports such educational beliefs and practices.

MI provides a framework for individualizing education by helping us to understand the full range of students' intellectual strengths. Traditional schooling has focused on developing only math and language as cognitive abilities. Teachers who use a multiple intelligences framework recognize other abilities—musical, bodily-kinesthetic—as cognitive, too. But opening one's eyes to thinking about these other competencies in new ways is not enough. We must also be prepared to test and support hypotheses about a student's strengths. Several research and development projects have explored ways to do this in the classroom.

Project Spectrum, a collaboration between Harvard Project Zero and Tufts University, is an approach to curriculum and assessment in early childhood that gives teachers tools for identifying and providing evidence for children's strengths in different areas (Chen, 1993; Krechevsky, 1998). Spectrum researchers devised assessments ranging from structured activities to observational checklists in such domains as movement, music, science, art, and social understanding to help teachers recognize the various ways students can use their intelligences. For example, Spectrum divides the movement domain into athletic and creative movement. Athletic movement abilities include power, agility, speed, and balance, and creative movement includes body control, sense of rhythm, expressiveness, and generation of movement ideas. This delineation helps teachers make sense of key aspects of a domain with which they may not be familiar. Once a student's strengths and interests have been reliably identified, they either can be nurtured further or used to engage students in areas of difficulty.

At the middle school level, students themselves can become recorders of their own strengths and can work with teachers to individualize their assignments. In the Practical Intelligence for School (PIFS) Project, a collaboration between Harvard Project Zero and Yale University, students are encouraged to learn about their own intelligence profiles and how to draw on their interests and strengths in carrying out their schoolwork (Gardner, Krechevsky, Sternberg, & Okagaki, 1994; Williams et al., 1996). PIFS is an effort to help students succeed in school in part by helping them understand the nature of school, why they attend, and how school activities can be useful in their current and future lives. One of the PIFS curriculum units introduces students to different notions of intelligence and encourages them to take more responsibility for their own learning. Students personalize their education by learning about how they learn best, reflecting on and sharing past experiences that reveal special talents and/or interests, and engaging in a set of problem-solving tasks and challenges that can be resolved in a variety of ways. These types of experiences and related discussion and reflection enable students to take more control of their education and build on their strengths by tailoring assignments to their own interests.

Decisions about whether to offer all students a broad education in many or all of the areas addressed by MI, or whether to tailor students' education to develop their strengths or remediate their weaknesses, may depend on the developmental level of the students. Many schools using MI choose to offer broad exposure early on, with increasing focus and specialization as students get older. One reason for adopting this approach is the belief that it is especially important in children's younger years to introduce them to many different forms of expression and meaning-making to provide them with experiences that are as rich as possible. But as students get older, going into depth in many different subject matters simply is not possible. Also, the pressures of college entrance exams and the job market demand that students be proficient in certain domains. Therefore schooling appears to become more focused. However, even with a more circumscribed curriculum, MI theory can be useful in helping students develop competence.

Teaching Subject Matter in More than One Way

MI leads to teaching subject matter in multiple ways, providing students with different points of entry into learning a topic. Gardner talks about experts as individuals who are able to represent and explain thoughts and concepts in more than one way. The more ways a teacher can explain or teach a topic or concept, the more likely that both the teacher and the students will understand it deeply. Because most teachers do not feel comfortable or knowledgeable enough to teach by drawing on a variety of intelligences, applying MI in the classroom often leads to team teaching or bringing in community experts to share their expertise. In one elementary school with three kindergartens, each teacher focused on developing her curriculum in two domains and then the children rotated among the three rooms. Classroom teachers often team up with the school's specialists to share knowledge and information about the children.

In his book, *The Unschooled Mind*, Gardner (1991) claimed that any substantive topic can be approached in at least five ways—through the use of narrative, logical analysis, hands-on experience, artistic exploration, and philosophical examination (Gardner has since added participatory/interpersonal experience). For example, students can learn about the theory of evolution by reading about Darwin and his trip on the Beagle (narrative); examining quantitative relationships in breeding dominant and recessive traits (logical); breeding fruit flies for certain characteristics (hands-on); looking for and drawing patterns of similarities and differences in fruit flies' wings (artistic); addressing fundamental questions such as whether evolution yields progress in all things (philosophical); or working together on a project where students assume different roles (interpersonal).

The experiences of two college-level English classes (one for students with learning disabilities) illustrate how students learn to articulate and craft arguments in writing using bodily kinesthetic and spatial techniques (Klein & Hecker, 1994). In these classrooms, teachers ask students to represent their arguments by walking across the room, changing directions to reflect shifts in logic. Students thought out loud as they stepped out their essays, asking themselves questions about where they wanted to go and how they could get there. New information was represented by a step forward, contradictory information by a step back, and additional examples by steps to the side. Having students step out their narratives seemed to trigger ideas, help word retrieval, and aid in the sequencing of events.

Another set of strategies entails asking students to build models of the relationships between their ideas using colored pipe cleaners, Legos, or Tinkertoys. Rather than generating a written outline for an essay, students created models with differently sized, shaped, or colored pieces that represent different components of the essay like the introduction, main points, and conclusion. Seeing concretely how different ideas are linked helped the students develop an overall sense for how the essay comes together. To bridge the spatial and linguistic domains, the teachers asked the students to describe and explain what they had built. Klein and Hecker reported that after several papers, students only had to imagine manipulating blocks or walking out an essay to write in a clear and organized fashion.

Project-Based Learning

Another natural partner of MI theory is project-based learning. As Katz and Chard (1989) pointed out, projects draw on a range of abilities, allow for multiple points of entry, and often reflect meaningful, complex work over time (see also Steinberg, 1997). Projects offer students the opportunity to solve problems or create products—the definition of intelligence according to Gardner. In project work, the intelligences function as means, rather than goals, i.e., they are used in service of completing the work of the project, not as ends in themselves. Since projects also frequently involve collaborative work, they help students both to develop their own interpersonal intelligence and to value the intelligences of their peers (see, e.g., Greeley, 1996b).

An example from the earlier grades is a first grade classroom's project to study the school itself (Kornhaber, 1994). Children investigated the history of the school and wrote both fiction and nonfiction books about the school. They explored the school's physical structure and created scaled floor plans out of blocks. They graphed the number of doors and windows in the school and drew pictures of the pipes they discovered in the basement. Two other classrooms in the school undertook projects studying the community. These projects included such activities as transforming the classroom into a model community complete with churches, banks, and beach pavilions, visiting a local restaurant and making pasta, conducting surveys of parents' occupations and graphing and posting the results, and drawing a mural of a passenger train. Many of these activities continued for 5 months or more.

Arts-Infused Curriculum

As we have seen, MI theory suggests that learning in and through the arts involves cognitive, problem-solving abilities just like more traditional subject matter. In many schools and classrooms influenced by MI, people turn to the arts and arts-based activities as a way to implement the theory in significant learning experiences. Teachers, parents, and students in MI-based classrooms value achievement in the arts as more than just frills.

Because many classroom teachers have not been trained as artists, they often find it useful to meet or team up with the school's arts specialists or artists from the community. One second grade arts team used dance and movement activities to help children understand place value. They asked children to create movement patterns to represent the 1s, 10s, and 100s places and then to represent their solutions physically (Kornhaber & Krechevsky, 1995). Teachers learned both from their own direct experience with the art form and from looking at student work under the guidance of a trained eye, learning to identify characteristics of unusual ability. The students got to experience first hand the passion and mastery of expert practitioners.

Schools often draw on local institutions and resources like museums and arts groups to provide experiences or apprenticeships that they are unable to offer themselves. Many schools and districts write grants to host artistic residencies or bring in mentors or experts from the community to work with teachers or students. One middle school teacher asked local experts to come into her class one hour per week to work with students and to look at and critique their work on a play about immigrant life in the textile mills of the 19th century. A parent who was a professional composer helped students compose original music for the play. A set designer brought in books about mills and took the students to the library to do historical research. Because the students' notions of research were based on linguistic rather than visual information, the students had not previously thought of set designers as needing to conduct historical research. The teacher also took the students to visit one of the local mills, where they recorded the sound of the machines in operation, again extending their ideas about the nature of research. Through writing music and designing sets, students deepened their understanding of the immigrant experience in industrial America (Greeley, 1996a).

Some Misuses of MI Theory

Before turning to the implications of MI theory for assessment, it might be useful to identify some of the questionable instructional practices that purportedly follow from MI. Although many of these practices are understandable as initial attempts to apply the theory, ideally, educators trying to apply MI will be able to learn from and deepen their efforts over time.

First, MI is not a mandate to teach every topic in seven or eight ways. Many of the lesson plans and grids that are created to help teachers apply MI in the classroom contain seven slots or boxes, implying that teachers need to fill in just as many learning activities for each unit or lesson. Yet, not all topics and concepts lend themselves to being taught in seven or eight ways, and trying to force-fit activities into each box often leads to well-intentioned but contrived lessons. Suppose, for example, that one of the learning objectives in a math unit is for students to understand fractions and their relationships. Asking students to sing a song about the operations they have learned, or playing classical music in the background during the lesson, are not particularly meaningful uses of music to support learning math. However, it may be that learning about different rhythmic structures will help those students who are more musically inclined, especially if the link back to the mathematics can be made explicit.

Second, many schools and classrooms that have adopted MI encourage teachers and students to identify and honor students' strengths. However, celebrating strengths is not enough; the strengths need to be connected to what students need to know and understand. In either a societal or an academic context, nurturing meaningful achievement in a domain or discipline matters much more than nurturing intelligences per se.

Third, many of us fall into the trap of applying MI by labeling children. Or we may think that children learning to label activities as involving one or another intelligence is the same as demonstrating understanding in the different intelligences. But students need to know that there are different standards of performance and products in different domains, so they can learn what is considered quality work. Depending on the learning goals of a project, standards from a range of disciplines may need to be identified and used to judge the students' work in various genres.

Finally, infusing domains like the arts into the regular curriculum avoids the potential artificiality of separating out MI-based activities from the classroom. Ideally, attention to multiple points of entry and authentic activities in different disciplines should occur throughout the school, not just in a specially designated MI "activity," "discovery," or "flow" room. Although such a setup has understandable appeal, if only for ease of implementation, it runs the risk of making MI something one "does," as opposed to a way of thinking about children, how they learn, and how best to teach them.

IMPLICATIONS OF MI THEORY FOR CLASSROOM ASSESSMENT

In this section, we consider principles for constructing or choosing methods to determine what children are learning and how they are progressing with their school work. We also explore some fundamental tools of assessment from an MI perspective. Throughout this discussion, we are primarily concerned with assessments that provide insight into the workings of children's minds. Although these are assessments, their purpose is instructional—that is, to help teachers consider how best to teach and to help students consider how to become effective learners.

Four Principles for Designing Assessments

Because, in MI theory, intelligences are potentials exercised only in the context of certain experiences and environments, it is especially important that classroom assessments be highly contextualized. Separating bits of knowledge from the contexts in which they have meaning, or separating the child from an environment with real problems to solve or materials to work with, is unlikely to demonstrate what a child has learned or can figure out. The following four principles focus on placing the child and the assessment in engaging situations with problems that have meaning within the context of particular disciplines or domains of work. (The assessment tools that correspond to these principles are discussed in greater detail later in this section.)

1. *Assessments have to be contextualized in order to be intelligence-fair.* Intellect cannot be assessed in the abstract. Assessment should be embedded in meaningful, ongoing, real-world activities and reflect the real-life behaviors and challenges experienced by actual practitioners in the field (Wiggins, 1989a). They should also draw on the materials and tools of the domain, rather than always relying on pencil-and-paper tests. In this regard, performance tasks are good examples of contextualized assessments.

   In classrooms influenced by MI theory, the active and contextualized nature of assessments are a primary reason why the lines between curriculum and assessment blur (Baron, 1990). Students are often engaged in authentic work—solving problems and carrying out projects that have importance not just in the world of school but in the world outside of school. Further, because MI theory says that important cognitive activity is going on all the time, informal assessment needs to be taken as seriously as formal assessment. Documentation of students' observations, questions, and solutions to all kinds of problems can provide critical insights into students' minds that might not emerge in more structured assessments.

2. *Assessments should allow for diverse modes of response or multiple ways to demonstrate understanding.* Portfolios are often full of examples of the diverse ways in which students represent their insights and ideas. They are a good reminder of the direct relationship between curriculum and assessment (Wolf, 1989). A portfolio of work from a classroom in which students have been allowed few choices and little flexibility in modes of expressing their thinking (a collection of worksheets, for example) is unlikely to meet the demands of this principle.

3. *Assessment should help to track the growth over time of children's ability to use their intelligences.* MI theory says that intelligences are educable. However, growth—especially when teachers try to recognize it in all its guises—can be subtle and hard to see on a daily basis. Collections of student work from the beginning of the year (or even across many years) provide a way of tracking and examining this growth (Gardner, 1993a; Wolf, 1989). Implementing this principle takes great effort and focus if one is to create a meaningful collection of work.

4. *Assessment is a fundamental part of the learning process. Through engaging in reflection and self-assessment, students can come to understand their own intelligences and how they work.* Gardner identifies two personal intelligences in his theory—intra- and interpersonal intelligence. A number of studies at Project Zero have focused on the importance of thinking about one's thinking and how one goes about one's work (see, e.g., Seidel et al., 1997; Winner, 1991). There are many ways to engage students in looking

at their own work and reflecting on its quality and value as well as what was learned in creating the work. This principle asserts the active role of students in assessment processes.

Tools of Assessment

In this section, the approaches to assessment noted in the principles—observation and documentation, performance tasks, portfolios, and student reflection and self-assessment—are described in greater detail. These are only a sample of the tools educators influenced by MI theory have experimented with in recent years, though they are by no means products of the theory. While these techniques have enjoyed considerable development in recent years, they certainly predate Gardner's statement of the theory in *Frames of Mind*.

Observation. Perhaps the most powerful assessment tool is careful observation of children at work and play. Observing children closely is a deceptively complex process (Cohen & Stern, 1974). What to look for is not always obvious nor is how to make sense of what has been seen. Keeping in mind Gardner's definition of *intelligence*, simply watching children as they encounter problems or try to make things can be instructive.

In classrooms in which students are controlled and passive with only very limited and prescribed assignments, such as worksheets, there is, admittedly, not much to watch. However, in classrooms in which students are given genuine and challenging problems to work on or projects to carry out, observation yields a wealth of information. In many classrooms, such problems are directly related to an academic discipline, like solving an algebraic equation or anticipating the result of mixing particular chemicals. Others are the spontaneous result of coincidences or social dynamics. One child, in her spirited dance improvisation, accidentally slaps her unsuspecting dance partner in the face, causing a total disruption to the work. What starts as an accident becomes an occasion for hurt feelings and embarrassment. How do these children work through this moment? Can they recover, restore dignity and order, and return to work? Careful observation can provide quite a bit of information about the ways these students use their intelligences.

Just as students constantly face problems, large and small, physical and psychological, abstract and concrete, they are displaying their intelligences at work in subtle and explicit ways. Keeping in mind the diversity of approaches to problem solving and making products that MI theory suggests will help sensitize teachers to intelligent behaviors that might otherwise go unnoticed. (It may also remind teachers of options they can suggest to children when they are especially frustrated.)

Here are a few things to look for:

- Notice children's choices when given options.
- Watch the roles they take when working together to complete a task.
- Observe how they handle unanticipated problems. Look for differences in their approaches to this problem solving.
- Note what captures one child's attention and passes another by. Observe when children lose or gain interest in a task.
- Try to name the particular problem-solving strategies each child offers.
- List the different ways in which children communicate ideas, under-standings, thoughts, and feelings to others. Look for patterns from each child.
- Pay attention to physical actions as well as to what a child says.

Documentation.   Most teachers have too many students to remember very many of the details of a child's life in the classroom. Keeping notes on students can be especially helpful to teachers as they seek to find patterns in the ways children use their intelligences. Teachers who keep anecdotal records focus these notes in many different ways. Some concentrate on frustration points for children in order to heighten their attention to moments when children's intelligences are challenged. Others focus on moments of delight and satisfaction with the idea that a child's particular intelligences will be most fully engaged. In either case, these descriptive notes help teachers use a child's emotional responses to indicate aspects of a child's strengths and needs.

In addition, some teachers keep notes of children's conversations as they listen for questions and ideas that arise spontaneously. One first grade teacher trained herself to listen for certain phrases, such as "What if ... " and "Why don't we.... " She identified these and other phrases as an-nouncements that a child was imagining the world as other than it appeared to be. She heard these comments as the beginning of creative solutions to problems encountered or alternative explanations for phenomena observed. Again, she was listening for minds at work—minds imagining possibilities not yet suggested.

Performance Tasks.   Observation and documentation are essentially in-formal forms of assessment. Performance tasks are like the part of the driver's test that is conducted in the car. One is given a task to perform and is assessed on one's performance. Performance tasks are appropriate tools for things that can be assessed only in action (see, e.g., Baron, 1990; Frederiksen & Collins, 1989; Wiggins, 1989b). In the early grades, teachers ask students to read a text aloud. Children may grasp the narrative of a story or make conclusions about the characters simply from the illustrations. Without asking students to perform the text, the teacher may have little information about how well they read and what they understand. Most performances in the arts or athletics are fine examples of authentic performance assessments, from appearing in a dance concert to testing one's strength, skills, and focus in a wrestling match. In both cases, various intelligences are required. In excellent dance and wrestling, a delicate balance of intelligences is at work.

Considerable work has been done in math and the sciences to construct significant and authentic performance tasks. Generally, these tasks have carefully designed constraints, such as specific problems to solve, materials to use, and a limited timetable. The New Standards Project developed a frequently cited math task that gives students a database with information about tropical fish—their costs, their sizes, which fish can coexist with other fish, and so on. Students are instructed that they have a certain amount of money to spend on the fish. What would they purchase and why? There is no single "correct" answer. In fact, there are countless solutions. The test here is about children's capacities to weigh different factors, consider alternatives, calculate accurately, and demonstrate reasoning (Resnick, Briars, & Lesgold, 1992). This task, like authentic work in any domain, requires far more than a single intelligence. Certainly, children's logical-mathematical intelligences are tested by this task. But their ability to write a clear statement of process and reasoning is also required.

Portfolios of Student Work. When students are given assignments that allow for diverse modes of response or multiple ways to demonstrate understanding, they often produce complex and striking work. Too often, however, our schools have devalued such products by encouraging a system in which student work is handed in or presented, graded by the teacher, handed back, and never looked at again. Portfolios of student work provide an opportunity for saving such work and returning to it at various points for assessment and reevaluation.

In work on Arts Propel, a project on assessment in music, visual arts, and imaginative writing, researchers repeatedly found that students revisiting their work some months after its completion had come to substantially different perspectives on its quality and significance (Walters, Seidel, & Gardner, 1994). Sometimes they saw qualities that impressed them and had been hidden before. More often they found the work to be far less accomplished than they previously thought, an indication that in the ensuing months they had actually raised their standards of quality in that domain. Through careful comparison of pieces across a body of work created in a term of a year or more (in schools where portfolios are kept across years), portfolios can provide vivid evidence of growth and development.

Collecting and examining bodies of work can also reveal other aspects of a student's mind at work. Particular interests and themes often emerge when a portfolio is read carefully. One student in an Arts Propel classroom who had been considered—and dismissed as—a class clown by his high school language arts teacher, emerged as a writer with a serious interest in comedy. His papers revealed consistent attempts to bring humor to his writing, especially his dramatic writing. Without looking across these pieces, his teacher simply thought this student was never getting serious about his writing (Walters et al., 1994). The portfolio made it possible for the teacher to see the student's deeper pursuit.

Portfolios, in themselves, are only collections of work. Assessment happens when teachers and students review those portfolios through particular lenses. Some portfolio reviews focus on the process of students' work. How do students approach and solve problems? How do they understand the methods of a particular academic discipline, demonstrate their capacity to use those methods, and make sense of their findings? How do they communicate their thoughts and perceptions most effectively? What seems to be problematic, and have they made progress in addressing those problems?

Other portfolio reviews look at a student's level of accomplishment. In Arts Propel, rubrics were developed to look at a range of dimensions within the disciplines of visual arts, music, and imaginative writing. Some of those dimensions include craftsmanship; invention; expression/point of view; capacity to make discriminations in works from a wide variety of genres; cultures, and historical periods; and ability to learn from other works of art within the domain (Winner, 1991).

Student Reflection and Self-Assessment.   The theory of multiple intelligences reminds us that thinking about oneself is one of the realms of intelligence. Traditionally, assessment and evaluation have been the domain of the teacher. Students hand in their work; teachers judge it. Certainly teachers do and must make judgments of student work. But this scenario misses a world of insight and instruction as both students and teachers can learn important lessons from engaging students deeply and regularly in reflecting on and assessing their own work.

Teachers have many ways in which they engage students in reflection on their work. Reflection can be written or verbal and can occur at the middle or end of a project, or even months after its completion. It can be a conversation or a monologue. Often teachers provide guiding questions that range from very open ("What have you learned from this project?") to quite specific ("Describe some of the mistakes you feel you made in doing your project. Show evidence in your drafts.").

In the Project Zero/Massachusetts Schools Network (PZ/MSN), a collaborative project of the Massachusetts Department of Education, 11 Massachusetts elementary and middle schools, and Project Zero, the goal of reflection activities is to encourage students and teachers to look back, take stock of where they are, and think ahead, identifying goals and plans for next steps. In the process of taking stock, teachers and students look at both internal and external standards. Looking inward, students think about what they are attempting to accomplish in their work and assess how they did in relation to those goals. Looking outward, students measure their own standards against those of the school and experts in the field. Through this process, they reconsider their standards and goals and prepare for their next project (Blythe & Seidel, 1996).

Once students are engaged in reflection and self-assessment, it becomes much easier to have conversations about their work. They come to their own opinions about their work and learn how to share them. These thoughts are an invaluable resource for teachers who want insight into how their students approach and think about their work. A meeting ground is created for teachers and students on which both consider ways to move forward in the process of teaching and learning.

IMPLICATIONS OF MI THEORY FOR PROFESSIONAL DEVELOPMENT

For many teachers, the curricular and assessment practices discussed in this chapter might be quite familiar, whereas for others they may represent a radical shift from their current practice. In either case, a thoughtful appraisal of the relation between a theory of intelligence and a set of classroom practices is an important exercise. The intellectual demands of teaching are considerable. Seeking clear and substantive connections between theory, research, and practice is a particularly challenging and core problem of professional development.

A multiple intelligences perspective has further implications for professional training and development. Each of the curricular practices discussed in this paper is complex and teachers, new or midcareer, have many questions about how to individualize instruction, design projects, approach subject matter in multiple ways, or infuse the arts into work in other disciplines. Such practices are easy to name and hard to make effective in the classroom. Teachers need models, materials, coaching, and support to develop the many skills, sensitivities, and sophistication that make these approaches work as well as clarity about their theoretical foundations.

The assessment tools discussed here are also complex practices that take time to develop into smooth and effective components of the classroom. As with virtually any changes in the conduct of assessment, the implementation of these tools—portfolios, performance tasks, student self-assessment—is likely to create some controversy. Many values and assumptions about how schools should work are embedded in the way assessment is carried out. In implementing these new approaches, roles shift, standards evolve, and what counts as evidence of learning and accomplishment changes. This is likely to create some confusion and anxiety for teachers, parents, and students. The rules of school can appear to be changing and, along with notions of intelligence, they are.

Any of these changes suggests a need to rethink aspects of professional training and development. In addition to opportunities to explore theories of intelligence and learning and links among those theories and the classroom, teachers need ways to become comfortable with new curricular, instructional, and assessment practices. Other needs arise as well. These include:

- sustained work on honing discipline-specific observation skills.
- opportunities to examine both children's and adults' work in different domains.
- the chance to work with experts or practitioners in different fields.

Good professional development can have many of the forms and settings traditionally associated with pre- and in-service programs, such as college courses, student teaching, training workshops, and summer institutes. Other learning situations also hold great promise. In the PZ/MSN, extensive professional development takes place within the school setting during the school day (Seidel, Veenema, Blythe, & Almeida, 1998).

In these schools, teachers meet in small groups during the school day, sometimes within and sometimes across grade levels to examine student work, discuss the success and challenges of new classroom practices, and reflect on the relationship of theory, research, and practice. These sessions are led by facilitators from outside the school (a district "coach" or a staff person from Project Zero or the Department of Education) or a member of the school faculty or administration. In most PZ/MSN schools, these sessions occur at least once a month and all faculty and many administrators participate. In this context, professional development becomes a part of teachers' work and not something done outside the school building on one's "own" time.

In addition, teachers in this network are encouraged to visit other network schools to talk with other teachers and to see how these practices look in different school settings. There are also network meetings three or four times a year. A regular focus of these meetings is the sharing of materials, ideas, experiences, and findings from classrooms and schools across the state as well as updates on relevant developments in theory and research.

CONCLUDING NOTE

The theory of multiple intelligences suggests that it may be more instructive to consider how people are intelligent rather than "how much" intelligence they have. Certainly, in classrooms, the prognosis for every child having a successful learning experience is greatly enhanced when the dominant paradigm is one in which all children are seen as having substantial ways of making sense of the world—including the worlds of academic disciplines—although those ways may not be immediately obvious to the teacher or the child. In part, the work of teaching, learning, and assessing is coming to understand such ways of knowing.

We have identified a number of approaches to curriculum and assessment, none of them entirely new, that reflect a perspective on intelligence that is consistent with the theory of multiple intelligences. Although their use is still far from widespread, most of these approaches have received considerable attention during the last decade of school reform. Some, like portfolios and project-based learning, have long histories of use in schools, especially in arts education. Yet these practices remain largely marginal in most schools in part because they reflect a view of intelligence that is still marginal. The paradigm of intelligence as a fixed, measurable quantity with limited forms of legitimate expression is convenient for certain models (e.g., transmission of knowledge through lecture) and functions (e.g., tracking and sorting by social class) of schooling. But it does not reflect what observation and empirical research indicate about the complexity of the human mind and the process of learning.

Those with alternative perspectives must take seriously the difficulty of implementing new practices in the classroom. In many schools, little time is devoted to explicit thinking through of how practice reflects theories and beliefs and how theory might inform practice. Whatever the practice—old, new, borrowed, or experimental—it is the responsibility of all practitioners and institutions to consider the beliefs and theories that justify what goes on in the classroom. Time must be allocated for the adults in a school to have reflective conversations, engage in such study, and share this thinking with parents and the community. (Theorists, of course, also have a responsibility to consider practical implications of their perspectives.)

Short of this kind of restructuring of the school schedule and redefining of a school's culture, individual teachers can pursue these links between theory and practice in the classroom. Simply looking carefully at one's own or the classrooms down the hall and asking how students are encouraged to think, solve problems, and express themselves is a good start. Some questions that are helpful to ask of curriculum, instruction, and assessment are the following:

- Are students given the opportunity to make choices that reveal their intellectual proclivities and ways of thinking?
- Are there opportunities for assignments and projects that allow students to pace themselves and make decisions that suit their individual profiles?
- Do the approaches to assessment help both teacher and student to learn about and recognize the full spectrum of the student's intellectual strengths or weaknesses? Do these assessments help teachers teach and learn more effectively in subsequent classes?
- What options and resources are available in the classroom so students can exercise a variety of intelligences?
- What are the teachers' own strengths as learners? Are provisions made for understanding and supporting students whose strengths differ from theirs?

Intelligence is only one aspect of theory and beliefs about teaching and learning that needs to be examined. But it is a crucial aspect and one that is, arguably, at the heart of the educational enterprise. From the first day of school, students bring working minds to class. The educator's job is to create the best possible working environment for those minds.

ACKNOWLEDGMENTS

Project Zero's work on applying MI in the classroom has been supported by generous grants from the William T. Grant Foundation, the Lilly Endowment, the James S. McDonnell Foundation, the Pew Charitable Trusts, Rockefeller Brothers Fund, the Rockefeller Foundation, and the Spencer Foundation. We are grateful to Tina Blythe, Howard Gardner, Sara Hendren, and Mindy Kornhaber, who gave many helpful comments on earlier drafts of this chapter.

REFERENCES

Astington, J. (1993). *The child's discovery of the mind*. Cambridge, MA: Harvard University Press.

Baron, J. B. (1990). Performance assessment: Blurring the edges among assessment, curriculum, and instruction. In A. B. Champagne, B. E. Lovitts, & B. J. Calinger (Eds.), *This year in school science: Assessment in the service of instruction* (pp. 127–148). Washington, DC: American Association for the Advancement of Science.

Blythe, T., & Seidel, S. (1996). *Reflective practice in the classroom*. Malden, MA: Massachusetts Department of Education.

Bronfenbrenner, U. (1979). *The ecology of human development: Experiments by nature and design*. Cambridge, MA: Harvard University Press.

Brown, A. L., Collins, A., & Duguid, P. (1989). Situated cognition and the culture of learning. *Educational Leadership, 18*(1), 32–42.

Campbell, B. (1992). Multiple intelligences in action. *Childhood Education, Summer, 68*(4), 197–201.

Carroll, J. (1993). *Human cognitive abilities: A survey of factor analytic studies*. New York: Cambridge University Press.

Ceci, S. J. (1990). *On intelligence ... more or less: A bio-ecological treatise on intellectual development*. Englewood Cliffs, NJ: Prentice Hall.

Chen, J. (1993, April). *Building on children's strengths: Examination of a Project Spectrum intervention program for students at risk for school failure*. Paper presented at the biennial meeting of the Society for Research in Child Development, New Orleans.

Cohen, D., & Stern, V. (1974). *Observing and recording the behavior of young children*. New York: Teachers College Press.

Comer, J. (1988). Educating poor minority children. *Scientific American, 256*(11), pp. 42–48.

Csikszentmihalyi, M. (1988). Society, culture, and person: A systems view of creativity. In R. J. Sternberg (Ed.), *The nature of creativity* (pp. 325–39). New York: Cambridge University Press.

Damasio, A. (1994). *Descartes' error: Emotion, reason, and the human brain*. New York: Putnam.

Dunn, K., & Dunn, R. (1978). *Teaching students through their individual learning styles: A practical approach*. Reston, VA: Reston Publishers.

Dunn, K., & Dunn, R. (1992). *Teaching elementary students through their individual learning styles: Practical approaches for grades 3–6*. Boston: Allyn & Bacon.

Eysenck, H., & Kamin, L. (1981). *The intelligence controversy: H. J. Eysenck versus Leon Kamin*. New York: Wiley.

Feuerstein, R. (1980). *Instrumental enrichment: An intervention program for cognitive modifiability*. Baltimore, MD: University Park Press.

Frederiksen, J. R., & Collins, A. (1989) A systems approach to educational testing. *Educational Researcher, 18*(9), 27–32.

Gardner, H. (1993). *Frames of mind*. New York: Basic Books. (Original work published 1983).

Gardner, H. (1991). *The unschooled mind*. New York: Basic Books.

Gardner, H. (1993a). Assessment in context: The alternative to standardized testing. In H. Gardner, *Multiple Intelligences: The theory in practice* (pp. 161–183). New York: Basic Books.

Gardner, H. (1993b). "Choice points" as multiple intelligences enter the school. *Intelligence Connections*. 3(1), 1,3, 7, 8.

Gardner, H. (1995). Reflections on multiple intelligences: Myths and messages. *Phi Delta Kappan, November, 77*(3), 200–209.

Gardner, H. (in press). Are there additional intelligences? The case for naturalist, spiritual, and existential intelligences. In J. Kane (Ed.), *Education, information and transformation*. Englewood Cliffs, NJ: Prentice-Hall.

Gardner, H., Krechevsky, M. Sternberg, R. J., & Okagaki, L. (1994). Intelligence in context: Enhancing students' practical intelligence for school. In K. McGilly (Ed.), *Classroom lessons: Integrating cognitive theory and classroom practice* (pp. 105–127). Cambridge, MA: MIT Press.

Greeley, K. (1996a). Making theater, making sense, making change. In D. Udall & A. Mednick (Eds.), *Journey through our classrooms* (pp. 27–52). Dubuque, IA: Kendall/Hunt.

Greeley, K. (1996b). Windows into students' thinking: interweaving curriculum and assessment. In D. Udall & A. Mednick (Eds.), *Journey through our classrooms* (pp. 89–101). Dubuque, IA: Kendall/Hunt.

Gregorc, T. (1985). *Inside styles: beyond the basics*. Maynard, MA: Gabriel Systems.

Guilford, J. P. (1967). *The nature of human intelligence*. New York: McGraw-Hill.

Hecker, L. (1997). Walking, Tinkertoys, and Lego: Using movement and manipulatives to help students write. *English Journal, 86*(6), 46–52.

Herrnstein, R. J., & Murray, C. (1994). *The bell curve: Intelligence and class structure in American life*. New York: Free Press.

Horn, J., & Cattell, R. B. (1996). Refinement and test of the theory of fluid and crystallized general intelligences. *Journal of Educational Psychology, 57*(5), 253–270.

Jensen, A., (1969). How much can we boost IQ and scholastic achievement? *Harvard Educational Review, 39*(1), 1–123.

Jensen, A. (1980). *Bias in mental testing*. New York: Free Press.

Katz, L., & Chard, S. (1989). *Engaging children's minds: The project approach*. Norwood, NJ: Ablex.

Klein, K., & Hecker, L. (1994). The "write" moves: Cultivating kinesthetic and spatial intelligences in the writing process. In A. Brand & R. Graves (Eds.), *Presence of mind: Writing and the domain beyond the cognitive* (pp. 89–98). Portsmouth, NH: Heinnemann-Boynton-Cook.

Kornhaber, M. (1994). *The theory of multiple intelligences: Why and how schools use it*. Qualifying paper, Graduate School of Education, Harvard University, Cambridge, MA.

Kornhaber, M., & Gardner, H. (1993). *Varieties of excellence and conditions for their achievement*. NCREST: Teachers College, Columbia University.

Kornhaber, M., & Hatch, T. (1996). *Advancing intelligent models for schools using the theory of multiple intelligences*. Proposal submitted to the Geraldine R. Dodge Foundation, Morristown, NJ.

Kornhaber, M., & Krechevsky, M. (1995). Expanding definitions of learning and teaching: Notes from the MI underground. In P. Cookson & B. Schneider (Eds.), *Transforming schools* (pp. 181–208). New York: Garland.

Krechevsky, M. (1998). *Project Spectrum: Preschool assessment handbook*. New York: Teachers College Press.

Lave, J. (1988). *Cognition in practice: Mind, mathematics, and culture in everyday life*. New York: Cambridge University Press.

Mann, C. (1996). *Integrating the multiple intelligences theory into classrooms*. Unpublished doctoral dissertation, Nova Southeastern University, Richmond, British Columbia.

McCarthy, B. (1982). *The 4Mat system*. Arlington Heights, IL: Excell.

Mann, C. (1996). *Integrating the multiple intelligences theory into classrooms*. Unpublished doctoral dissertation, Nova Southeastern University, Richmond, British Columbia.

McCarthy, B. (1982). *The 4Mat system*. Arlington Heights, IL: Excell.

Myers, I. B. (1980). *Gifts differing*. Palo Alto, CA: Consulting Psychologists Press.

Pea, R. (1990, April). *Distributed intelligence and education*. Paper presented at the annual meeting of the American Educational Research Association, Boston.

Perkins, D. N. (1993). Person plus. In G. Salomon (Ed.), *Distributed cognitions: Psychological and educational consideration* (pp. 88–110). Cambridge: Cambridge University Press.

Perkins, D. (1995). *Outsmarting IQ: The emerging science of learnable intelligence*. New York: Free Press.

Rauscher, F., Shaw, G. L., & Ky, X. N. (1993, October 14). Music and spatial task performance. *Nature, 365*, 611.

Resnick, L. (1987). Learning in school and out. *Educational Researcher, 16*(9), 13–20.

Resnick, L. (1991). Shared cognition: thinking as social practice. In L. Resnick, J. M. Levine, & D. Teasley (Eds.), *Perspectives on socially shared cognition* (pp.1–20). Washington, DC.: American Psychological Association.

Resnick, L., Briars, D., & Lesgold, S. (1992). Certifying accomplishments in mathematics: The New Standards examining system. In I. Wizup & R. Streit, (Eds.) *Proceedings of the Third University of Chicago Mathematics Project International Conference. Vol. 3., Developments in school mathematics education around the world*. Reston, VA: National Council of Teachers of Mathematics.

Resnick, L. B., Levine, J. M., & Teasley, S. D. (Eds.). (1991). *Perspectives on socially shared cognition*. Washington, DC.: American Psychological Association.

Rogoff, B., & Lave, J. (Eds.). (1984). *Everyday cognition: Its development in social context*. Cambridge, MA: Harvard University Press.

Salomon, G. (Ed.). (1993). *Distributed cognitions: Psychological and educational considerations*. Cambridge, England: Cambridge University Press.

Seidel, S., Veenema, S., Blythe, T., & Almeida, C. (1998) Alligators can't walk on water: Learning through reflective practices in schools [Working Paper]. Cambridge, MA· Project Zero.

Seidel, S., Walters, J., Kirby, E., Olff, N., Powell, K., Scripp, L., & Veenema, S. (1997). *Portfolio practices: Thinking through the assessment of children's work*. Washington, DC.: NEA Publishing Library.

Sizer, T. (1984). *Horace's compromise: The dilemma of the American high school*. Boston: Houghton Mifflin.

Sizer, T. (1992). *Horace's school: Redesigning the American high school*. Boston: Houghton Mifflin.

Spearman, C. (1961). The proof and measurement of association between two things. In J. J. Jenkins & D. G. Patterson (Eds.), *Studies in individual differences: The search for intelligence*. (pp. 59–73). New York: Appleton-Century-Crofts. (Original work published 1904)

Spearman, C. (1927). *The nature of intelligence and principles of cognition*. London: Macmillan.

Steinberg, A. (1997). *Real learning, real work: School-to-work as high school reform*. New York: Routledge.

Sternberg, R. J. (1985). *Beyond IQ: A triarchic theory of human intelligence*. New York: Cambridge University Press.

Sternberg, R. J. (1988). *The triarchic mind: A new theory of human intelligence*. New York: Viking.

Thurstone, L. L. (1938). *Primary mental abilities*. Chicago: University of Chicago Press.

Vernon, P. E. (1950). *The structure of human abilities*. London: Methuen.

Vygotsky, L. S. (1978). *Mind in society: The development of higher psychological processes*. Cambridge, MA: Harvard University Press.

Walters, J., Seidel, S., & Gardner, H. (1994). Children as reflective practitioners: Bringing metacognition to the classroom. In J. Mangieri & C. Collins Block (Eds.), *Creating powerful thinking in teachers and students: Diverse perspectives* (pp. 290–303). Orlando, FL: Holt, Rinehart, & Winston.

Wiggins, G. (1989a). A true test: Toward more authentic and equitable assessment. *Phi Delta Kappan, 70*(9), 703–713.

Wiggins, G. (1989b). Teaching to the (authentic) test. *Educational Leadership, 46*(7), 41–47.

Williams, W., Blythe, T., White, N., Li, J., Sternberg, R. J., & Gardner, H. (1996). *Practical intelligence for school*. New York: Harper Collins.

Winner, E. (Ed.). (1991). *Arts propel: An introductory handbook*. Harvard Project Zero and the Educational Testing Service.

Wolf, D. P. (1989). Portfolio assessment: Sampling student work. *Educational Leadership, 46*(7), 35–39.

Wolf, D. P. (1990). Assessment as an episode of learning. In R. Bennett, & W. Ward, (Eds.), *Construction versus choice in cognitive measurement: Issues in constructed response, performance testing, and portfolio assessment*. Hillsdale, NJ: Lawrence Erlbaum Associates.

CHAPTER 3

Intelligent Schooling

Roger C. Schank

Diana M. Joseph
Northwestern University

You are six years old, and a great lover of animals. For your birthday, you receive a fishtank and a tiny goldfish, the first pet that is entirely your responsibility. You want the little fish to grow, so that you'll know it's healthy. You are certain that small animals need to eat a great deal in order to grow. Therefore, you drop food into the tank several times a day. To your great surprise and disappointment, the fish does not thrive, and in fact it dies before the week is out. You ask your parents what went wrong, and they tell you that fish died because there was too much uneaten food in the water. A few weeks later, you feel ready to care for another fish, and this time, you are very, very careful with the amount of food.

INTELLIGENT SCHOOLING

Is this child intelligent? In one sense, she did not behave very intelligently. After all, many animal-lovers know that overfeeding fish is a bad idea, and this child did not know that. Many people would try to find out as much as possible about caring for fish in advance, and this child did not do that, either. Intelligence, according to this point of view, is a quantity that can be measured and compared with that of other people. It has to do with performance on certain tasks, often some form of objective test. Somehow, this view of intelligence does not seem satisfactory. Think about people you know who have very high IQs and yet do not seem to know how to take care of themselves. Is it fair to say that they are intelligent?

In day-to-day conversations, people often use the word *intelligent* to describe people who seem to learn well or quickly or both and who apply what they have learned when they make choices. By this standard, the child depicted in this passage does seem intelligent. Would it not be wonderful if schools promoted this kind of intelligence?

In this chapter, we do not talk about ways that one person might be more or less intelligent than another. Instead, we talk about how intelligence works. All human memories use certain processes to allow a person to learn from experiences. These processes are the bedrock of human intelligence, and we all have them. The question is this: How can we use this view of intelligence to improve schooling?

In this chapter we describe the theory of human intelligence used at the Institute for the Learning Sciences (ILS), and how it can be used in the classroom. We begin by describing and explaining what happened in the mind of our young fish enthusiast. Based on that process, we suggest some principles for schooling. We will describe *goal-based scenarios*—the approach we and our colleagues at the ILS use to apply the principles for schooling in context. Finally, we provide some examples of how the principles might be used in classrooms for particular subject areas. We hope that after reading this chapter, readers will want to explore the application of these ideas in their own classrooms and see for themselves how they work.

INTELLIGENCE: A MATTER OF MEMORY
AND LEARNING

Fundamentally, there are five issues involved in intelligence: goals, expectations, surprises, mental stories, and explanations. These interact with each other in a constant cycle, resulting in constant reorganization of the memory. This reorganization is what we call learning (Schank, 1982).

Very generally, a learning experience looks like this: You have a certain goal with regard to a particular circumstance in your life. You have certain expectations about that circumstance and about the goal, that is, you expect the world to behave in a certain way, and to respond in a certain way to your actions. Some of these expectations turn out to be wrong in real experience. This mistake, or surprise, gives you a need to figure out what went wrong.

When you figure out what went wrong, you revise your expectations. Just about any learning experience can be thought of this way.

The Fish Experience Explained

Using these terms, we can describe what happened in the mind of the young fish keeper, while learning not to overfeed the fish.

Goal

To start with, as soon as she realized that she owned a fish, the child had a goal: "I want my fish to be healthy." She probably had a lot of other goals too, like "I want to impress my parents," and "I want to learn more about animals," but let us concentrate on the first goal for the sake of the example.

Expectation (Generalization)

At the moment the fish arrived, the child had a lot of general background expectations. For example, she probably expected that "chocolate cake will taste good," and "if I clean my room I will get my allowance." But these particular expectations would not come to mind in relation to her goal of seeing her fish grow.

The goal she had in this particular situation—getting the fish to grow—helped her mind to focus on the specific expectations that could be useful in understanding her situation. These expectations might include these: "Fish swim in water," "pets need to go to the veterinarian once in a while," and "if a small animal eats a great deal of food, it will grow." This is the expectation we will talk about in this example.

Surprise (Expectation Mismatch)

When the child applied her prior expectations to her actions, that is, when she fed the fish a lot of food, it did not grow. In fact, it died. Her experience of losing the fish demonstrated undeniably that something was wrong with her original expectation. Either she had applied it to something that it should not have applied to (perhaps fish are different from other small animals), or she was wrong about the expectation in the first place (perhaps eating and growing have nothing to do with each other—it's just a coincidence that some animals both grow and eat). Either way, there was a mismatch in her mind between her original expectation and what really happened. Her mind demanded an explanation for this mismatch. In other words, she was deeply curious about what had gone wrong.

This is a pretty negative kind of surprise. Some surprises are positive, of course. The little girl might also have learned about feeding fish if she had forgotten to feed hers for a few days, and found to her surprise that it survived just fine. Or, she might have been surprised if the fish grew well even without a lot of food.

Positive and negative surprises are both associated with a lot of emotion, and that emotion probably has something to do with why we feel so strongly compelled to learn and remember based on surprise. This sense of curiosity is a very powerful human drive.

Explanation

The child felt compelled to solve the mystery, both because it was surprising, and because she did not want to make a mistake again. That is, she felt compelled to find an explanation for the mismatch between her original expectation and her actual experience. Her strategy for finding an explanation was to ask her parents. Often, people figure out or invent their own explanations when they are surprised in the way we have described. Sometimes they seek more formal sources, such as books or experts. (Schank, 1986)

Mental Stories and Getting Reminded

The idea of mental stories is probably the most complicated of the five mental issues in learning. However, before we delve into the explanation of mental stories, we give here some background about how our minds create stories based on our experiences. We will get back to the fish example momentarily.

Creating Mental Stories.   What form do our experiences take in our memories? We could not possibly treat every tiny detail of our experience with the same importance. If we tried to do that, we would not be able to draw borders in our minds between one experience and the next. Our memories would consist of one long, muddy streak of impressions—images, sounds, feelings, all mashed together.

When you think about your own memories, you may notice that they generally take the form of narratives (with images) about your experiences. Your own particular goals define what you think is important in an experience and determine the form of the stories your mind creates about that experience.

We learn from stories by creating and revising expectations based on them.

Generalizing From Mental Stories to Create Expectations.   Let us think back for a moment to the child's original expectation—small animals grow if they eat a lot. Where did this expectation come from? It was based on stories already in her mind. Here is one way that the original expectation might have been made:

The child's parents probably told her often that she needed to eat well so that she would be healthy and grow. She might have heard them tell her younger brother the same thing. She might have seen the family dog eat a tremendous amount of food and grow from a tiny puppy into a rather large dog in a fairly short period of time. Her mind sorted these stories together, based on what seemed to be the most important elements, as her parents described them—the goal of getting little things to grow and the approach of giving lots of food. All of those similar stories together allowed her to make a generalization: When small creatures eat a lot of food, they grow, and that is what healthy creatures do.

The links among the stories in our memories form complex structures in our minds that allow us to be reminded of relevant stories when those remindings would be the most useful (Schank, 1982).

Getting Reminded of Older Stories.   Our mental stories keep track of the most important elements of our experiences, based on our particular perspectives. These important elements include our goal(s), the surprises we experienced, and the explanations for them. Perhaps also, depending on the experience and the experiencer, the other people involved, the emotions, important objects, or the outcomes might be included. All of these elements become labels that aid us in being reminded.

For example, when you first read the example at the beginning of this chapter, you might have been reminded of a time when you were responsible for something and you caused a problem through overeagerness, or perhaps of a time when a loved pet died accidentally. That is because when you first had the experience of which you were reminded, your mind created a story, labeled with some elements that turned out to be similar to our description of the little girl's experience with the fish. Those labels might be a similar goal (I want to show how responsible I am) and a similar surprise (I did what I thought was right, but it turned out to be too much), or a similar character (a loved pet), and a similar outcome (accidental death; Schank, 1990).

The Little Girl's Mental Story About the Fish.   Now let us shift back to the little girl's experience and how she might turn it into a story in her mind. The entire complex event, beginning with receiving the fish and ending with its death, had a huge number of elements in it while it was occurring. In the moment, the child was aware of everything from the weight of the food in the shaker to the daily change in color of the water, the sound of the filter bubbling, perhaps to the voice of her parents calling her to her own dinner, her dreams about the fish. But most of these elements might not seem to her to have much to do with the goal of making the fish healthy. It would not be efficient for her mind to keep track of all of those details in the long term. Instead, her mind might use the goal (getting the fish to grow) and the prior expectation (food leads to growth) to determine which parts of the experience would be built into the story.

The child's new story might look something like this: "I wanted the fish to grow and be healthy (goal), so I gave it a lot of food (action based on expectation). But it wasn't healthy; instead it died (surprise). The reason was that fish need to have clean water more than they need a lot of food (explanation)."[1] This story would be linked with the others based on the same labels. But the presence of those stories requires a revision of the original expectation. The new expectation might be something like: animals need food, but they also need a clean living space.

This expectation is probably incomplete, too, but she will need to have more experiences in order to enrich the expectation and focus it accurately on the right kinds of situations.

Reorganization (Learning)

To summarize the example, the child had expectations based on old stories with similar goals, similar actions, and similar outcomes. These stories resulted in a generalization, or expectation, about the relationship between small animals and food. The fish's death became a new story that was sorted together with the old ones because of the similar goal and the similar action. But because the fish's death was a surprise, the child had to find out why. She used the story about this experience to reconstruct her expectation to better suit the reality of her experience. She will remember this new expectation well, both because of the surprise involved, and because she maintains the goal of wanting her fish to thrive. Altogether, she learned a memorable lesson.

In other words, the five factors—goals, expectations, stories, surprises, and explanations—interact continually to result in learning. Learning takes place in the reorganization of stories and expectations based on personal goals, through the action of surprise and the search for explanations.

PRINCIPLES FOR INTELLIGENT INSTRUCTION

School has to tap into the process of learning in a sensible way. That means that students need cognitively appropriate goals and experiences that tie those goals together with the expectations school is intended to build. They also need to be surprised—to have their curiosity piqued. And they need access to good explanations. Finally, they need to have the opportunity to

---

[1]The story probably does not take this linear form in the child's memory most of the time, although she can recall it that way when she needs to. Probably it is more like a series of connected images. The exact form is not important for understanding how stories interact with the other elements in intelligence.

think about and reflect on their experiences, to give their minds the time and space to reorganize.

We can derive six rules of thumb from the five elements in the theory of learning discussed here:

1. Center learning around cognitively appropriate *goals* the students have
2. Choose learning objectives based on important and sensible *expectations* (including background knowledge, generalizations and skills) that students should acquire
3. Pique the students' curiosity (*surprise* them)
4. Provide access to *explanations* exactly when the students need them
5. Provide experiences that relate the goals to the learning objectives, so that students will build useful *stories*
6. Provide opportunities for reflection, so that students have time and space to *reorganize* their memories.

Center Learning Around Cognitively Appropriate Goals

The school system expects students to believe in and be motivated by goals such as test scores, grade level requirements, college entrance, and acquisition of adult work skills. These are all very long-term goals. We all know how difficult it is to delay gratification, and yet we seem to expect young people to manage it better than adults do. We tend to do our best learning when we have goals that are directly and immediately related to the work we are doing. The little girl in our example learned because her experiences were directly related to her immediate goal, not because she was expecting a future reward.

Like it or not, these long-term goals are not the most important ones that young people have on their minds. This mismatch of goals is a serious problem in education. Unmotivated students will be unwilling to work or to concentrate, let alone stay in school. The public high schools in Chicago have a graduation rate of less than 50%. Perhaps part of the reason is that the schools are not helping some students achieve goals they care about. We believe students must be motivated in order to learn, either in school or not.

Getting students to attend school is important, but it is not enough. If we expect young people to learn skills and background expectations they can use in their regular lives, we must base their work in goals that fit the cognitive bill—goals that are sensible to the students, so that they can fit the stories built through those goals into the complex webbing of stories they have in memory. Stories built for the purpose of goals about which students do not care will be left unconnected and unrecallable.

What kinds of mental stories do students who care about grades build? Remember that they label the goal, the outcome, the surprise, and not much else, and that those labels determine whether and when they can be reminded of the story. A story about a grade-centered social studies lesson might be something like "I wanted an A; I was quiet in class; I learned a list of terms long enough to recite them when I was called on; I got an A for the day." If, on the other hand, the goal was to win the Lincoln–Douglas debate, her story might be much richer and more complex. "I wanted to beat Douglas; I needed to find out what Lincoln and Douglas really disagreed on and what their supporters thought; I looked up the original debate to find out what Lincoln really said; I added a modern tone to it," and so on. Participating in such a debate would be an unforgettable experience. The story the student would create out of the debating experience would be far more useful in her future life than a story about preparing for an exam.

The long-term, reward-and-punishment goals that are so important in the structure of the schools (grades, test scores, etc.) create a strange mental context for creating stories. In these stories, skills and knowledge are not used for a meaningful, experience-based purpose—they are used only to acquire rewards or avoid punishments. Stories like this have labels that are unlikely to be activated again, no matter how good the grade was in the original experience. Students who do not care about or feel competent to acquire rewards such as grades tend to simply accept poor performance in school.

In a cognitively sound learning environment, goals are based in things students care about in both the short-term and the long term. Designing and operating such learning environments requires understanding what different goals students really have, based on their interests, and then creating experiences for them that allow them to learn in the context of those interests. This is no simple task, but it is not impossible. Later in the chapter we suggest ways of designing intelligent learning environments of this kind, even given the difficult circumstances in many schools.

It is very difficult for teachers to begin to focus on students' real goals rather than grades. Everyone involved—students, parents, teachers, administrators—is used to the grade-based way of doing things. Perhaps eventually we can make a change. In the meantime, this principle may help you add to student-centered goals in your classroom in addition to grading.

Learning Objectives Should Center Around Building and Revising Expectations (Including Background Knowledge and Skills)

What kinds of learning objectives do you have for your students? The standardized tests your students are required to take may lead you to focus on a few very specific skills (reading, arithmetic) and a lot of quite specific facts (learning that George Washington was the first president, for example). We will talk about fact-centered learning later in this chapter. Here, we recommend that schools focus on learning skills. We recommend that schools take into account the expectations (including skills) that students enter with and focus on revising those expectations and forming new ones.

Skills Are Small-Scale Expectations.   We should explain first that in the terms of the theory we discuss in this chapter, skills are a form of expectation. That may seem far-fetched at first, but let us explain further. Let us think of a very simple skill, like tying shoes. How did you learn to tie your shoes? Chances are, someone showed you, and then you tried to tie them, over and over again, creating a little mental story out of each attempt. You formed little expectations—"if I move the end of the string like this, the shoe will be tied." The expectations failed to match the reality some of the time—"Well, the shoe isn't tied when I moved the string in what I thought was the right way, so I guess I was wrong." You sought explanations for the mismatch—"Maybe I did the steps in the wrong order," and ultimately, you got explanations or stories from someone else. Finally, after cycling through the usual mental processes, over and over again, you ended up with a collection of successful shoe-tying stories, and a correct generalization (expectation) about how to tie a shoe. So a skill is a kind of expectation, in a sense. Skills work the same way expectations do, so we can treat them similarly from the standpoint of intelligence and learning.[2] (Schank & Cleary, 1995).

The skills people learn in school, such as reading or doing multiplication or doing research, work exactly the same way as tying shoes—you make many attempts (forming and sorting mental stories), and they do not work out the way you thought they would (surprise). You try to figure out what went wrong and somebody helps you (searching for explanation), and finally, you start to get it right most of the time. You build your generalization about how to do the skill so that it fits the needs of real experience.

Take Prior Expectations Into Account.   All people have their own unique sets of background knowledge and skills developed over their lifetimes. If that is the case, then every student in school has a different set of expectations and will react differently to forms of content, instruction, social interactions, and so on. To the extent possible, educators need to take students' backgrounds into account. What kinds of skills, habits, and

---

[2]Of course, there is a physical skill involved also. This theory does not address the physical side of skills, but its stands to reason that the kind of practice involved in creating the mental skill would also result in improved physical skill.

background expectations do your students have? If your students are fairly similar in terms of these kinds of expectations, you may have an opportunity to use that similarity to make the content or the structure of school more effective for your students.

Choose Skill-Based Learning Objectives. Learning objectives should be based on the skills, strategies, and knowledge students use in their lives now and are likely to use in their lives later. Education can go far beyond the three *R*s.

Learning objectives can include, for example, the following:

- Communication: discussion, speaking, listening, debate, conflict resolution, reading, writing.
- Leadership: critiquing, persuasion, personal responsibility, followership, collaboration, mentoring.
- Problem solving: brainstorming, problem selection, planning, follow-through, reflection, research.
- Resource management: budgeting, scheduling, delegating, research, arithmetic.
- Technology: media production/comprehension, computer literacy.

This sounds like a very long list, and indeed it is. Remember that we are talking about a lifetime of learning—this list is not something that one teacher has to cover for every student. We simply raise the idea that all of these skills are suitable for education, because they are difficult and because students will need them in their future lives.

Pique the Students' Curiosity (Surprise Them)

For a memory to sort a new story or skill into a useful place in the structure of the mind, the learner needs to have a question or an expectation mismatch that incites his or her memory to do the kind of reorganization we describe. That is, the learner needs to be curious about something. The trick in education is to answer students' own curiosity whenever possible. Teachers also need to get students to be curious about the answers we want them to hear.

There are a couple of different ways to focus student curiosity usefully. One is to set the learning in as real a context as possible, so students run up against the complexity of reality. Such a situation almost has to result in curiosity that is related to that situation. For example, if students take on a task such as organizing a picnic (for younger students) or running a small business (for older students), real life is bound to surprise them with unexpected logistical challenges. If the teacher wants them to learn to cope with unexpected logistical challenges, these projects are wonderful for inciting the right kind of curiosity.

Another possibility is to arrange to surprise students about something in particular. For example, science teachers often arrange to do experiments whose results run against expectations generated by ordinary experience.

Not all surprises need to be as dramatic as the ones we discuss here. An error is a perfectly useful surprise, as long as the student recognizes it as an error. Sometimes students need feedback in order to understand the real nature of an expectation mismatch. For example, a beginning reader might simply ignore a misread word unless a more adept reader points out the error. In other words, a student might need support to understand when a surprise has happened.

Provide Access to Explanations Exactly When the Students Need Them

Once you pique your students' curiosity, it is crucial for them to have a variety of relevant information sources at their command. Having students memorize a single answer to a question *dampens* their curiosity. Students need to develop the habit of questioning the explanations they get. That is, they need to try out multiple possible reorganizations when they learn something, so their mental structures become as flexible as possible. If we try to get them to accept pat answers, they may end up with rigid mental structures that cannot respond well to surprise.

Experts are important sources of explanations. Expert stories are preferable to reference texts, precisely because they take the form of stories. Although experts' stories are second-hand sources, our minds are primed to use and remember them in a way that they are not primed to use and remember isolated information.

In addition to providing valuable explanations, experts can also help to arrange learning environments in ways that accurately portray their real-life work. In other words, they can create settings that are likely to inspire students to develop rich and accurate expectations about a particular field.

Provide Experiences That Relate the Goals to the Learning Objectives, so That Students Build Useful Stories

We have already seen three reasons for using realistic work to center student learning—to develop realistic expectations, to create useful expectation mismatches, and to tie learning to realistic goals. A fourth reason is that we want children to build stories that are related to real life, so that those stories become accessible when similar things happen to them in the future.

All learning, according to this theory of intelligence, is learning by doing—by creating, sorting, and generalizing from stories about real experience. That means the experiences students have in school determine what they learn. If their experiences have to do with preparing for a test, they learn to prepare for a test. If their experiences have to do with choosing strategies for solving complex life problems, than that is what they learn.

Educators need to arrange learning environments so that goals students genuinely believe in and care about provide a focus for learning skills and knowledge we want them to have. This means we need to develop experiences for them in which the path to an interesting goal is through learning a new skill or generalization.

Provide Opportunities for Reflection, so Students Have Time and Space to Reorganize Their Memories.

It stands to reason that students need to be able to think about what they learn. They also need feedback on their work in order to confirm the explanations they come up with and do the kind of reorganization about which we have been talking.

Reflection can be supported through writing about, making art about, or discussing experiences with peers and teachers. It is important also that students have time to learn—deadlines can be useful for motivation, but they can also mean that students have wonderful experiences in a setting that is so intense that they learn less than they should.

INTEGRATING THE PRINCIPLES

Ideally, all learning environments would address these principles in an integrated fashion. The centerpiece of such an integrated environment is learning by doing. Whenever possible, we should try to make the goals, the learning objectives and the experiences students have in school meaningful and connected with real life. We want to describe now the learning environments we have been building at ILS, based on the principles we have been discussing.

Goal-Based Scenarios (GBSs)—The Principles In Practice

The ILS is engaged primarily in building goal-based scenarios (GBSs)—learning environments based on the principles we have been discussing. GBSs always have a goal, some learning objectives, and a realistic task that allows the student to reach the goal through working with the learning objectives. The structure of a GBS provides a *cover story*—a real or imaginary (but realistic) setting for the task—and a *mission* that describes the task (including the work with the learning objectives) in detail. Often, the student has a special *role* that, in the context of the mission, helps the student to focus on particular learning objectives (Schank, Fano, Jona, & Bell, 1993).

Let's look at how GBSs use the principles described above to create cognitively sound learning environments.

Goals

The students' goal in a GBS is carefully selected to be something students genuinely want to do—write a rap lyric, make a video, raise fish. It can be something imaginary that they would want to do if they could—advise the President, for example. Students also have learning goals that can be used as primary goals in GBSs. For example, some students may be curious about fire fighting. Currently, ILS has GBSs with all of the above goals—except for the one about fish. But there's nothing to stop a GBS designer from using that one.

Expectations

The expectation-based learning objectives in a GBS can be just about anything that seems important for students to learn. Some of the GBSs at ILS teach reading, fire safety, evidence-based reasoning, and conflict resolution.

Stories, and Learning By Doing

GBSs use the *cover stories* and *missions* to create a learning-by-doing situation. The student must do something that relates both to real goals the student has and to important learning objectives. The following examples come from programs built by our colleagues at ILS.

In Broadcast News, the students' goal is to make a news video starring themselves. The learning objectives involve habits of writing and media literacy. The *cover story* is that the students are working at a news studio.

The *mission* is to edit some prepared news copy and then shoot a video based on that copy. This mission brings together a goal students genuinely enjoy and a task that genuinely requires work on desired skills. The Broadcast News software provides feedback on writing and ideally would provide feedback on the video production as well (Kass, Dooley& Luksa, 1993).

Learners in GBSs can be given roles that give them even more specific focus on particular learning objectives. In Broadcast News, for example, the same student plays two different roles—editor and reporter. Students might be asked to focus on only one of these roles if their weaknesses were concentrated in that area. Note that roles can be used to allow students to work on weaknesses or strengths, as the particular students needs dictate.

The experiences students have in GBSs create rich mental stories in which feedback is embedded. The lessons learned are recallable and applicable in a way that experiences that are less contextualized are not.

Surprise

GBSs pique student curiosity by arranging opportunities for the student to make mistakes. Students quite naturally make mistakes in exactly the places where they are most likely to need help. GBS designers anticipate these moments and arrange to support them. For example, young readers often misread a word that begins with the same letter as another familiar word. Say Say Oh Playmate has a mission (writing the lyrics to a familiar clapping game) that allows young students to make this kind of mistake. The program responds with immediate feedback and eventually provides a solution to the error if the student is unable to discover a solution alone (Pinkard, 1998).

Explanations

A common way that GBSs provide explanations is through expert stories. Software GBS designers collect videotaped stories about work and working difficulties from experts in the field of the particular GBS mission. These stories provide explanations in the form of second-person experiences, in the same way that another child might learn something from hearing our example about the little girl who lost her fish.

Fire Commander, designed for elementary grade students, provides explanations in the form of videotaped stories from real fire fighters, based on real events. The student's mission in Fire Commander is to direct a team of firefighters in putting out a house fire. The events in the simulated house fire are also based on fire-fighters' knowledge and experience. This mission is quite difficult, and expert stories are a great help. Whenever students make a mistake, or whenever they need help, explanations are available (Towle, 1998).

Reflection

Advise the President, a GBS built for high school students, is intended to teach evidence-based reasoning skills through a mission in which students seek out evidence to support their advice in a touchy diplomatic situation. Students collect their evidence in a notebook to which they can return at any time. This notebook provides one form of support for reflection. The report the learner submits to the "President" at the end of the interaction provides another form of support (Korcuska, Herman, & Jona, 1996).

Passion Curricula—Live GBSs in K–12 Schooling

All of the GBS examples so far have been about software GBSs. Recently, we have begun to build school-based GBSs that embody the same principles. Interest-based GBSs for K–12 education, called Passion Curricula, are designed to capture the importance of student interest as the defining characteristic in these curricula. Ultimately, we hope to create a design framework that educators can use to create interest-centered curricula.

We implemented the first ILS passion curriculum, the Video Project, in a fifth-grade urban public school classroom. Following are details about this project and its design, which give a sense of how these principles might operate in the K–12 classroom (Joseph, 1998).

In the Video Project, 35 students in teams of 5 to 10 created talk shows, music videos, sitcoms, "live" sports coverage, and a variety of other pieces. In the process of making these videos, they worked on skills such as planning, conflict resolution, writing, media literacy, and media production. At the end of the project, each student received a copy of a variety-show video edited from footage shot by the class and edited by the teachers.

Goal. The goal of the video project was one we were quite certain would be appealing to youngsters—making videos. Another approach to building a passion curriculum would be to interview students to elicit their deep interests and create a custom curriculum for those students who had a common interest. The problem with this approach, however, is that it would not be sustainable. It would be all but impossible to get the resources together to create an infrastructure that required a separate curriculum for every few students. Instead we compromised by choosing a theme in which most students seem to be quite interested.

Expectations. The video project addressed planning, reflection, personal responsibility, conflict resolution, and writing as target skills.

Passion curricula are intended to take background expectations into account by creating communities of common interest. Although students may have vastly different experiences, they can be guided to forming some similar expectations through the work they all genuinely want to do.

Stories And Learning By Doing

The video project used several different structures to define the mission in a way that would keep students focused. In particular, some tasks were created simply by determining the social arrangements, some were defined by worksheets, and some were defined by student roles.

Guiding the Task With Social Arrangements.   The video project's mission, making a video, included a number of different tasks. Some of the tasks had to do with the structure of the work—for example, we created a context for working on conflict resolution simply by asking students to work in groups. The reality of working in groups led naturally to conflict, which students could then work on resolving.

Guiding the Task With Artifacts   Other tasks were organized via worksheets—one worksheet listed all the steps students were expected to go through (brainstorm ideas; plan the beginning, middle and end of the video; make a storyboard; shoot a practice video; watch and critique the practice video; shoot a final video). Other worksheets provided guidance for each step. For example, one worksheet was a table for keeping track of shots in the practice video.

In the next version of the video project, every task will have a guiding worksheet associated with it. The video critique worksheet, for example, will list questions based on issues the students jointly deem important for thinking about videos. The worksheets leave the teacher free to focus on teaching individual students or answering surprises as they come up, rather than guiding activities from moment to moment.[3]

Guiding the Task With Roles.   Students in the video project chose specific roles—conflict arbitrator, camera director, script writer, props and costumes director, or performance director. In future passion curricula, rather than having students choose their own roles (at least at this age), we will assign roles so that each student works in an area in which they have strength and in an area in which they are challenged.

Surprises.   In the video project, surprises generally arose through real experience. In addition to the conflict resolution issues just described, students commonly learned to use the video equipment especially well because of the mistakes they made—it only takes one ruined video to help students remember that they need to check the sound before they begin to shoot, for instance.

---

[3]No doubt this kind of guidance will be necessary some of the time, especially at the beginning of a project.

Explanations.   Due to resource constraints, explanations in the video project were provided mainly by the teacher, with guidance from outside experts. In future versions, expert video-makers will participate in the project on a weekly basis. In addition to providing help to the students, they will also model video-making by creating a documentary of the video project experience.

Teaching.   Because there is no lecture component to a GBS, teachers can spend their time focusing on individual student needs. Ideally, the teacher tracks the level of each student's ability on each planned learning objective. Then, each student is directed toward work that focuses on his or her particular needs, either through an appropriate role or through spontaneous opportunities. Grasping spontaneous opportunities for teaching a skill is a subtle art. Such opportunities depend on the students involved and the particulars of their work in a given moment.

The teacher in the video project had many opportunities to work with particular students on particular needs. For example, one group of students developed a script that required a narrator and asked the teacher to narrate. The teacher was able to ask honest questions about the clarity of the script that raised issues about spelling and standard English grammar. The students *had* to learn these lessons in order to produce a video that would be satisfactory to themselves.

BRINGING THE PRINCIPLES INTO THE TRADITIONAL CLASSROOM

We now discuss what bringing these ideas into classrooms might be like. The theoretical ideas about intelligence and the principles described here are intended to help classrooms to better suit the way people learn, with or without a shift to fully GBS-based curricula.

Before we talk about teaching particular subjects, we caution a bit against fact-based learning. Most schools are used to a way of teaching that emphasizes many facts and few skills. We begin by talking about facts and how they have traditionally been addressed in classrooms and then about what classrooms might look like if they took the principles of intelligence we have described into account.

Fact-Centered Education

Facts are a very hot topic these days. School has always had a lot to do with getting students to collect a lot of facts in their minds, and lately, writers such as Hirsch (1988) have been pushing fact-based learning even more to the forefront of thinking about education.

Our position is that the time for schooling based on fact-based learning has passed. Once it made sense to define an educated person as one who had read every good book in the world—that was during the centuries when there were only a few, or a few hundred, books available. But now, the world is changing at breakneck speed. How can we possibly predict which facts will be useful in adulthood for people who are in high school now, let alone elementary school?

Students will inevitably learn and remember exactly and only those facts that are relevant to them. Think about, for example, your high school biology class. How many facts do you remember from that class? Could you pass the exam if you had to take it now? Most people have little or no recollection of these kinds of details memorized years ago. The point is, we human beings are simply not very good at remembering facts except when we use them in a context that is meaningful to us.

What would a meaningful context look like? Well, Roger, for example, knows a lot of facts about football, because he cares about football, and he needs those facts when he plays or talks about it. Diana knows a lot of facts about music, because she cares about music, and she needs those facts when she talks about or plays music. Neither of us has ever needed to sit down and memorize these facts. They enter our minds as part of the stories we collect in our minds during our work within our interests, in the same way that the little girl learned the fact that fish die from polluted water. There is no need to do any special work to learn facts separately from the experiences of which they are a part.

Let us think about facts learned in school for a moment. Most of us were asked to memorize the state capitals a long time ago, and no doubt, memorized them without too much trouble. Few of us can remember very many of them now, except when they are cities we have visited. The information is there somewhere, tied to a mental story about sitting in school memorizing things. That story does not have many interesting labels on it, so it is not often recalled. Some adults who were particularly driven to memorize the information may have spent so much time going over and over the list that they can still recall it in exactly the order they memorized it. Their recall of the information, however, might be strange. They might have to go through the entire list in order to find any particular capital. Their only mental story about the capitals contains the entire list in order, rather than each city tied to a context. On the other hand, people who have been to state capitals can remember them well and when they need them, because the names are a part of experiential stories that are richly labeled and therefore easily recalled.

The bottom line is, we did not really need to know all of the capitals in order, and we do not need to know them now. If we suddenly do need to know a particular capital that we cannot remember, it is quite easy to look it up. So why were we asked to memorize them? Because somebody decided a long time ago that all American children need to memorize this set of facts. Perhaps the reason was that it seemed like people need to understand the idea of state capitals—what they are and what purpose they serve. But that is not the same thing as knowing the names.

We are not arguing that students do not need to know anything—we are arguing that they do not all need to know the same things, and above all, we are arguing that school does not need to emphasize fact learning. Instead, it should emphasize learning sensible expectations and generalizations.

It could be argued that there are some facts that everyone needs to know, for example, the name of the President, or of a local lawmaker. But these facts, like all others, are better learned in context than via memorization. *Why* would someone want students to know the President's name? Probably for a reason that has to do with something other than the name itself, such as so that the students do not sound foolish during conversations, or because they need to know the President's name in order to participate in elections. Why not teach these skills by providing support for students to participate in the processes of intelligent conversation about democracy rather than asking students to memorize names out of context? Actively working on these skills will lead to the formation of sensible stories and skills, with the names conveniently contained within those easily recallable, and therefore useful, stories (Schank & Cleary, 1995).

Intelligent Classrooms

Think back to the six principles once again:

1. Center learning around cognitively appropriate goals the students have
2. Choose learning objectives based on important and sensible expectations (including background knowledge, generalizations and skills) that students should acquire
3. Pique the students' curiosity (surprise them)
4. Provide access to explanations exactly when the students need them
5. Provide experiences that relate the goals to the learning objectives, so that students will build useful stories
6. Provide opportunities for reflection, so that students have time and space to reorganize their memories.

Any of these principles can be applied to any classroom for a cognitive benefit to the students. You may already be using some of these principles in your classroom, whether you have thought about them this way or not.

Although you may not be able to select learning objectives because of mandated requirements, you may be able to think of ways to pique the students' curiosity about those learning objectives. Although it may be impossible to provide multiple, interesting, story-based explanations, you may nevertheless be able to use your students' goals to determine the content of the work you do. We talk about a few school subjects here. The issues addressed under one subject may be applicable to others that are listed here, and others that are not listed here.

English.   The teaching of English in schools is a good place to see students learning by doing. That is, they learn to write by writing and getting feedback. This element could be made even stronger by making sure that the writing was set in a meaningful context. For example, students might adapt a novel for performance, publish a book, or write a script for a television show. Any of these activities would help the work to fit in with the mental structures students already have in place.

If it is impossible to create a real context for the work students do in English class, student interests can still be brought into the work. Allowing students to choose what they read, and what they write about, can be tremendously helpful in ensuring that the goals of the work are cognitively appropriate.

Mathematics.   Mathematics courses, by their nature, have to include a great deal of practice. This practice could be motivated very well by providing a context for the work. Some math courses do at least some contextualizing, but others we have observed seem to emphasize memorization of the algorithms students need to learn, to the detriment of providing a sense of real-life usage for those algorithms. Could this be a cause of widespread math phobia? It is very difficult for people to understand mathematical exercises that do not have an obvious purpose.

Children might very well take a real or imaginary trip to the grocery store in preparation for, say, a class picnic, and find a way to make a small budget stretch a long way. This project would require students to learn about resource management, as well as estimation and arithmetic skills. High school students might take an architecture course that required and taught complex mathematical understanding. At the very least, either an elementary or high school math course might include small projects that contextualize the particular mathematical issues.

Science.   Science teaching is a good example of an arena in which many teachers consistently set up surprising moments through demonstrations. One problem with some science classes is that they do not allow these surprises to arise naturally. When experiments are a part of the course, the "experiments" tend to be like workbook exercises—a series of prescribed steps leading to a pat outcome. You might say that they are an attempt to *keep* students from being surprised.

Instead, students should be allowed to work through any mismatch between the expected result and the actual outcome. This requires tremendous expertise on the part of the teacher, because he or she needs to be able to respond expertly to *any* mismatch, not just the one in the prepared lesson. The best learning sometimes takes place when the teacher does not know what went wrong. This is an opportunity for the teacher to model his or her own approach to untangling a mystery.

Social Studies. Social studies teaching, like some science teaching, tends to be based in lecture and textbook work and tends to be fact-centered. Some of these conditions may be unavoidable. Adding events like role playing, debates, and public presentations can reset student work to more cognitively appropriate goals. Another strategy would be to allow students to select their own content for required projects.

Social studies provides many opportunities for piquing student curiosity. For example, an invited presentation and question and answer session by a Native American activist might be an excellent introduction to or culmination of an elementary social studies unit on Native Americans.

A FEW WORDS ABOUT ASSESSMENT

We have not yet addressed the question of assessment. The most common school assessment, the standardized test, is completely incompatible with the kind of intelligent instruction we discuss here. It creates cognitively poor goals for learning. In comparing students to each other, it denies the significance of students' differing background knowledge and skills. The mental stories students create about their experiences with objective tests are at best dull, at worst traumatic, and almost certainly not useful in later life. In short, standardized tests are a root cause of schools *not* taking the processes of human intelligence into account.

We do, of course, need a way to understand how students are doing with regard to the things we want them to learn. A number of researchers are working to develop performance- and portfolio-based assessment forms. Adoption of these assessments requires very different ways of thinking about schools.

You may be able to develop some form of performance or portfolio assessment in your own classroom. If you must use tests, use them to discover what kind of challenges each student needs, rather than to compare students with each other. You can use the information you get from tests to understand each students' needs, and challenge them appropriately, without stigmatizing them. Consider grading on the basis of improvement, rather than, or in addition to, ability level. Consider providing feedback in the form of nonpunitive comments rather than grades. Consider providing feedback in the form of real consequences—for example, if students are planning a class picnic, the success or failure of the event is its own best feedback, especially when the students can see how their work plays into the entire project.

CONCLUSION

In this chapter, we have described a view of intelligence, and suggested six principles for education based on that view. We have talked about our methods for implementing these principles in an integrated way in goal-based scenarios for software and for live learning environments. And we have suggested some ways of using these ideas in your own classrooms.

If we have a short take-home message it is this: Wherever possible, strengthen the cognitive soundness of your classrooms by providing interesting, contextualized work, focused on each student's strengths and weaknesses. Given your real circumstances, you have developed techniques that are highly effective. Many of these techniques can remain effective even while making content and context more cognitively appropriate. This approach may or may not affect test scores, but it will certainly affect your students' life skills in a positive way.

We have tried to make this chapter embody the educational ideas it contains, as much as possible—we used a realistic situation (the fish story) to tie together all the ideas in a sensible way, we tried to surprise you with some of our views, we offered explanations and expert stories, and we asked reflective questions. A book chapter is not a very good way of doing this kind of educational work because we can only encourage you to do things; we cannot create an environment in which you do them. As teachers, however, you have the ability to take hold of any ideas that intrigue you and try them out in your own learning and in the learning environments you direct.

REFERENCES

Hirsch, E, D., Jr. (1988). *Cultural History: What Every American needs to know.* New York: Vintage Books.

Joseph, D. M. (1998) *Passion as a driver for learning: Formative evaluation of a curriculum design framework*. Poster presentation as part of the session "Analysis of Learning and Instruction," AERA annual meeting. San Diego, CA.

Kass, A., Dooley, S., Luksa, F. (1993) *The Broadcast News Project: Using broadcast journalism as a vehicle for teaching social studies* (Tech. Rep. No. 40). Evanston, IL: Northwestern University, The Institute for the Learning Sciences.

Korcuska, M., Herman, J., Jona, M. (1996) Evidence-based reporting [Short paper], Boston, MA: Ed-Media.

Pinkard, N. (1998). Leveraging background knowledge: Using popular music to build children's beginning reading skills. Doctoral dissertation in progress, Northwestern University, Evanston, IL.

Schank, R. C. (1982). *Dynamic memory: A theory of reminding and learning in computers and people*. Cambridge, England: Cambridge University Press.

Schank, R. C. (1986). *Explanation patterns*. Hillsdale, NJ: Lawrence Erlbaum Associates.

Schank, R. C. (1990). *Tell me a story: A new look at real and artificial memory*. New York, NY: Scribner's.

Schank, R. C., & Cleary, C. (1995). *Engines for education*. Hillsdale, NJ: Lawrence Erlbaum Associates.

Schank, R. C., Fano, A., Jona, M., & Bell, B. (1993). *The design of goal-based scenarios* (Tech. Rep. No. 39). Evanston, IL: Northwestern University, The Institute for the Learning Sciences.

Towle, B. T. (1998). Reusable architectures for complex educational simulations. Doctoral dissertation in progress, Northwestern University, Evanston, IL.

CHAPTER 4

Learnable Intelligence
and Intelligent Learning

Heidi Goodrich Andrade

David N. Perkins
Harvard Graduate School of Education

To those who believe that intelligence is a fixed, inborn trait, the term *learnable intelligence* is an oxymoron: One either is born with brains or not, and any attempt to alter the unalterable is futile at best, maybe even cruel. Recent research, however, suggests that human intelligence is not simply a matter of gray matter but also a matter of what is put in it and how it is used (e.g., Baron, 1985; Chipman, Segal, & Glaser, 1985; Nickerson, Perkins, & Smith, 1985; Perkins, 1995; Segal, Chipman, & Glaser, 1985; Sternberg, 1985). This chapter presents an analysis of intelligence that acknowledges not only one's neuronal makeup but also the role of experience and thinking patterns. This analysis argues that a significant portion of human intelligence is, in fact, learnable.

The conception of intelligence presented here is less concerned with standard measures of IQ than with the practical side of intelligence—the kind that allows people to learn better, to perform their jobs better, to live better. As applied to school-based teaching and learning, the research on learnable intelligence permits two relatively bold claims:

1. Students can be taught to behave more intelligently.
2. Teaching for intelligence can lead to improvements in academic achievement.

Educators tend to find this more generous take on intelligence appealing. After all, what teacher would not like to help his or her students behave more intelligently and do better in school? A common and understandable concern, however, springs from the fact that many teachers need to cover content, leaving little time for much else. Happily, teaching for intelligence and covering a curriculum need not be conflicting endeavors. Imagine, for example, the following scenario: A class full of students is bent over first drafts of persuasive essays in which they argue for or against a rule requiring school uniforms. In preparation for this draft they have interviewed other students, teachers, parents, and administrators in order to uncover all of the relevant issues and familiarize themselves with the arguments on either side of the case. On each student's desk is a scoring rubric that lists the criteria for the essays as well as descriptions of levels of quality for each criterion, from *excellent* to *poor*. The criteria on the rubric address the full spectrum of characteristics the teacher expects in a good essay, including organization, details, voice, mechanics, and reasoning. The reasoning criterion requires students to provide a clear and accurate treatment of the evidence in support of their claim as well as a careful discussion of evidence that potentially weakens their claim and why it does not completely undermine it.

The students are in the process of assessing their own work on the essay. They have done this kind of self-assessment many times by now, so they know that when they are done they should begin to revise their drafts to build on the strengths and eliminate the weaknesses they just identified. They are surprisingly willing to revise, perhaps in part because the rubric provides clear direction for improvement. Several students ask the teacher for advice on how to resolve a particular problem with their work. The teacher also checks the work of the one student who consistently overestimates his progress. The other students, she knows from experience, tend to evaluate their work more severely than she does, so she just lets them work.

This is a relatively ordinary scenario, one that can be played out in virtually any classroom, and the results can include increases in students' abilities to think and act intelligently (Claim 1) and in the quality of student work (Claim 2). Let us take these claims one at a time. Concerning the first claim, a recent study showed that self-assessment can prompt some students to be more metacognitive as they work (Goodrich, 1996a). Being metacognitive means being aware of and controlling one's own thinking in order to think and learn better. For instance, asking yourself if you are paying attention as you read this chapter or if you are trying to relate what you read to your own teaching practice are both metacognitive acts, because they have to do with how well you are thinking right now. Metacognition is a central aspect of learnable intelligence. Research shows repeatedly that students who monitor and regulate their own thinking tend to be better at solving problems, writing, reading, even playing games (Brown, 1978; Flavell, 1987). The study on student self-assessment shows that many students who were asked to assess their own work were significantly more metacognitive than students who did not do so.

The second claim applied in this case says that having students assess their own work and revise it before handing it in to the teacher improves the quality of their work. Such a claim is based on anecdotal evidence collected over several years of working with hundreds of teachers who consistently report that giving students an opportunity to assess their own work according to clearly articulated criteria (a key component of student self-assessment) results in a high level of quality they have never before seen. We recently began a research project that tests this claim formally.

This introductory example provides just one window on the diverse and challenging world of bringing together teaching for intelligence and teaching the subject matters. In the pages to come, we present our particular take on that world, based on more than a decade of experience in developing programs and working with a wide range of teachers and students at ages from kindergarten through college. The next section presents a theory of intelligence that makes a place not only for the raw intelligence human beings are born with but also for the kinds of intelligence that can be and have been taught and learned. We present five key areas of attention in teaching intelligence: strategies, metacognition, thinking dispositions, distributed cognition, and transfer. A series of examples drawing on our in-school experiences illustrates how ideas about intelligence can translate into enriched learning opportunities for students of all ages in any subject.

WHAT IS INTELLIGENCE? CAN WE TEACH IT? HOW DOES IT SUPPORT LEARNING?

A vision of students behaving more intelligently in their studies and in their everyday lives is alluring indeed. But pursuing such a vision means coming to grips with one of the most puzzling issues in the history of psychology—the nature of intelligence. With educational aspirations in mind, three fundamental questions have to be considered: What is intelligence? Can we teach intelligence? How does intelligence support learning?

All three questions look back to the very beginnings of the science of intelligence. In 1904, the minister of public education in France asked the well-established psychologist Alfred Binet to devise a way to identify school children in need of special help (Gould, 1981). The minister and Binet in his turn found themselves worried over a puzzle all teachers face—some children learn much better than others. Imagine two children called Abby and Betty. Abby always seems to be ahead of the game in school. She solves the story problems in the math text, has good recall of geography facts and figures, writes well, and even engagingly. Betty, by contrast, always seems to be a bit behind the game. We take such differences for granted, but why do they occur? To be sure, some youngsters are better motivated than others, but some youngsters seem just plain more *able* than others at school learning. It was this difference that Binet sought to understand.

Binet developed puzzle-like tests to try to separate the Abbys from the Bettys, emphasizing questions that depended only on everyday knowledge and not school knowledge. The idea of intelligence and later IQ developed out of such tests. Along the way, Binet arrived at answers to the three questions raised earlier. What is intelligence? In Binet's view, it was a grab bag of diverse abilities that together equipped youngsters to perform better or worse in school. Can we teach intelligence? Binet thought so. He wrote of "mental orthopedics" that would build up students' will, discipline and attention (See Binet & Simon, 1911). And how does intelligence support learning? More will, discipline, attention, and related skills make the student a more systematic and focused learner.

At about the same time a very different perspective on the nature of intelligence also emerged. The great American statistician and psychologist Spearman published a key paper in 1904 that gave his view of intelligence (Gould, 1981). Spearman observed that people who do well on one intellectually challenging task tend to do well on others. He developed a statistical way of measuring this common trend and called it *g* for general intelligence. Spearman thought of general intelligence as a biologically based trait, reflecting some kind of neural energy that pervaded the brain. The Abbys of the world had more of this energy available, the Bettys less, with most people in the middle. Could this general intelligence be taught? No, but it had a lot to do with learning, because a brain suffused with this neural energy operated more effectively, like a car engine with greater horsepower.

If those are the roots of the science of intelligence, what is intelligence today? Binet and Spearman both began with behavior, with how students performed and how people solved problems. Today's ideas about intelligence honor the same point. They all aim toward accounting for behavior in the world rather than performance on abstract tests. Just as teachers encounter Abbys and Bettys and the in-betweens, everyone meets up with the phenomenon of more or less intelligent behavior in the world. Indeed, part of our culture is an informal conception of intelligence that has little to do with IQ or tests. Research conducted by Sternberg, Conway, Ketron, and Bernstein (1981) identified the kinds of characteristics that people typically have in mind when they speak of someone as intelligent. These characteristics include solving problems well, reasoning clearly, thinking logically, using a good vocabulary, drawing on a large store of information, balancing information, sustaining a goal orientation, and showing intelligence in practical, not just academic ways.

To sum up the informal conception, people judged intelligent by our culture know a lot and think well with what they know. This puts them in a better position to learn more. Formal theories of intelligence of quite diverse character try to honor this idea one way or another. For instance, the kinds of items included on IQ tests often probe reasoning, logical thinking, and vocabulary. Even so, this leaves a remarkable amount of room for diversity in theories of intelligence. The contrast between Spearman's one general intelligence and Binet's bundle-of-abilities conception of intelligence remains today. Indeed, much of the contemporary debate has focused on how many and what intelligences there are, from the classic g to Sternberg's (1985) three broad categories in his triarchic theory of intelligence (analytic, creative, and practical intelligence), to Gardner's (1983) theory of seven, and perhaps more, multiple intelligences (linguistic, logical–mathematical, musical, visual–spatial, bodily kinesthetic, interpersonal, and intrapersonal) to as many as 150 components proposed by Guilford (1967).

To help organize the diversity, Perkins (1995) identified three broad trends in the kinds of psychological resources people offered to explain the differences in intelligence between the Abbys and the Bettys: a *neural* viewpoint, an *experiential viewpoint,* and a *reflective viewpoint.* Although many theories are a mix of these, the three provide a useful way to stake out basic positions because they give quite different answers to the three questions raised earlier.

The neural viewpoint usually identifies intelligence with IQ. Advocates of the neural position take IQ most fundamentally to be an index of some kind of information-processing efficiency at a biological level in the neural system, although general education also influences IQ (Herrnstein & Murray, 1994; Jensen, 1983). Can we teach this kind of intelligence? Not in any straightforward way. According to the neural position, true changes in intelligence have a basic physiological character. In keeping with this, efforts to teach intelligence in the sense of raising IQ have shown at best limited success. Gains are generally modest, tend to favor high testing ability although they sometimes spill over to general school performance, and tend to dwindle away in a few years (Brody, 1992; Herrnstein & Murray, 1994; Jensen, 1983). By and large, the Bettys stay Bettys, although in one well-documented case, 7 years after an intervention, children sustain modest gains in IQ and school performance (Campbell & Ramey, 1994). As to the connection between intelligence and learning, the idea is that better neural equipment makes for better learning. In terms of predictiveness, IQ turns out to be fairly predictive of success in school learning. It tells you who the Abbys and Bettys are likely to be, although not who they are for sure because many other motivational and cultural factors come into play as well.

Many reservations can be advanced against the neural position. For example, advocates of the neural position are not generally neuroscientists but psychologists making rather indirect arguments for a neural basis for IQ. None of the arguments have proved compelling (Brody, 1992; Ceci, 1990). Sternberg (1985), Gardner (1983), Perkins (1995) and many others have argued that IQ tests neglect important dimensions of intellectual functioning such as creativity, critical thinking, practical functioning in the world, and important kinds of mental ability such as musical or interpersonal intelligence. Although efforts to raise IQ directly have not been overwhelmingly successful, they have shown some limited worthwhile impact (e.g., Campbell & Ramey, 1994). These and other challenges make plain the need for other ways to account for the differences between the Abbys and the Bettys. Both the experiential and the reflective viewpoints mentioned earlier have their own accounts.

Those ascribing to the viewpoint of experiential intelligence foreground what those ascribing to the IQ tradition seeks to filter out by their test designs that intelligence reflects knowledge and experience in the domain in question. The auto mechanic, physicist, or dancer who solves problems best is in trend the one who draws on a rich and diverse body of knowledge and experience (Bereiter & Scardamalia, 1993; Ericsson & Smith, 1991). Supporting this position are findings that, although IQ predicts how well people learn in the long term, knowledge of the challenge at hand predicts best how people perform (Hunter, 1986). Also supporting it is a large body of research accumulated over the past 30 years about what makes experts good at what they do. As already said, not general thinking ability but a rich repertoire of knowledge is the answer.

To the question, "How does intelligence support learning?" there is a ready answer from the experiential viewpoint: Prior knowledge and experience in an area are excellent preparation for further learning, because they provide the learner with hooks on which to hang new knowledge. Abby handles new knowledge better than Betty because Abby already has more foundational knowledge than Betty, perhaps by way of help from supportive parents or older siblings or a habit of reading at home.

Finally, from the experiential viewpoint, the answer to the question, "Can we teach intelligence?" is easy: Yes, by providing the kinds of experiences that build an active, involved expertlike understanding or, for school children, that at least gesture in that direction. However, easy to say, this is not so easy to do. The rich authentic experiences of doing math, history, science, or literary interpretation that step toward what an expert does do not much resemble what happens in typical classrooms. Critics have pointed out that all too often teaching in the subject matters involves a very artificial version of disciplines that emphasizes facts and routines but neglects inquiry and understanding (Brown, Collins, & Duguid, 1989; Gardner, 1991; Perkins, 1992). Building up experiential intelligence calls for creating cultures of learning that pay more attention to inquiry and understanding.

The viewpoint of reflective intelligence offers a third perspective. In significant part, intelligence consists of good mental management (e.g. Baron, 1985, Baron & Sternberg, 1986; Chipman et al., 1985; Nickerson, 1989; Nickerson et al., 1985; Perkins, 1995; Segal, Chipman, & Glaser, 1985; Sternberg, 1985). Abby thinks and learns better than Betty because she attends to her thinking, monitors it, directs it and redirects it. Abby more than Betty resists impulsiveness, brainstorms options, thinks ahead, ponders the other side of the case, looks for multiple causes, tries to keep an open mind, and makes the other kinds of moves that would generally be considered good thinking practices. Can we teach this kind of intelligence? Certainly, by teaching strategies, cultivating self-monitoring and self-assessment, and in other ways to be discussed. Finally, from the reflective viewpoint, how does intelligence support learning? Here one of the most fundamental principles identified by a wide range of research on learning comes to the fore: *Learning is a consequence of thinking* (Perkins, 1992). Real learning that builds good retention of knowledge, genuine understanding of it, and the active use of knowledge in other situations, emerges from active thoughtful engagement with the content being learned. Abby, with her greater reflective repertoire, is in a better position to engage thoughtfully with school content than is Betty.

In the perpetual debate concerning human intelligence, the neural, experiential, and reflective viewpoints often have been expressed as opposing stances. However, Perkins (1995) suggested that they each capture an important part of the truth. Neurological endowment, experience in a domain, and the reflective use of one's mind all contribute to the edge the Abbys have over the Bettys. We do not know exactly how much each counts for—indeed their relative influence would be very hard to measure accurately. But we do know that experiential and reflective intelligence count for a lot. And perhaps we can help Betty get a promotion. Experiential and reflective intelligence are learnable. In and out of school, we can cultivate both experiential intelligence—through rich experiences of thinking in areas of concern—and reflective intelligence—through fostering reflective management of one's thinking. The door to learnable intelligence is, in principle, open.

TEACHING INTELLIGENCE
BY REORGANIZING THINKING

The door may be open, but walking through it requires some finesse. A common attitude toward teaching thinking makes an analogy with the development of physical abilities: Exercise can "practice up" the target skill, be it thoughtful decision making or high diving. Practice makes perfect, or at least advances along the path toward perfection.

Plausible as it may sound, this idea is mistaken. Although plenty of practice helps, the notion of simply practicing complex skills does a disservice to the development both of physical and mental skills. Research on the development of physical skills in sports and in musical performance suggests that a regimen of routine repetitive practice does not lead far. The greatest attainments come to those who engage in what has been called *deliberate practice*, meaning a systematic effort to examine one's performance, analyze strengths and shortcomings, and improve by focusing attention on the shortcomings (Ericsson & Charness, 1994). In other words, effective practice reorganizes performance.

The same lesson holds for successful efforts to improve various kinds of thinking. Effective initiatives are emphatically reorganizational in nature. They do not just exercise up mental processes to be stronger and faster but introduce new more powerful patterns of organization. Students learn to attend to matters they previously neglected—the other side of the case, alternative causes, long-term consequences. They learn to rein in patterns of mental conduct that previously did mischief—impulsive decision making, disorganized thinking, a narrow viewpoint. Moreover, explicitness about the targeted reorganization turns out to be important. Studies have compared interventions that were explicit about reorganization and similar interventions that simply illustrated without explaining (Brown & Palincsar, 1989; Schoenfeld, 1979). Directness paid off. Unsurprisingly, learners benefit from knowing what patterns of reorganization they are striving to attain.

If a reorganizational approach is the path to take, what kinds of reorganization of thinking are called for? It is useful to identify five broad categories of reorganization prominent in various combinations in a number of efforts to cultivate learners' intelligence. We call these five the CORE categories. CORE is an acronym standing for categories of COgnitive REorganization. Here they are in brief, with more detailed accounts of each to come:

- *Strategies.* Strategies that redirect thinking (thinking about the other side of the case, brainstorming, looking for long-term consequences, etc.) are powerful tools for reorganizing thinking.

- *Metacognition.* Metacognition is a technical term for monitoring and directing one's thinking. The habit of doing so can have a powerful reorganizing influence on one's thinking.
- *Dispositions.* Dispositions contrast with abilities. A thinking disposition is a tendency in one's thinking, for instance, the tendency to be open minded, to look for reasons, or to find and articulate problems. Reorganizing learners' thinking means not just making them more able but encouraging and inspiring them to invest their minds in fruitful directions.
- *Distributed cognition.* Most of human thinking does not occur solo. It involves social interaction, physical supports from pencil and paper to computers, and specialized terminology (*hypothesis, evidence*), diagrams, and other such devices. All these can help to reorganize thinking.
- *Transfer.* Transfer of learning occurs when a person acquires knowledge and understanding in one context and carries it over to other contexts, sometimes quite similar ones (near transfer) and sometimes remote ones (far transfer). Transfer of learning often does not occur spontaneously. Effective reorganization of thinking requires promoting the transfer of the new patterns of thinking learned across a range of contexts.

The CORE categories offer handy tools for appraising commercial or home-grown approaches to teaching intelligence. Under each of the five, one can ask, "Does this approach attend to this category? If not, how can I supplement it to do so?" Of course, a particular approach need not honor all five evenhandedly, but neglect of several certainly constitutes a warning sign.

The five CORE categories also provide a useful framework for discussing several approaches developed by us and our colleagues at Harvard Project Zero over the past several years. These approaches illustrate what the categories mean and how they translate into practice. Some teachers may wish to look more closely at the specific approaches discussed. But proactive teachers of students of any age can easily pick up on the general pattern and adapt it to their own students and their own needs.

COGNITIVE REORGANIZATION IN THE CLASSROOM

If the reorganization of thinking is so important, what are the implications for classroom practice? The following sections take up each of the CORE principles in turn and illustrate how it might play out in classroom contexts, drawing on programs and approaches we have developed, including strategies, curriculum, and assessments.

CORE Category 1: Strategies in the Classroom

Many formal approaches to teaching thinking teach strategies—step by step procedures that guide thinking. For instance, a typical problem-solving strategy involves articulating a clear definition of the problem, brainstorming possible solutions, indentifying pros and cons promising solutions, selecting a likely solution, and testing it. Students can employ such a strategy as a way of exploring subject matter content. For example, students can think through how they might have handled the situation that led to the Boston Tea Party and then evaluate how the American colonists dealt with it, or they can examine how to deal with an outbreak of cholera in a third-world setting, synthesizing information about medicine and social organization.

Understanding is a fundamental objective in most kinds of learning. Students are endlessly challenged by topics from the meaning of fractions to the meaning of poems. Figure 4.1 shows a thinking strategy called the *Understanding Through Design* strategy (Perkins, Goodrich, Tishman, & Mirman Owen, 1994). It is intended to teach students how to take a careful, deep and thorough approach to understanding a theme or concept. (For a detailed discussion of the theoretical and practical underpinnings of the strategy see Perkins, 1986).

We focus on this particular example because of its relevance to school, where students are asked to understand things many times a day. The Understanding Through Design strategy enables students to better understand anything that was designed with purposes in mind, including objects (compasses, clavicles, cleats, and covered wagons, for example), concepts (democracy, diets, documentary, and the diatonic scale), and human events or procedures (evacuation plans, empirical methods, elections, equation, and acts of ecoterrorism).

The Understanding Through Design strategy teaches students to ask three fundamental questions key to building a deep understanding of something:

1. What are the purposes of the design, or what is it for?
2. What are its features and the reasons for them; that is, how is it designed to do whatever it is supposed to do?
3. How well does it work and how could it work better?

The strategy also provides standards or guides that help students think carefully about the answers to each question. The strategy can be used in a variety of ways. Teachers generally begin by leading whole class discussions of the answers to the three questions. Then, when students have grasped

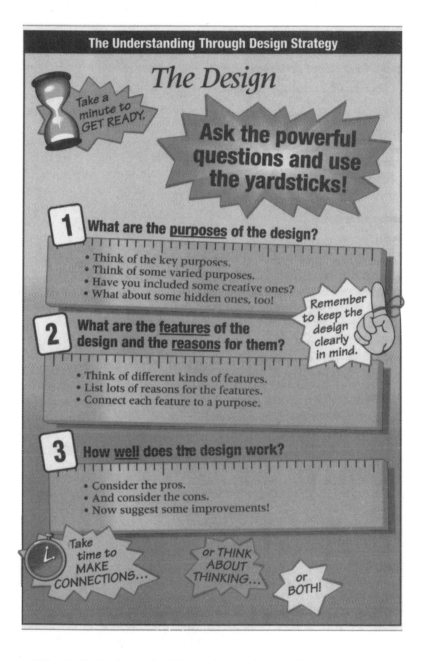

FIG. 4.1. The Understanding Through Design Strategy. From Perkins, Goodrich, Tishman, and Owen (1994). Reprinted by permission of Addison-Wesley.

the strategy, teachers have them use it in small groups or even as written homework.

By answering the three Understanding Through Design questions in a careful and systematic manner, students advance their understanding of the design they are studying. With repeated practice, this should also help them develop a more intelligent and reflective approach to studying in general. Thus, the use of a strategy can help students to behave more intelligently in the service of increasing their disciplinary knowledge and understanding. There are many examples of thinking strategies that can serve the same purposes. The problem solving strategy briefly described above is one. A decision making strategy included in *Thinking Connections*, the book that discusses the Understanding Through Design strategy, is another. There are also effective reading strategies (Brown, 1980; Brown & Palincsar, 1982; Palincsar & Brown, 1984, 1986, 1988), writing strategies (Flower & Hayes, 1981; Scardamalia & Bereiter, 1983, 1985; Scardamalia, Bereiter, & Steinbach, 1984), mathematical problem solving strategies (Schoenfeld, 1983, 1985, 1987), and study strategies (Weinstein, 1994), to name but a few types. Providing instruction in such strategies is an important step in helping students boost their reflective intelligence and their disciplinary knowledge.

CORE Category 2: Metacognition in the Classroom

The second element of cognitive reorganization is metacognition. To be metacognitive is to be aware of your own thinking and to ensure that you are thinking well. Learners' awareness and control of their thought processes is important in every subject matter, in and out of school. Dozens of studies have shown that one of the defining characteristics of successful thinkers and learners is the tendency to be metacognitive (Armbruster, Echols, & Brown, 1982; Brown, 1978; Flavell, 1987; Flower & Hayes, 1981; Schoenfeld, 1983; Weinert, 1987).

There are many ways to promote the development of metacognition in students. Asking them to assess their own work products and processes according to clearly articulated criteria is one way. In the research on student self-assessment mentioned in the introduction, students were asked to create a classification system for a collection of arthropods (lobsters, spiders, centipedes, bees, etc.) and to assess their work and their thinking as they progressed. The task involved reading a page of information about arthropods, using the information to create a classification system, then sorting the animals and explaining the system to the researcher. Students in the experimental group were stopped and asked to assess their work at each step. The criteria by which they were to evaluate themselves were contained in the rubric in Figure 4.2.

1. I read the page about arthropods carefully to make sure I understood it.

  4. I read carefully and checked my comprehension of the page as I read. I feel that I have a good understanding of the information presented and that I have learned something new.

  3. I read carefully and feel I understand the passage.

  2. I read the passage but did not check my understanding of it. I feel there are probably gaps in my memory and understanding of the information.

  1. I skimmed the page and do not remember or understand most of it.

2. I checked the page about arthropods to make sure my classification system is accurate.

  4. I reread the page about arthropods to make sure my system is consistent with the information on the page. If I left something out or found errors, I corrected my work in a way that improved its quality.

  3. I reread the page to make sure my work is accurate. I corrected errors if I found them.

  2. I reread the page but not thoroughly. I missed some errors and failed to correct others.

  1. I didn't reread the page to make sure my classification system is accurate. I made little effort to find errors or correct my work.

3. I specified useful categories for the arthropods

  4. I created categories based on important physical characteristics of the arthropods. Each arthropod can only fit in one category.

  3. I created categories that make me think about important characteristics of arthropods.

  2. I created categories that allow me to classify but don't really make me think about the important characteristics of arthropods.

  1. I created categories that use only unimportant characteristics of arthropods.

4. I accurately placed the arthropods in the categories

  4. I placed each arthropod in the correct category and checked to see that it only fits in that one category.

  3. I placed each arthropod in the correct category.

> **2.** I made some mistakes when I placed arthropods in categories.
>
> **1.** I made many errors when placing arthropods in categories.
>
> **5.** I described accurate and complete rules for deciding which arthropods go in each category.
>
> > **4.** I clearly and completely described the rules for deciding which arthropods go in each category; I described these rules in a way that would allow some one else to put the arthropods in the same categories I did.
> >
> > **3.** I clearly described rules for deciding which arthropods go in each category.
> >
> > **2.** I described the rules for deciding which arthropods go in each category, but I left things out and created confusion, or I included information about the categories that does not really help put the arthropods in correct categories.
> >
> > **1.** I listed rules, but they do not describe the categories.

FIG. 4.2: Scoring rubric for arthropod classification task.

The arthropod classification task and the accompanying requests to assess themselves cued metacognitive attention to learning. An examination of think-aloud protocols revealed that many students in the experimental group, particularly girls, were significantly more metacognitive than the control group students who were not asked to assess themselves. In addition, students in the experimental group appeared to learn more about arthropods and classification from the task, as evidenced by higher scores on a posttest of content knowledge. Self-assessment, therefore, has the potential to promote metacognition and to improve knowledge and understanding in the disciplines.

Another more directive approach to fostering metacognition can be found in *The Thinking Teacher's Guide to the Visual Arts* (Remer & Tishman, 1992). Several members of our group were involved in the design of this intervention. *The Thinking Teacher's Guide* infuses the teaching of thinking into instruction about artistic techniques such as creating the illusion of depth, using color to create a mood, focusing attention by framing, and so on. The guide teaches students to be metacognitive by asking them to answer "Think about Thinking Questions" after each lesson.

The "Think about Thinking Questions" are designed to make students more aware of their own thinking as well as to help them think of ways to improve it. For example, a lesson on how linear perspective can create the illusion of depth ends with several questions intended to heighten students' metacognitive awareness: "How does looking at a picture with linear perspective affect your thinking? If you were to draw a deep picture of your thinking during any of the activities in this theme, what would it look like? What methods for creating depth would you use?" The lesson also includes a series of questions intended to focus students' attention on improving their understandings and their skills: "How well do you think you understand linear perspective now? What still puzzles you? How can you get better at noticing and drawing in perspective?"

Each of the questions listed above could easily be adapted to other disciplines. This kind of attention to metacognition can increase students' reflective intelligence by making them more able to monitor, evaluate and regulate their own thought processes.

CORE Category 3: Dispositions in the Classroom

Teaching thinking strategies and metacognitive techniques like those discussed above can give students the *ability* to think well, but that's not all there is to it. Good thinking also involves certain attitudes and habits. The attitudes and habits possessed by good thinkers are referred to as *dispositions* (Baron, 1985; Ennis, 1986; Perkins, Jay & Tishman, 1993; Tishman, Jay, & Perkins, 1993). A person with a good repertoire of thinking dispositions not only knows how to think well but also notices when good thinking is important and has the inclination or motivation to follow through by using the thinking tools and strategies he or she knows.

Students often know how to think well but fail to mobilize their knowledge (Langer, 1989; Perkins, Farady, & Bushey, 1991; Perkins et al., 1993). For this reason, *Keys To Thinking* (Perkins et al., 1994), a collection of 56 lessons written for South African township schools, was designed to attend to students' dispositions. Through stories, activities and homework assignments, this stand-alone course on thinking encourages students to develop four broad thinking dispositions—the dispositions to *give thinking time*, to *make thinking broad and adventurous*, to *make thinking clear and careful*, and to *make thinking organized*.

Keys to Thinking uses stories to show students how good thinking is useful in real life situations and to sensitize them to occasions when good thinking is important—one element of good thinking dispositions. For example, one story explains how a young girl learned how the concept of democracy applies to her own life by being clear and careful in her thinking. Other stories provide similar examples of when good thinking is opportune.

The inclination side of dispositions can seem challenging to attend to in the classroom. What are teachers to do when they know their students can think well and can recognize opportunities to think but still choose not to bother? One solution to this problem is to make thinking count. What is assessed by a teacher sends a clear message to students about what counts, and too often thinking does not count. Including thinking-related criteria in scoring rubrics used by both students and teachers to evaluate student work can make thinking count and increase students' inclinations to think well. (For a fuller discussion of rubrics see Goodrich, 1996b.) Table 4.1 shows a rubric that explicitly requires a clear demonstration of good thinking in verbal, written or graphic reports on student inventions—inventions designed to ease the westward journey for 19th century pioneers, or to solve a local environmental problem, or to represent an imaginary culture and its inhabitants, or anything else students might devise. Based on the Understanding Through Design strategy discussed earlier, the rubric informs students that their reports must explain (a) the purposes of the invention, (b) the features or parts of the invention and how they help it serve its purposes, (c) the pros and cons of the design, and (d) how the design relates to other things past, present and future. The rubric could easily include criteria related to presentation style and effectiveness, the mechanics of written pieces, and the quality of the invention itself as well.

The criteria in the rubric in Table 4.1 are intended to demonstrate how students' thinking can be assessed through their products. If a child creates an impressive looking invention with expensive materials and the latest technology but cannot explain the purposes, features, pros, cons, and connections of the invention, he or she has not fulfilled the requirements of the task. If, on the other hand, he or she can articulate clear and convincing statements about each of these criteria, he or she has demonstrated good thinking on the subject and earns high marks.

Including thinking-oriented criteria in scoring rubrics is one way to make thinking count and boost students' inclinations to think well. Influencing students' thinking dispositions requires attention to a combination of formal and informal assessments, including but not limited to rubrics, written narratives, and verbal feedback.

Core Category 4: Distributed Cognition in the Classroom

There is a strong tendency both in psychological theorizing and classroom practice to treat learners as solo minds. Each learner does his or her own work and accumulates knowledge and skills that serve individual performance. However, this view can be challenged. A number of authors have pointed out that human beings do not usually function as brains in boxes (see the collection edited by Salomon, 1993). People reach beyond their immediate mental resources in at least three ways: (a) physically, utilizing pencil and paper, computers, and other devices to support and guide com-

TABLE 4.1

Scoring Rubric for Student Inventions

Criteria	Levels of Quality			
Purposes	The report explains the key purposes of the invention and points out less obvious ones as well.	The report explains all of the key purposes of the inventions.	The report explains some of the purposes of the invention but misses key purposes.	The report does not refer to the purposes of the invention.
Features	The report details both key and hidden features of the invention and explains how they serve a variety of purposes.	The report details the key features of the invention and explains the purpose(s) they serve.	The report neglects some features of the invention and/or the purposes they serve.	The report does not detail the features of the invention or the purposes they serve.
Critique	The report discusses the strengths and weaknesses of the invention and suggests ways in which it can be improved.	The report discusses the strengths and weaknesses of the invention.	The report discusses either the strengths or weaknesses of the invention but not both.	The report does not mention the strengths or the weaknesses of the invention.
Connections	The report makes appropriate connections between the purposes and features of the invention and a wide variety of different kinds of things or phenomena.	The report makes appropriate connections between the purposes and features of the invention and one or two other things or phenomena.	The report makes unclear or inappropriate connections between the invention and other things or phenomena.	The report makes no connections between the invention and other things.

plex thinking about a topic; (b) socially, collaborating with others to understand, solve problems, and pursue projects; and (c) symbolically, drawing on a range of general purpose and special purpose symbol systems that help to organize thought and understanding, including such ordinary language terms as hypothesis, theory, or evidence. This broadened perspective has been called *distributed cognition* or *distributed intelligence* to emphasize how complex cognition typically reaches beyond the solitary learner and thinker.

The principal recommendation that follows from the idea of distributed cognition is straightforward: Schools should make the physical, social, and symbolic distribution of cognition more of a presence in students' learning (Perkins, 1992). Writing, for example, should serve not just for final statements to be graded but as an exploratory medium, a tool of thinking. Well-designed formats of collaborative learning can help students to cope with challenging topics. Explicit attention to the language of thinking can sharpen students' conceptions of key aspects of thinking. What is a hypothesis? How does it contrast with a guess? What kinds of evidence are needed to test a hypothesis about the meaning of a poem versus the need of plants for sunlight? What is the difference between evidence and proof? An exploration of such distinctions, not as dictionary definitions but in a real context of inquiry, can empower students to see the demands of inquiry more clearly.

Often, effective thinking strategies and dispositions can be expressed in an amalgam of graphic representation and labels sometimes called *graphic organizers* (Jones, Pierce, & Hunter, 1988–1989; McTighe & Lyman, 1988; Swartz & Parks, 1994). By helping students to externalize, track, critique, and elaborate their patterns of thinking as they work on a problem or pursue a project, such graphic organizers also provide for metacognition. In summary, distributed cognition serves all the categories already discussed, helping each of them to do their job better.

An example of distributed cognition comes from an afterschool program we developed for third-, fourth-, and fifth-grade students in an urban elementary school. The program focused on relatively complex, long-term projects such as creating a newspaper, writing Big Books, or organizing field trips (see Goodrich, Hatch, Wiatrowski, & Unger, 1995). Early in the life of the program, it was difficult for students to keep the ultimate goal of a project in mind as they engaged in the myriad of tasks that led up to it. As a result, the projects tended to lose momentum. In order to provide a continual reminder of the "big picture," program staff created a large poster with a generic problem-solving strategy relevant to every project, shown in Figure 4.3. Called *Smart Thinking*, the strategy has eight steps, six with accompanying guidelines for good thinking. Each step of the strategy has an accompanying icon such as a storm cloud raining down ideas to represent brainstorming, or an exaggerated ear receiving compliments and criticisms to represent feedback.

By referring to the poster, teachers in the program helped students orient themselves and understand their progress through a project. In effect, the

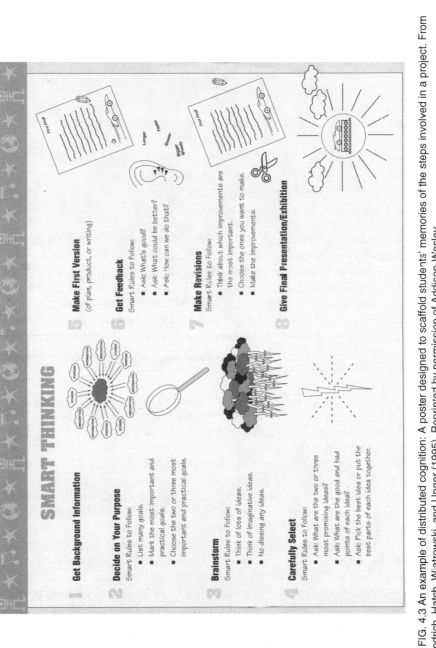

FIG. 4.3 An example of distributed cognition: A poster designed to scaffold students' memories of the steps involved in a project. From Goodrich, Hatch, Wiatrowski, and Unger (1995). Reprinted by permission of Addison-Wesley.

poster served as a container for students' understandings of the path of the projects: When their understanding faltered, it could easily be scaffolded by the guidelines on the poster. Some teachers used the icons from the poster on daily handouts, making it even clearer to students how what they were working on contributed to the goal of the project. By representing a problem solving strategy, the poster also taught students to work and think strategically. Finally, by using the language of thinking, the poster taught vocabulary and concepts associated with high level thinking. The posters included in the *Thinking Connections* materials can serve the same purposes. Taken together, these examples suggest that even remarkably "low tech" approaches to distributing cognition can provide a lot of educational leverage.

CORE Category 5: Transfer in the Classroom

The term *transfer* refers to the act of applying knowledge or skills gained in one context, like school, to another context, such as a job. Most instruction takes transfer for granted, assuming that students reliably apply what they learn in one class to other classes and to their lives outside of school. Yet transfer is anything but certain. Witness the science teacher who laments her students' lack of math skills. On questioning the math teacher, she learns that not only have her students been exposed to the mathematics they need, they even took a series of tests on the subject and passed with flying colors. The problem, she now realizes, is not lack of knowledge or skill, it is lack of transfer.

If students fail to transfer knowledge and skills from one classroom to another, the prospects for applying their understandings outside of school years later seem quite poor. Research confirms that transfer is hard to come by, particularly transfer across disciplines and to other quite different contexts, usually called *far transfer* (Detterman & Sternberg, 1993; Salomon & Perkins, 1989). More often than not, knowledge and skills are inert, meaning that students possess them but do not think to use them unless they are explicitly instructed to do so (Bereiter & Scardamalia, 1985; Bransford, Franks, Vye, & Sherwood, 1989). However, Salomon and Perkins (1989) argued that transfer can happen when at least one of two conditions are met. One condition is thorough practice on deliberately diverse cases. This condition attends to transfer by actually demonstrating the variety of contexts in which a skill is useful. The other condition, called mindful abstraction, involves actively making connections between ideas and multiple contexts in one's mind.

The example of transfer given here is of the second kind, mindful abstraction. It is part of the first thinking strategy in the *Thinking Connec-*

tions collection, called the Mental Management strategy. Figure 4.4 shows the complete strategy, which was designed to teach students to be metacognitive and to attend to transfer. The strategy has three steps, one that is done before a task, such as writing an essay, studying for a test or even using the Understanding Through Design strategy, and two that are done afterwards. The first and third steps, Get Ready and Think About Thinking, are metacognitive in nature. They help students to mentally prepare for a task and to improve their thinking on future tasks.

Step 2 of the strategy is the transfer step. It asks students to make connections between what they just worked on or studied and other things they know, do and study. That may sound simple enough but students generally find this to be the most challenging step of the strategy. Making connections becomes easier with practice, however, and is worth the effort, particularly when the alternative—thorough practice in diverse contexts—is too time consuming to be feasible.

Of course, there are many ways that instruction can foster transfer. Figure 4.5 shows a brief compendium drawn from Fogarty, Perkins, and Barell (1992).

CREATING A CULTURE OF THINKING

You may have noticed by now that many of the examples presented here serve more than one CORE element. The Mental Management strategy attends to metacognition and strategies as well as transfer, the Smart Thinking poster attends to strategies as well as distributed cognition; and rubrics were recommended in order to promote metacognition, strategies and thinking dispositions. Although each CORE element can be defined and described independently of the others, they are related. Attention to several at once comes naturally.

Taken together, the five CORE elements represent a comprehensive reorganization of students' thinking to impart learnable intelligence. From this point of view, uncomplicated yet powerful techniques like assessing one's own persuasive essay on school uniforms or making connections between math and science can, over time, help students behave more intelligently and increase their academic achievement.

One key to the whole enterprise of teaching for intelligence is to ensure that all five CORE elements get some attention, if not at the same time then at least over the course of a day or a week. But a greater challenge is to infuse the CORE elements throughout regular classroom instruction. That is not to say that it is inappropriate to teach thinking just for the sake of teaching thinking from time to time. In our view, however, a deeper approach is in

FIG. 4.4. The Mental Management Strategy. From Perkins, Goodrich, Tishman, and Owen (1994). Reprinted by permission of Addison-Wesley.

Approach 1: *"Hugging." Make the learning experience more like the ultimate applications. Students do and feel something more like the intended applications.*

1. *Setting expectations:* Simply alert learners to occasions in which they can apply what they are learning directly, without transformation or adjustment. *Example:* "Remember, you'll be asked to use these pronouns correctly in the essay due at the end of the week."

2. *Matching:* Adjust the learning to make it almost the same experience as the ultimate applications. *Example:* In sports, play practice games. In drama, full costume rehearsals.

3. *Simulating:* Use simulation, role playing, acting out, to approximate the ultimate applications. *Example:* Simulated trials, simulated senate discussions, and so on, as preparation for understanding and participating in government as a citizen.

4. *Modeling:* Show, demonstrate rather than just describing, discussing. *Example:* A math teacher demonstrates how a problem might be solved, "thinking aloud" to reveal inner strategic moves.

5. *Problem-based learning:* Have students learn content they are supposed to use in solving problems through solving analogous kinds of problems, pulling in the content as they need it. *Example:* Students learn about nutritional needs under different conditions by planning the menu for a desert trek and a long sea voyage, getting nutrition information out of their texts and other sources as they work.

Approach 2: *"Bridging" Make conceptual connections between what is learned and other applications. This is more cerebral and less experiential. Students generalize and reflect.*

6. *Anticipating applications:* Ask students to predict possible applications remote from the learning context. *Example:* After students have practiced a thinking skill or other skill, ask, "Where might you use this or adapt it? Let's brainstorm. Be creative." List the ideas and discuss some.

7. *Generalizing concepts:* Ask students to generalize from their experience to produce widely applicable principles, rules, and ideas. *Example:* After studying the discovery of radium, ask, "What big generalizations about scientific discovery does the discovery of radium suggest? Can you support your generalizations by other evidence you know of?"

8. *Using analogies:* Engage students in finding and elaborating an analogy between a topic under study and something rather different from it. *Example:* Ask students to compare and contrast the structure of the human circulatory system with the structure of water and waste services in a city.

9. *Parallel problem solving:* Engage students in solving problems with parallel structure in two different areas, to gain an appreciation for the similarities and contrasts. *Example:* Have students investigate a (nonsensitive) problem in their home environment and a study problem in school, using the same problem solving strategy. Help them to draw out the parallels and differences.

10. *Metacognitive reflection:* Prompt and support students in planning, monitoring, and evaluating their own thinking. *Example:* After a quiz or indeed any thought-demanding activity, have students ask themselves, "What went well, what was hard, and how could I handle what was hard better next time?"

FIG 4.5. Ten ways to teach for transfer.

order—a cultural transformation in which thinking through content becomes the mainstay of the way learning happens in classrooms.

One way to organize our efforts as teachers around such an enterprise is to work with a simple model of culture. Tishman, Perkins, and Jay (1995), in their book *The Thinking Classroom*, discussed how a natural process of enculturation occurs in any setting from classroom to playground to workplace to family. The models we see around us, the explanations others offer, the way we interact with people, and the feedback we receive directly and indirectly all help to draw us into a culture. Therefore, creating a culture of thinking in a classroom means providing models or examples of good thinking, clear explanations of how, when and why to think well, interactions with other people and class assignments that require good thinking, and informative feedback about students' thinking and how it can be improved.

What would it mean to take such an encompassing approach? Recall the persuasive scene sketched in the introduction, in which students were assessing their essays on an impending school uniform rule. Aiming to create a classroom culture in which students think critically about the quality of their own work and their own thinking, the teacher spent part of one period demonstrating how she evaluated her own draft of a piece she was writing for a professional publication. She began by explaining her process, which included listing the criteria for the piece, then comparing her draft to those criteria and noting its strengths and weaknesses. She then engaged in the evaluative process out loud, modeling her thinking for her students. Several days later, when students had written drafts of their school uniform essays, she instructed them to assess their own drafts and have another student assess it as well. Pairs of students then talked together about any differences in their evaluations of the same draft, providing reasons for their assessments and sorting out any disagreements. The teacher asked each student to staple a copy of his or her own assessment of their paper to the final papers when they handed them in. After grading the students' work according to the same rubric they used, the teacher compared her assessments to theirs and gave written comments on the similarities and differences.

In terms of the four cultural forces, this teacher provided an explanation of the self-assessment process, presented a model, had students engage in interactions around self-assessment, and lastly, gave them feedback about the accuracy of their assessments. She takes a similar approach to other CORE elements, sprinkling models of strategic thinking into her lessons, explaining the need for transfer and sharing a few techniques for making connections, arranging students in small groups with clear roles for each student in order to encourage distributed cognition, and providing both formal and informal feedback about their abilities, sensitivities and inclinations toward intelligent behavior. Of course, creating a culture of thinking does not happen in a day, a week, or even a month. Teachers setting forth on this road need not feel rushed. Small comfortable steps—a strategy introduced here, a graphic organizer there, a rubric later, then a set of key dispositions, with a fair amount of business as usual in between—can begin the journey. As time goes on, it is worth attending to each of the four cultural forces systematically. If the road toward full transformation is long, the goals are worthy—keep alive a spirit of intellectual vibrancy in the conviction that each student can learn to think and think to learn.

REFERENCES

Armbruster, B., Echols, C., & Brown, A. (1982). The role of metacognition in reading to learn: A developmental perspective. *Volta Review, 84*(5), 45–56.

Baron, J. (1985). *Rationality and intelligence.* New York: Cambridge University Press.

Baron, J. B., & Sternberg, R. S. (Eds.). (1986). *Teaching thinking skills: Theory and practice.* New York: Freeman.

Bereiter, C., & Scardamalia, M. (1985). Cognitive coping strategies and the problem of inert knowledge. In S. S. Chipman, J. W. Segal, & R. Glaser (Eds.), *Thinking and learning skills, Vol. 2: Current research and open questions* (pp. 65–80). Hillsdale, NJ: Lawrence Erlbaum Associates.

Bereiter, C., & Scardamalia, M. (1993). *Surpassing ourselves: An inquiry into the nature and implications of expertise.* Chicago: Open Court.

Binet, A., & Simon, T. (1911). *A method of measuring the development of the intelligence of young children.* Lincoln, IL: Courier Company.

Bransford, J. D., Franks, J. J., Vye, N. J., & Sherwood, R. D. (1989). New approaches to instruction: Because wisdom can't be told. In S. Vosniadou & A. Ortony (Eds.), *Similarity and analogical reasoning* (pp. 470–497). New York: Cambridge University Press.

Brody, N. (1992). *Intelligence.* New York: Academic Press.

Brown, A. L. (1978). Knowing when, where, and how to remember: A problem of metacognition. In R. Glaser (Ed.), *Advances in instructional psychology, Vol.1* (pp. 77–165). Hillsdale, NJ: Lawrence Erlbaum Associates.

Brown, A. L. (1980). Metacognitive development and reading. In R. Spiro, B. Bruce, & W. Brewer (Eds.), *Theoretical issues in reading comprehension* (pp. 453–481). Hillsdale, NJ: Lawrence Erlbaum Associates.

Brown, J. S., Collins, A., & Duguid, P. (1989). Situated cognition and the culture of learning. *Educational Researcher, 18*(1), 32–42.

Brown A. L., & Palincsar, A. S. (1982). Inducing strategic learning from texts by means of informed, self-control training. *Topics in Learning and Learning Disabilities, 2*(1), 1–17.

Brown, A. L., & Palincsar, A. S. (1989). Guided, cooperative learning and individual knowledge acquisition. In L. B. Resnick (Ed.), *Knowing, learning, and instruction: Essays in honor of Robert Glaser* (pp.3 93–451). Hillsdale, NJ: Lawrence Erlbaum Associates.

Campbell, F. A., & Ramey, C. T. (1994). Effects of early intervention on intellectual and academic achievement: A follow-up study of children from low-income families. *Child Development, 65,* 684–698.

Ceci, S. J. (1990). *On intelligence … more or less: A bioecological treatise on intellectual development.* Englewood Cliffs, NJ: Prentice-Hall.

Chipman, S. F., Segal, J. W., & Glaser, R. (Eds.). (1985). *Thinking and learning skills, Vol. 2: Research and open questions.* Hillsdale, NJ: Lawrence Erlbaum Associates.

Detterman, D. K., & Sternberg, R. J. (Eds.) (1993). *Transfer on trial: Intelligence, cognition, and instruction.* Norwood, NJ: Ablex.

Ennis, R. H. (1986). A taxonomy of critical thinking dispositions and abilities. In J. B. Baron & R. S. Sternberg (Eds.), *Teaching thinking skills: Theory and practice* (pp. 9–26). New York: Freeman.

Ericsson, K. A., & Charness, N. (1994). Expert performance: Its structure and acquisition. *American Psychologist, 49*(8), 725– 747.

Ericsson, K. A., & Smith, J. (Eds.). (1991). *Toward a general theory of expertise: Prospects and limits.* Cambridge, England: Cambridge University Press.

Flavell, J. H. (1987). Speculations about the nature and development of metacognition. In F. Weinert & R. Kluwe (Eds.), *Metacognition, motivation, an understanding,* (pp. 21–30). Hillsdale, NJ: Lawrence Erlbaum Associates.

Flower, L. A., & Hayes, J. R. (1981). The pregnant pause: An inquiry into the nature of planning. *Research in the Teaching of English, 15*(3), 229–243.

Fogarty, R., Perkins, D. N., & Barell, J. (1992). *How to teach for transfer.* Palatine, IL: Skylight Publishing.

Gardner, H. (1983). *Frames of mind.* New York: Basic Books.

Gardner, H. (1991). *The unschooled mind: How children think and how schools should teach.* New York: Basic Books.

Goodrich, H. (1996a). *Student self-assessment: At the intersection of metacognition and authentic assessment.* Unpublished doctoral dissertation, Harvard University, Graduate School of Education. Cambridge, MA.

Goodrich, H. (1996b). Understanding rubrics. *Educational Leadership, 54*(4), 14–17.

Goodrich, H., Hatch, T., Wiatrowski, G. & Unger, C. (1995). *Teaching through projects: Creating effective learning environments.* Reading, MA: Addison-Wesley.

Gould, S. J. (1981). *The mismeasure of man.* New York: Norton.

Guilford, J. P. (1967). *The nature of human intelligence.* New York: McGraw-Hill.

Herrnstein, R. J., & Murray, C. (1994). *The bell curve: Intelligence and class structure in American life.* New York: The Free Press.

Hunter, J. E. (1986). Cognitive ability, cognitive aptitudes, job knowledge, and job performance. *Journal of Vocational Behavior, 29,* 340–362.

Jensen, A. R. (1983). The nonmanipulable and effectively manipulable variables of education. *Education and Society, 1*(1), 51–62.

Jones, B. F., Pierce, J., & Hunter, B. (1988–1989). Teaching students to construct graphic representations. *Educational Leadership, 46*(4), 20–25.

Langer, E. J. (1989). *Mindfulness.* Menlo Park, CA: Addison-Wesley.

McTighe, J., & Lyman, F. T. (1988). Cueing thinking in the classroom: The promise of theory embedded tools. *Educational Leadership, 45*(7), 18–24.

Nickerson, R., Perkins, D. N., & Smith, E. (1985). *The teaching of thinking.* Hillsdale, NJ: Lawrence Erlbaum Associates.

Nickerson, R. S. (1989). On improving thinking through instruction. *Review of Research in Education, 15,* 3–57.

Palincsar, A. S., & Brown, A. L. (1984). Reciprocal teaching of comprehension-fostering and comprehension-monitoring activities. *Cognition and Instruction, 1,* 117–175.

Palincsar, A. S., & Brown, A. L. (1986). Interactive teaching to promote independent learning from text. *The Reading Teacher, 39*(8), 771–777.

Palincsar, A. S., & Brown, A. L. (1988). Teaching and practicing thinking skills to promote comprehension in the context of group problem solving. *Remedial and Special Education, 9*(1), 53–59.

Perkins, D. N. (1986). *Knowledge as design.* Hillsdale, NJ: Lawrence Erlbaum Associates.

Perkins, D. N. (1992). *Smart schools: From training memories to educating minds.* New York: The Free Press.

Perkins, D. N. (1995). *Outsmarting IQ: The emerging science of learnable intelligence.* New York: The Free Press.

Perkins, D. N., Capdevielle, B., Chonco, S., Cilliers, C., Goodrich, H., Sibisi, S., Tishman, S., van Heusden, M., & Viljoen, R. (1994). *Keys to thinking.* Johannesburg, South Africa: UPTTRAIL Trust.

Perkins, D. N., Farady, M., & Bushey, B. (1991). Everyday reasoning and the roots of intelligence. In J. Voss, D. N. Perkins, & J. Segal (Eds.), *Informal reasoning* (pp. 83–105). Hillsdale, NJ: Lawrence Erlbaum Associates.

Perkins, D. N., Goodrich, H., Tishman, S., & Mirman Owen, J. (1994). *Thinking connections: Learning to think and thinking to learn.* Reading, MA: Addison-Wesley.

Perkins, D. N., Jay, E., & Tishman, S. (1993). Beyond abilities: A dispositional theory of thinking. *The Merrill-Palmer Quarterly, 39*(1), 1–21.

Perkins, D. N., & Salomon, G. (1989). Are cognitive skills context-bound? *Educational Researcher, 18*(1), 16–25.

Remer, A., & Tishman, S. (1992). *The thinking teacher's guide to the visual arts.* New York: Learning Designs.

Salomon, G. (Ed.). (1993). *Distributed cognitions.* New York: Cambridge University Press.

Salomon, G., & Perkins, D. N. (1989). Rocky roads to transfer: Rethinking mechanisms of a neglected phenomenon. *Educational Psychologist, 24*(2), 113–142.

Scardamalia, M., & Bereiter, C. (1983). The development of evaluative, diagnostic and remedial capabilities in children's composing. In M. Martlew (Ed.), *The psychology of written language: A developmental approach* (pp. 6–95). London: Wiley.

Scardamalia, M., & Bereiter, C. (1985). Fostering the development of self-regulation in children's knowledge processing. In S. F. Chipman, J. W. Segal, & R. Glaser (Eds.), *Thinking and learning skills, Vol. 2: Research and open questions* (pp. 563– 577). Hillsdale, NJ: Lawrence Erlbaum Associates.

Scardamalia, M., Bereiter, C., & Steinbach, R. (1984). Teachability of reflective processes in written composition. *Cognitive Science, 8,* 173–190.

Schoenfeld, A. H. (1979). Explicit heuristic training as a variable in problem solving performance. *Journal for Research in Mathematics Education, 10*(3), 173–187.

Schoenfeld, A. H. (1983). *Problem solving in the mathematics curriculum: A report, recommendations, and an annotated bibliography.* Washington, DC: Mathematical Association of America.

Schoenfeld, A. H. (1985). *Mathematical problem solving.* New York: Academic Press.

Schoenfeld, A. H. (1987). What's all the fuss about metacognition? In A. Schoenfeld (Ed.), *Cognitive science and mathematics education* (pp. 189–215). Hillsdale, NJ: Lawrence Erlbaum Associates.

Segal, J. W., Chipman, S. F., & Glaser, R. (Eds.). (1985). *Thinking and learning skills, Vol. 1: Relating instruction to research.* Hillsdale, NJ: Lawrence Erlbaum Associates.

Spearman, C. (1904). General intelligence, objectively defined and measured. *American Journal of Psychology, 15,* 201–293.

Sternberg, R. J. (1985). *Beyond I.Q.: A triarchic theory of human intelligence.* New York: Cambridge University Press.

Sternberg, R. J., Conway, B. E., Ketron, J. L., & Bernstein, M. (1981). People's conceptions of intelligence. *Journal of Personality and Social Psychology, 41*(1), 37–55.

Swartz, R. J., & Parks, S. (1994). *Infusing the teaching of critical and creative thinking into elementary instruction: A lesson design handbook.* Pacific Grove, CA: Critical Thinking Press and Software.

Tishman, S., Jay, E., & Perkins, D. N. (1993). Thinking dispositions: From transmission to enculturation. *Theory Into Practice, 32*(3), 147–153.

Tishman, S., Perkins, D. N., & Jay, E. (1995). *The thinking classroom.* Boston: Allyn and Bacon.

Weinert, F. E. (1987). Introduction and overview: Metacognition and motivation as determinants of effective learning and understanding. In F. Weinert & R. Kluwe (Eds.), *Metacognition, motivation, and understanding* (pp. 1–16). Hillsdale, NJ: Lawrence Erlbaum associates.

Weinstein, C. (1994). Strategic learning/strategic teaching: Flip sides of a coin. In P. Pintrich, D. Brown, & C. Weinstein (Eds.), *Student motivation, cognition and learning* (pp. 257–273). Hillsdale, NJ: Lawrence Erlbaum Associates.

CHAPTER 5

The Practical Use of Skill Theory in Classrooms

Jim Parziale

Kurt W. Fischer
Harvard Graduate School of Education

All teachers hope to change the way that their students think. They want students to gain knowledge and skills, new thinking structures. Kindergarten teachers hope that children will learn among a host of other skills to recognize that numbers represent quantities, whereas high school English teachers hope that students learn to read passages for subtext as well as other techniques.

Hope is necessary in these cases because of the uncertain nature of learning and development. Several pertinent questions frame some of this uncertainty:

- What can, and should, children learn at different ages?
- How can teachers determine if their lessons are stimulating new thinking skills?
- How can teachers confirm if a student is using a new thinking structure?

- How can teachers follow the changes in thinking that their students are going through?
- In what ways are thinking skills dependent on each other? What older skills are part of newer skills? How are thinking skills sequentially ordered?
- How can teachers use the potential of innate learning mechanisms to more effectively foster change?

Educators have used many diverse theoretical frameworks in seeking answers to these questions. Three families of these frameworks are most notable, those of Piaget, Vygotsky, and the behaviorists.

Piaget, in *Science of Education and the Psychology of the Child* (1970a), proposed that teachers become experimenters to answer questions such as those listed above. His theory provides educators with two main conceptions to aid them in their research: constructivism and stage structures (Piaget, 1970b). Piaget's constructivism encourages teachers to appreciate the active role that students play in their own development, and his stages define how children's general abilities change through discrete and discontinuous steps.

Vygotsky focused on the role of adults, including teachers of course, in providing thinking structures to children. Like Piaget, Vygotsky believed that children have an important role in the construction of their own understandings, but unlike Piaget he emphasized how children learn by observing others (Vygotsky, 1962). His concept of internalization describes how thinking tools are appropriated by children for their own use. Vygotsky also thought that children's thinking could be extended by support from adults along a zone of proximal development (Vygotsky, 1978). This zone explains the scaffolding effect that carefully crafted lessons have in supporting children's thinking.

Behaviorist theories also strongly emphasize the role of the environment in learning (Bandura & Walters, 1963; Skinner, 1938). This focus on learning environments is reflected in concepts from behaviorism, such as reinforcement, punishment and practice that continue to be useful in the design of effective learning environments.

This chapter describes another developmental framework, skill theory (Fischer, 1980). Skill theory, like Piagetian theory, focuses on children's construction of their own understandings. Rather than using Piaget's generalized schema, skill theory posits thinking structures that children control in specific contexts. These thinking structures, skills, provide a balance between Piaget's child-centered conceptions, and Vygotsky's and the behaviorists' environment-centered approaches. This balance is achieved by equally specifying the contribution of both the child and the environment when the skills are defined. The environmental specificity of skills can be used to predict and explain the role of educational environments in children's learning.

Unlike most other theories, skill theory predicts many observations that teachers commonly make about learning and development:

- Children learn along varied pathways (Fischer & Knight, 1990; Fischer & Silvern, 1985).

- Individual performance levels depend on the degree of support (Fischer & Pipp, 1984).

- Development occurs simultaneously and unevenly across and within domains, as a web-like process, rather than a linear one (Fischer & Granott, 1995).

- To understand process-oriented learning, dynamic assessment is necessary (Parziale, 1997).

In order to explain this balanced and detailed perspective, this chapter first describes the basic units of skill theory and then demonstrates how these skills are organized during development. Examples from classrooms are used to make the practical aspects of the theory obvious and useful to the reader. Because of this emphasis on the theory's practical use, later in the chapter, stepwise instructions are given for analyzing a learning unit using the theory. A second section reviews the most educational significant features of the theory. Finally, the conclusion suggests some specific ways that skill theory can inform future educational practice.

A SKILL THEORY PRIMER

Skill theory is a neo-Piagetian theory that combines elements of cognitive and behaviorist theories to provide tools for the prediction of developmental sequences and synchronies. The theory focuses on children's ability to control variation in what they think or do. These abilities are described by abstract structures, skills, that contain elements of both the thinking person and the context that they are thinking in. Developmental levels define the ages during which skills of varying complexity can be constructed by children. These levels organize skills into a series of increasing complexity, from sensorimotor to representations and then to abstractions. People develop continuously and gradually through these levels across a great many domains. In domains in which they are highly practiced, people can also show stagelike shifts in their understanding. A set of transformation rules explains how skills are combined or modified, but its consideration is beyond the scope of this introductory chapter (see Fischer, 1980; Fischer

& Farrar, 1987). Skill theory can be used to study development during very short as well as long time periods, and across cognitive, social and language domains.

Skills

The skill theory perspective centers on thinking structures, skills, that represent what a student does in a narrow context. These skills are defined in terms of sets of thinking structures. For example, when a child measures the length of a line with a ruler, a specific skill is being used, but this skill is composed of many smaller skills coordinated together forming a single thinking structure. To teach a child how to measure a line means helping a child bring together the necessary skills—understanding the ruler as a number line and coordinating the length of the line to the ruler. Each of these skills is composed of other less complex skills that are linked together into working wholes. Reflex actions are the simplest of skills and form the base structures of these and all other skills.

Any classroom task or student action can be straightforwardly defined in skill theory terms as skills.

Skills in a Classroom Activity

Skills are best understood when they are described for a specific task because skills are the control of activity in specific domains and contexts (Bidell & Fischer, 1992). For example, in a study of an elementary science lesson (Parziale, 1997), skill theory was used to analyze the progression of learning of fifth- and seventh-grade students during a specific design activity following a method of skill theory adaptation pioneered by Granott (1993). Children built bridges across an 11-inch gap between tables using only mini-marshmallows and toothpicks. The limited materials stimulated the students to be creative in their design approaches in order to build structures that would not quickly sag and fall.

In any classroom lesson or activity evidence can be found of changes in thought in many domains. Skill theory expects changes to occur at different rates and levels along various strands of development. During the bridge activity there was evidence of changes in thinking in various domains, such as socially oriented perspective taking and strategy use. However, the purpose of the analysis was to examine only those changes that were directly related to the lesson's goal of teaching children how to design stable structures.

Simple task related skills involved understanding the individual components that could be used to make the bridges, for example, knowing the relative strength of a marshmallow or the length of a toothpick. These simple skills were constructed by student actions on the components. Children then coordinated those skills together, understanding how the components' qualities allowed them to be combined. In this way they quickly learned to connect marshmallows with toothpicks and their bridges began to grow. As these physical components were linked together newer understandings were constructed about the connections and about variations in those connections. For example, the angle of the toothpicks in marshmallows was varied resulting in different building units, such as triangles and squares.

Skill Progression

Because skills are most often composed of simpler skills coordinated together to form more complex skills, skills are sequential. In fact, development occurs as skills are combined through a series of hierarchically ordered levels. In the development of the concept of density, a student who determines the volume and mass of a solid cube understands the density of the object by relating these factors during a lesson. This student is coordinating the two simpler skills into a more complex understanding. A qualitative change in thought occurs because the student understands the relationship between mass and volume rather than considering the concepts as being separate. This qualitative change indicates a shift of understanding from one level of thought to a new higher level of complexity, although students typically vacillate between understanding and not understanding for a time before they consolidate a stable skill. These shifts are the guideposts that teachers can use to measure student progress from one moment to the next.

Framework of Levels

Because each classroom lesson requires its own skill sequence adapted to the goals and environment of the lesson, it is important to understand clearly the way that skills are related in sequences. Skill theory defines skill sequences by organizing skills in a hierarchical framework. These sequences predict the skills and skill progressions for learning concepts, such as density and bridge structure. A spatial metaphor, shown in Fig. 5.1, is useful in understanding how skills are composed of coordinated skills from previous levels.

The dots in the diagram are specific skills and the lines connecting them represent a coordination of these skills. Note that the coordinations of skills are not at all random. These coordinations follow a pattern of growth that all task sequences for lessons and activities will follow.

In the example of the concept of density, both mass and volume can be represented as single sets which are developed separately. These two skills

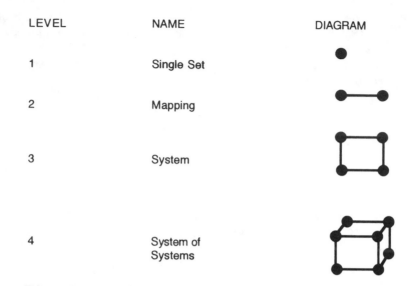

LEVEL	NAME	DIAGRAM
1	Single Set	
2	Mapping	
3	System	
4	System of Systems	

FIG. 5.1. A metaphor for the cycle of four levels.

could be represented as unconnected dots. When these ideas are understood as being linked together in the concept of density a qualitative shift occurs. This change can be represented by connecting the dots with a line. A student who fully understands the concept of density knows how mass and volume vary in relationship to one another. Mass and volume are then fully coordinated as a system and could be represented by the square figure. In this figure the vertical lines represent the variation in each concept and the horizontal lines the relation between each concepts' variation. If a student links another system to the density system, this new thinking complex could be represented by the cube. When a student understands the relationship between molecular kinetics and density such a system of systems is operating.

Learning Linked to Long Term Development

The pattern of skill coordinations made by children in classrooms is the same as the pattern of changes in long-term development. This pattern repeats through four tiers—reflex, action, representational, and abstract—forming 13 levels of development.

Table 5.1 provides the general definitions for the levels through the last three tiers, the most important in classrooms. The cycle overlaps between tiers so that the system of systems level ending one tier is the first single set level of the next tier. Table 5.1 also provides age periods during which people can construct skills at each level. This table represents a long-term develop-

TABLE 5.1

Definition of Developmental Skill Levels

Level	Definition	Age Period of Emergence
Action 1 Single Sets	A child understands how to act on specific things in the world but cannot relate different ways of acting on them	4–6 months
Action 2 Mappings	A child uses one action to bring about a second action.	6–7 months
Action 3 Systems	A child controls complex variations in means and ends.	1–2 years
Action 4 or Representation 1 System of Systems	A child represents simple properties of objects, events, and people, or of their own immediate actions.	Early preschool
Representation 2 Mapping	A child relates variations in one representation to variations in a second representation.	Late preschool
Representation 3 Systems	A child relates subsets of two or more representations but cannot think of objects in the abstract.	Grade school years
Representation 4 or Abstract 1 System of Systems	A person abstracts an intangible attribute that characterizes broad categories of objects, events or people.	Late grade school early high school
Abstract 2 Mappings	A person relates one abstract concept with another	Late high school
Abstract 3 Systems	A person relates subsets of two or more abstract concepts.	Early adulthood
Abstract 4 System of Systems	A person coordinates two or more abstract systems to form a principle.	Early adulthood

mental sequence against which task sequences of short-term (classroom) development can be compared. Skill theory, therefore, offers a way of connecting the activities designed by teachers with children's development.

Levels in the Bridge Building Task

The bridge task skills were arranged in a sequence based on this concept of progression through levels as shown in Table 5.2. Note that the skill levels described for the bridge task are always composed of skills from the previous level. In this way skills are not just dependent on simpler skills, but they are coordinations of those simpler skills.

TABLE 5.2
Bridge Building Activity Task Sequence

Level 1

Definition	A student acts on marshmallows and toothpicks and observes the characteristics of these objects as reflected in his or her actions, but does not yet understand how the actions can affect the objects
Examples	1. 03:01 Pam *"Look at this toothpick, it's like warped."*
Skill	**A student observes variation in the straightness of a toothpick.**
	2. 06:33 Mary *"The marshmallows aren't that strong either."* (Mary is squeezing a marshmallow between her fingers.)
Skill	**Mary feels the relative strength of a marshmallow.**

Level 2

Definition	A student understands how his or her actions affect the components of the bridge.
Examples	1. 10:05 Will *"Not that way, Josh, you're going to crush it."* (Will is warning Josh that the way he is moving the bridge is crushing it.)
Skill	**Will connects his partner's actions with a change in the bridge.**
	2. 09:45 Pam *"What we could do is we could put on here one, one and one and ... "* (Pam is indicating where on the growing structure more toothpicks could be placed.)
Skill	**Pam understands that adding more toothpicks will cause the bridge to enlarge.**

Level 3

Definition	A student understands how a variation in their action relates to a variation in a single aspect of the form or function of the bridge.
Examples	1. 22:34 Mary *"Let's just add on here and see if it works."* Beth *"No ... that will weigh it down."*
Skill	**Beth understands that changing the number of components changes the weight of the bridge.**
	2. 28:32 Sue *"I'm looking for a square right? I stick these things* (toothpicks) *in at an angle.... Like this."* (Sue shows two toothpicks stuck in the same marshmallow at 90 degrees to each other)
Skill	**Sue understands that changing the angle of toothpicks stuck in marshmallows changes the form of the bridge.**

Level 4

Definition	A student describes a property of his or her bridge, and relates, simultaneously, two building systems to form a representation.
Example	28:28 Will *"We don't need to double up this part, OK, because triangles are strong enough anyway. Get this out. But now we have to double up these, OK? So we have stuff here."* (Will explains that some sections of the bridge are already strong enough, so extra toothpicks should be moved to weaker sections.
Skill	**Will judges the variation in different section's strength and work to balance the strength of these sections** *(strength distribution).*

In the classroom study, the sequence described in Table 5.2 was used as a ruler to measure student progress. Teachers, in the school district where the study took place, for many years believed that children smoothly progressed in understanding about structures through this bridge building activity. However, the study based on the sequence in Table 5.2 proved that progress was not very smooth or extensive.

Teachers realize the importance of sequences like that in Table 5.2 and have similar progressions in mind when lessons are designed and used. In the alternate example of density, when students are having difficulty, teachers know that they need to review the basic skills of mass and volume. Skill theory provides a coherent and practical means of defining and identifying the skills and sequences in learning activities.

Skill Diagrams

Skill theory represents skills diagrammatically to precisely define the nature and context of skills. Table 5.3 provides an outline of this diagraming method that parallels the generalized definitions from Table 5.1.

In Table 5.3, the capital letters are single set skills and the brackets at each level enclose the structure of previous skills that are coordinated as new skills. Level 1, the beginning of the cycle, presents just single set skills (which are composed of system of systems skills from the previous tier). At Level 2 the straight line between the letters represents the mapping together of two single set skills. Cause and effect relationships, such as knowing that a marshmallow stuck with a toothpick will make a larger unit, are forms of mappings. The double-ended arrows in the Level 3 diagrams represent the system that is formed between variation in one side of a mapping and variation on the other side. For example, a student understands that there is a relationship between the number of components and the mass of the bridge. A Level 4 structure is formed when two such Level 3 systems are coordinated together, represented by the double lined arrow in the diagram.

Table 5.4 demonstrates the diagramming system as it was adapted for the bridge building study.

Using Skill Theory—Constructing a Task Sequence

A skill theory task sequence, as in Tables 5.1 and 5.4, predicts the pattern of short-term development during a lesson or an activity. To create this tool, teachers need to follow a series of steps.

1. List the task-related qualitative changes in thinking that the lesson is expected to stimulate. (This step will help ensure that certain changes in

thought are not just hoped for but are actively being encouraged by the lesson.)

2. Define these changes as skills by specifying the actions that are controlled by the students. (This step focuses the analysis on the skill theory concept of a person acting on and in a specific environment.)

3. Diagram these changes by the method shown in Table 5.3, and in the example from Table 5.4. (In this way, teachers can define the skills that are being constructed with precision and consistency.)

4. Sequence these diagrammed skills according to the cycle of levels in Figure 5.1. (The sequence will reveal what essential skills are missing from consideration in the design of the lesson.)

5. Compare this sequence to the developmental levels in Table 5.1. (This comparison allows the developmental appropriateness of the lesson to be judged.)

6. Use the sequence to observe student actions, including: conversations, physical acts, and qualities of any product. (The sequence is a ruler against which patterns of progression can be measured.)

Skill theory tools, such as the task sequence for building bridges, provide teachers with direct means to describe and predict development as it occurs in their classrooms. However, the tools provided must be adapted to the context and goals of each lesson. This investment in a teacher's time and effort is necessary because skill theory takes into consideration the effect that different contexts and goals have on learning. In other words, skill theory can explain development as it is directed and influenced by teachers.

TABLE 5.3

Skill Theory Method of Diagramming

Level	Description	Diagram
1	Single set	[W] or [X]
2	Mapping	[W — X]
3	System	$[W_{A,B} \longleftrightarrow X_{C,D}]$
4	System of systems	$\begin{bmatrix} W \longleftrightarrow X \\ \Updownarrow \\ Y \longleftrightarrow Z \end{bmatrix}$ or [M]

TABLE 5.4

Skill Diagrams for the Bridge Building Activity

1	A student observes that marshmallow are relatively massive.	marshmallows have significant mass
2	A student understands that adding more toothpicks will cause the bridge to enlarge.	adding components ⟷ bridge grows
3	A student understands that changing the angle of toothpicks stuck in a marshmallow changes the form of the building units.	90° CONNECTION ANGLE 60° ⟷ squares BRIDGE SECTION triangles
4	A student can judge the variation in different sections' strengths and work to balance the strengths of these sections —*strength distribution.*	building triangular sections ⟷ observed to be strong sections ⇕ doubling toothpicks ⟷ seen to make strong sections

EDUCATIONALLY SIGNIFICANT FEATURES

Many unique opportunities are provided when skill theory is adapted to the specifics of a classroom lesson. This section discusses four especially important ones:

- The mutual effects of classroom learning and long-term development can be understood
- Student progress from one moment to the next can be closely examined
- Uneven development from domain to domain can be measured and explained
- The range of performance within learning domains can be predicted.

Learning Linked to Development

Skill theory explains both long- and short-term development by using the same framework. In this way, task sequences created by teachers to explain short-term development stimulated by classroom lessons (example in Table 5.2) can be compared against the skill theory developmental sequence (Table 5.1).

This connection between classroom learning and developmental change allows teachers to set the learning expectations of their lessons and activities to appropriate developmental levels. In the example of the bridge building activity, the task sequence (Table 5.2) provides a ruler against which student progress can be measured. This ruler also can be compared to the developmental expectations given in Table 5.1. Such a comparison will show that children as young as early preschool can make such a bridge. Preschool children, however, would have to be performing at their optimal level of thinking ability to complete a stable bridge successfully.

If the skill levels required by the task are more complex than the children of that age are expected to coordinate, the lesson goals can be modified to match lower skill levels. If the lesson skill levels are near the optimal developmental levels of the students, the teacher can make sure that significant support and practice is given for success. Learning expectations can, therefore, be set to children's development making instruction more efficient and effective. Also spared is much needless frustration on the part of both teachers and students.

Skill theory also can demonstrate the contribution of teacher-designed lessons to students development. Unlike Piaget's view of mental development limited by biological development, skill theory is hopeful about the teacher's role. Skill theory suggests that both environment and biology contribute together in mental development. Teachers can set goals for lessons to stimulate the development of students. A lesson can guide children through a skill sequence that leads to the coordination of skills at a child's present optimum level or just beyond. For example, if preschoolers were building stable marshmallow and toothpick bridges, they would be controlling a Level 4 skill. A Level 4 skill, coordinating two systems of design variation, would be at the leading edge of their overall thinking development.

For the first time teachers have analytic tools that directly link their work in the classroom to their students' development.

Microanalysis

Classroom teachers need tools that can describe learning as it happens under their direction, in classrooms full of children. Skill theory offers just such tools, focused to the immediate changes that happen during lessons:

- Skill structures, defined with aspects of both the student and the environment, consider the amount of support provided by the instructor and peers. Teachers can, therefore, describe and analyze each step in learning a concept as it occurs in the classroom.

- Skills can be placed in a sequence that aids in identifying poorly supported changes in thinking, the degree of student progress, and unexpected patterns in learning.
- Student actions, conversations, and the products of lessons (written material or physical objects) can be used as evidence of the coordination of skills.

Skills and sequences allow teachers to take a close and direct look at the activities of students, and to make a microanalysis of their step-by-step progress. Before the study of the bridge task was made, teachers who had been using the lesson for years believed that students made steady progress in understanding bridgelike structures. However, these teachers had previously measured progress only by the quality of the bridge that was produced. The skill-based study, by identifying step-by-step changes in thought during the activity, proved that progress was not smooth or extensive. The analysis of student conversations showed that the individual students understood much less than the teachers expected for two reasons. The first is that students constructed understandings in groups rather than as individuals. The second was that students used a trial and error form of strategy, limiting the degree that component interaction was understood.

As a result of these findings, the building unit was modified to stimulate more individual complex thought. These modifications included having children build other types of structures and by having individuals report on the similarities of successful designs. These added lessons stimulated children to reflect on, and to use again in building, the more complex ideas observed in their marshmallow and toothpick bridges. The extended lessons made the complex relationships between physical components in bridges more overt to both students and their teachers.

The same type of microanalysis is possible for lessons in any subject by analyzing student actions, conversations, or the students' developing products. Teachers no longer need to infer the extent of learning only from tests or final products. This also means that teachers can more equitably assess students who lack test taking skills or those who have difficulty in producing a finished product.

Uneven Development

Teachers have long observed, although most theories do not predict, the uneven development of students. In skill theory terms, a student might be able to control Level 8 skills in writing but might not perform tasks in math that require only Level 6 skills. This sort of uneven development was a great source of concern for Piaget because of his conception of thinking structures working across domains. Skill theory, however, predicts uneven development, not just across large domains, but even in narrower ones. For example, a student might be able to count a large number of beans from a jar but be unable to count the number of his classmates.

According to skill theory, development occurs unevenly along a vast number of interconnected strands similar to a web. Teachers know from experience that some children demonstrate great variation in their cognitive abilities across subject areas. During the bridge study it was a challenge to focus the coding of conversation on the bridge building task because students showed evidence of skills at work in so many domains simultaneously. For example, these students actively switched from one approach to problem solving to another, demonstrating development along a strategy-making strand. However, mostly they evidenced development of the social aspects of being middle-school students.

Even when only conversations about the bridge designs were selected out for analysis from videotapes, it could be seen that students were working out several different design aspects simultaneously rather than following one element of design to fruition. For example, two girls alternated between a discussion of triangles as building units, and the quality of the connections that they were making with marshmallows. Skill theory analysis made it possible to view the way that students worked on many strands of development during the lesson.

The results of the bridge-building study leads to the question of just what strands of development are important in a classroom, and how progress can be managed on so many fronts. With skill theory, teachers can make an analysis to begin to sort out the dynamics of their classroom's web of development, perhaps for the first time.

Range of Performance

A large part of a teacher's job is to provide enough support for his or her students to construct new understandings. Teachers know well that a student's range of performance is directly related to this degree of support. Skill theory holds that understandings are not static modules that reside in a person's brain. Instead, understandings are viewed as being reformulated in the interaction of student and environment as they are needed. Student performance must, therefore be expected to range greatly, with optimal levels possible only under supportive conditions with significant practice. The skillful construction of these conditions and practice mark the work of effective teachers.

Often, teachers make notes to their peers, or to their students, that the performance expected during a lesson did not occur. Unfortunately, too many teachers are too quick to either blame the students for their lack of effort, or themselves for lack of teaching skill. This classroom inconsistency is rarely recognized as a positive feature of instruction and learning. However, many research studies using a skill-based analysis of both children and adults solving problems show that a form of regression in skills occurs when people of any age start a new project or activity (Granott, 1993). This regression is a natural mechanism of adjustment. When people find themselves in a new situation they can not maintain the higher levels of thinking complexity that they can use in familiar domains. They efficiently adjust the complexity of their thinking to the point where what they do in the new situation matches the complexity of the way they can think about the new situation.

An example of adaptive regression can be seen in the discrepancy between the developmental levels expected of the fifth and seventh graders (Table 5.1) and the performance levels of the students during the bridge building task (Table 5.2). The students who participated in the study could be expected to control Level-1 abstract skills in contexts in which they had significant experience, perhaps in social and language domains. However, when these students worked on building a bridge, they regressed to simpler action level skills that they could control in this new context. The students efficiently adapted the complexity of their thinking to the novelty of the context.

By using a skill theory analysis teachers can begin to understand the effect of support and practice on range of performance. The range of performance observed during lessons that might have been used for many years suddenly can be understood and controlled.

CONCLUSION

The results of skill-theory-based analysis of learning and problem solving are not very different from the observations that teachers make in their own classrooms. Skill theory, however, can help teachers understand and predict these common observations:

- The regression to basic skills when students seem to be capable of higher level thinking
- Students' development along varied pathways rather than along a single course
- Students' great range in performance across learning domains and even within narrow ones.

By using skill theory teachers do not need to rely so much on hope in designing lessons and assessing student work. Teachers can analyze the actual course of learning that occurs in classrooms with skill theory. They can watch as their lessons shape the way that children learn and develop. Teachers can evaluate their lessons and assess student progress much more directly than through the use of testing. They also can begin to view the potential of natural mechanisms such as regression and development along multiple strands (Granott, Fischer, & Parziale, 1997). Perhaps by activating, instead of constraining, these natural learning mechanisms teachers can make classrooms even more productive learning environments.

REFERENCES

Bandura, A., & Walters, R. H. (1963). *Social learning and personality development.* New York: Holt, Rinehart & Winston.

Bidell, T. R., & Fischer, K. W. (1992). Cognitive development in educational contexts: Implications of skill theory. In A. Demetriou, M. Shayer, & A. Efklides (Eds.), *The neo-Piagetian theories of cognitive development go to school* (pp. 11–30). London: Routledge & Kegan Paul.

Fischer, K. W. (1980). A theory of cognitive development: The control and construction of hierarchies of skills. *Psychological Review, 87,* 477–531.

Fischer, K. W., & Farrar, M. J. (1987). Generalizations about generalizations: How a theory of skills development explains both generality and specificity. *International journal of psychology, 22,* 643–677.

Fischer, K. W., & Granott, N. (1995). Beyond one-dimensional change: Parallel concurrent distributed processes in learning and development. *Human Development, 38,* 302–314.

Fischer, K. W., & Knight, C. C. (1990). Cognitive development in real children: Levels and variations. In B. Z. Presseisen (Ed.), *Learning and thinking styles: Classroom interaction* (pp. 43–67). Washington, DC: National Education Association.

Fischer, K. W., & Pipp, S. L. (1984). Processes of cognitive development: Optimal level and skill acquisition. In R. J. Sternberg (Ed.), *Mechanisms of cognitive development* (pp. 45–80). New York: Freeman.

Fischer, K. W., & Silvern, L. (1985). Stages and individual differences in cognitive development. *Annual Review of Psychology, 36,* 613–648.

Granott, N. (1993). Patterns of interaction in the co-construction of knowledge: Separate minds, joint effort, and weird creatures. In R. H. Wozniak & K. W. Fischer (Eds.), *Development in context: Acting and thinking in specific environments.* (pp. 183–207). Hillsdale, NJ: Lawrence Erlbaum Associates.

Granott, N., Fischer, K. W., & Parziale, J. (1997). *Bridging to the unknown: A fundamental transition mechanism in learning and development.* Manuscript in preparation, The cognitive Development Laboratory, Harvard University.

Parziale, J. (1997). *Microdevelopment during an activity based science lesson.* Unpublished doctoral dissertation. Harvard University, Cambridge, MA.

Piaget, J. (1970a). *Science of education and the psychology of the child.* New York: Orion Press.

Piaget, J. (1970b). Piaget's theory. In P. H. Mussen (Ed.), *Carmichael's manual of child psychology* (Vol. 1, pp. 5–24)). New York: Wiley.

Skinner, B. F. (1938). *The behavior of organisms.* New York: Appleton-Century-Crofts.

Vygotsky, L. S. (1962). *Thought and language.* Cambridge, MA: MIT Press.

Vygotsky, L. S. (1978). *Mind in Society: The development of higher psychological processes.* Cambridge, MA: Harvard University Press.

CHAPTER 6

The *g* Factor
and the Design of Education

Arthur R. Jensen
University of California, Berkeley

A scientific theory of intelligence, in the true sense of the term, cannot be translated directly into a prescription for practice. In any case, a real theory of intelligence does not yet exist. If it did exist, it would describe the anatomical, neural, and chemical processes in the brain that govern the types of behavior that are claimed to characterize intelligence. The major aim of present-day cognitive neuroscience is to achieve this kind of understanding of how brain mechanisms produce intelligent behavior, but as yet we have no comprehensive account of how the brain does this. After all, the human brain is the most complex structure known to modern science, and the technology needed for probing the living brain in action, such as the measurement of evoked electrical potentials by electroencephalography, or of the metabolic rates in specific regions and structures of the brain by positron emission tomography (PET) scan, or mapping localized functions by magnetic resonance imaging (MRI), are all of fairly recent origin in the history of scientific instrumentation. Hence, scientists are just beginning to investigate how the living brain performs the cognitive functions subsumed under the term *intelligence*.

Throughout the 20th century, however, psychologists have discovered many important facts about the nature of intelligent behavior itself. Some of the most well-established of these facts are realities of human nature that can be recognized and taken account of by our educational policies and practices to increase the benefits of education for every student in the school population. Ignoring these facts, I believe, limits the benefits of education to only some fraction of a nation's total population.

The most fundamental of these realities, as concerns public education, is the fact that there is an exceedingly wide range of individual differences in cognitive abilities in the school population. Indeed, the most troublesome concern of present-day universal public education seems to be the problem of how to deal with the conspicuous variation in ability. Before suggesting ways for the educational system to take account of this phenomenon successfully, I should spell out what we know of its most important aspects.

THE FIELDS OF RESEARCH ON MENTAL ABILITIES

Ability here simply means a response that any organism can make to some form of stimulation, either external or internal, that is not an innate or hard-wired reflex and for which the organism's response can be objectively assessed, for example, in terms of its magnitude, latency (i.e., the time interval between stimulus and response), appropriateness (e.g., effective–ineffective, or correct–incorrect), and consistency. An ability is a *mental* ability only if individual differences in the ability are not mainly the result of individual differences in sensorimotor functions, such as visual and auditory acuity or physical strength and agility. This definition of *mental ability* is open-ended in that, for human beings at least, there is no theoretical limit to the number of different abilities that may exist, because there is no conceivable limit to the number of different things that persons may be able to do in the bounds of this definition of mental ability.

Behavioral research on human mental abilities has five major branches: (a) psychometrics, or the technology of measuring abilities; (b) differential psychology, or the study of the variety and correlational structure of individual and group (e. g., age, race, sex, social class) differences in abilities; (c) behavioral genetics, or study of the relative influences of genetic and environmental factors as causes of variation in abilities; (d) cognitive development, or the study of how abilities emerge, mature, differentiate, and develop throughout the individual's life span; and (e) instruction, or the applied psychology of inculcating knowledge and specific cognitive skills.

The first three of these branches are closely interrelated, but each one also constitutes a large and highly developed discipline in its own right;

together they constitute an important branch of behavioral science. Their aim is mainly scientific, that is, exploratory and explanatory, by proposing theories that suggest empirically testable hypotheses, performing studies and experiments that could disconfirm an hypothesis, and, if so, revising the theory. Much, or perhaps most, of the explanatory power that we now possess in this field, however, is of such a nature as to have little direct relevance to the main mission of education.

Research on mental ability has been mainly concerned with understanding the causes or sources of variance in many different behavioral measures and describing their covariance structure. *Variance* is simply a precise statistical measure of the degree of dispersion of individual differences in a particular measurable variable in a specified group of individuals or in a representative sample of some population. Covariance structure refers to the degree to which various measurements covary (or correlate) with one another. A particular variable, X, might have some part (or component) of its total variance in common with another variable, Y, for example, and both X and Y might also have components of variance in common with variable Z. If one and the same component of variance is common to all of the different variables (X, Y, and Z), it is called a *common factor*. The mathematical technique for analyzing a matrix of correlations among various measurements (for example, scores on a variety of tests) to determine the number of common factors and the proportion of the total variance accounted for by each factor is known as factor analysis.

One point of interest to the psychometrician is the number of independent common factors that exist among a large number of different tests that superficially appear to measure different mental abilities. Psychometricians are also interested in the relative "size" of each of the common factors, as indicated by the proportion of variance in all of the tests that is accounted for, or "explained" by, each factor.

The correlations among various measures of scholastic performance (e. g., spelling, reading comprehension, arithmetic, and knowledge of scholastic subject matter), along with measures of various nonscholastic mental abilities (such as various types of nonverbal IQ tests), can be analyzed together by means of factor analysis to discover their covariance structure. Finding the components of variance (i.e., individual differences) in scholastic performance and discovering their genetic and environmental sources of variance by the analytic methods of behavioral genetics are extremely different aims from those of research on the psychology of instruction, which tries to discover the best means for helping pupils attain maximum personal benefit from the time they spend in school. Yet, I believe educators need to know something about the results of factor analysis and behavior–genetic analysis to be more effective in the conduct of instruction throughout the whole educational process. So I try here to abstract from the research in psychometrics, differential psychology, and behavioral genetics what I consider the now well-established empirical findings that seem most relevant to the educational system's responsibility for dealing with the ubiquitous problem of individual differences in scholastic performance. These findings can be listed as a series of points. Then I indicate their implications for education and how they might be implemented in practice.

THE PRIMACY OF THE g FACTOR IN SCHOLASTIC PERFORMANCE

The number of mental abilities (as defined earlier) is unlimited, but the number of independent common factors is relatively small. In other words, if we factor analyzed a great many different tests that were devised to measure as many seemingly different kinds of abilities as test constructors are able to imagine, we would find that, because of the great amount of correlation among the various tests, there are only a limited number of common factors represented in the whole lot. Without going into the technical details of factor analysis, it can be noted that the common factors differ greatly in their generality, that is, the number of different tests that reflect a particular factor and the amount of the tests' variance that is accounted for by a given factor. Factors that enter into only certain groups of tests based on a particular type of content are called *group factors*.

The more general group factors are labeled *verbal* (tests containing verbal material, such as vocabulary, reading comprehension, sentence completion, deciphering scrambled sentences), *spatial visualization* (tests based on non-verbal figural or puzzlelike problems, block designs, paper-folding, block counting), *numerical reasoning* (tests containing arithmetic problems, estimating quantities, number series), *mechanical reasoning* (tests based on problems involving the workings of balances, levers, cogwheels, gears, weights, and pulleys; see Carroll, 1993), and *memory* (tests requiring the recall of specific previously acquired information). There are also other factors of lesser generality, some of which may be called special talents, such as musical and artistic abilities (Carroll, 1993).

Over and above all of these group factors there exists one large superfactor that enters not only into tests of a particular type but into a great variety of tests of mental abilities, regardless of their specific knowledge content or required skills. There are few tests of mental ability that do not reflect this superfactor to some degree. A great deal of empirical evidence suggests that it may well be that the case that any test of mental ability, as defined earlier, reflects this superfactor to some degree, however slightly, when it is factor analyzed among a large and diverse collection of cognitive tests given to a large and representative sample of the general population (Carroll, 1993; Jensen, 1987, 1998).

This generalization is impossible to prove, because not every conceivable mental test can be tried. The generalization could be disproved, however, simply by discovering or constructing a test that qualified as a reliable measure of a mental ability under the foregoing definition, which, when factor analyzed under the conditions just specified, fails to show a statistically significant correlation with the superfactor, that is, a nonzero loading on the general factor of the highest order of the matrix of correlations among a large and diverse collection of mental tests. This has been attempted, but, to the best of my knowledge, no such demonstration has yet been accomplished (Alliger, 1988).

This ubiquitous superfactor is appropriately called *general mental ability*. It is a common source of variance across a great many cognitive tests of every description. Its existence was originally hypothesized in the mid-19th century, even before the invention of psychometric tests, but it was not discovered empirically until early in the 20th century, when, in 1904, the British psychologist Charles Spearman (1863–1945) invented a method of factor analysis that could prove the existence of a factor of general mental ability, which he labeled simply *g* (Spearman, 1927). The general factor in a battery or collection of conventional mental tests is typically referred to as *psychometric g*. It has proved to be one of the fundamental constructs of psychometrics and differential psychology.

Whatever is the ultimate cause of *g*, still the subject of ongoing research, its existence is manifested throughout positive correlations among diverse measures of cognitive ability. All positive correlations among various tests means that an individual's level of performance on any one test statistically predicts to some degree that individual's level of performance on any other test. Here are a number of things I think educators should know about the *g* factor.

Most important from the standpoint of education is the fact that *g* is the largest measurable source of common factor variance in scholastic performance, whether it is assessed by teacher's grades or by objective tests of scholastic achievement (Jensen, 1993a). In considering the entire school population, rather than just some restricted segment, it is a fact that *g* accounts for at least half of the total variance in scholastic achievement, which is far more than any other single source of variance independent of *g* (Cronbach & Snow, 1977; Gedye, 1981). The other measurable sources of variance that play second fiddle to *g* include all of the group factors of ability, special talents, specific non-*g* disabilities (e. g., dyslexia), personality variables, and students' socioeconomic status, sex, race, and national origin. By its very nature, the educational process, when it encompasses almost the entire population, highlights the effects of individual differences in level of *g* probably more than any other aspect of life in the modern industrialized world.

The strong relationship between individual differences in *g* and in occupational status and income in our society is largely mediated by the even stronger relationship between *g* and educational attainments (Jensen, 1993a; Snow & Yalow, 1982). We all take delight, of course, in stories of school failures or dropouts who go on to become billionaires or win Nobel Prizes, but these exceptional cases can by no means contradict the statistics based on large representative samples of a nation's population.

Although the *g* factor accounts for considerably more of the variance than any one of the group factors in a large number of diverse mental tests, it accounts for no more than about one third of the total variance in all of the wide variety of tests known to psychologists and that have been factor analyzed.

Unlike any specific ability or any group factor, *g* cannot be described in terms of the informational content or the types of skills called upon by the tests that are loaded with *g*. Vocabulary and block design tests, for example, are about equally *g*-loaded, yet they superficially have nothing in common. The block design test, for example, is a completely nonverbal test in which the participant is shown pictures of simple 2-dimensional designs and is asked to create a copy of the design using a set of colored blocks. The fact that g is loaded to varying degrees in every type of mental test implies that it cannot be described in terms of any one type of test.

Although all tests of mental ability are loaded on *g*, some tests have much larger *g* loadings than others; on a scale of 0 to 1, the *g* loadings of virtually all existing mental tests of any kind range continuously between about .20 and .90 (i.e., from 20% tp 90% of the total variance in different tests).

The degree of *complexity* (but not necessarily the difficulty) of the mental operations required by a test (or task of any kind) generally distinguishes between those tests with high *g* loadings and those with low *g* loadings (Jensen, 1987).

Not only formal psychometric tests but also many kinds of real-life activity that make cognitive demands, such as thinking, remembering, judging, decision making, reasoning, learning from experience, recalling relevant acquired knowledge or skills, and the like, are *g* loaded to varying degrees. Therefore *g* is reflected in a great many aspects of life, not just those generally thought of as scholastic, academic, or intellectual (Gordon, 1997; Gottfredson, 1997).

Individual differences in the best practical measures of *g*, such as the IQ obtained from a battery of diverse tests (e. g., the Stanford-Binet Intelligence Scale [Thorndike, Hagen, & Sattler, 1986] or the Wechsler Intelligence scales [Matarazzo, 1972], or the Kaufman Assessment Battery for Children [Kaufman & Kaufman, 1983) are approximately normally distributed in the population. These widely used test batteries are individually administered by a trained psychologist; each battery consists of a dozen or more diverse subtests designed to measure ability factors such as verbal, numerical reasoning, spatial reasoning, and memory; and about half of the subtests in each battery are performance tests, that is, they do not require reading or any overt use of language. In these tests' standardization sample, the scores, scaled as IQ, form the familiar bell curve, which means that most of the population is clustered around the middle (or average) of the distribution curve, with gradually decreasing percentages of the population showing increasingly below-average or above-average scores. On the IQ scale, with the average IQ set at 100 and the standard deviation set at 15, 50% of the population falls between IQs of 90 and 110, whereas 25% falls below an IQ of 90 and 25% falls above an IQ of 110.

The g construct does not reside in the tests or in test items, which merely serve as vehicles for measuring individual differences in the level of whatever causal factors are reflected by scores on highly g-loaded tests. Because tests having nothing superficially in common that would cause them to be correlated because they possess elements of knowledge and skills in common, it is reasonable to infer that the basic causal factors reflected by g are not intrinsic to the tests or to the methodology of factor analysis but are a property of the brain, specifically those neural processes involved in information processing and which cause differences between individuals in their speed and efficiency of information processing.

I have presented this view in detail elsewhere (Jensen, 1987, 1992, 1993b, 1997b). In brief, my view is that cognition is a form of information processing, and the g factor reflects individual differences in information processing as manifested in functions such as attending, selecting, searching, internalizing, deciding, discriminating, generalizing, learning, remembering, and using incoming and past-acquired information to solve problems and cope with the exigencies of the environment. These properties are obviously critical determinants of the individual's response to any educational experience, either formal or incidental. Other views of the nature of g based on less elemental processes than I have hypothesized emphasize metaprocesses, which are hypothetical constructs that serve an executive or controlling function in the deployment of the more elemental information processes, such as planning, selection of appropriate schemata for various kinds of problem solving, and monitoring, and evaluating one's own performance (Sternberg & Gardner, 1982). There are even more radically different views of the nature of human intelligence, but it is beyond the scope of this chapter to describe each of them. A fair and brief treatment of these can be found in an article by Wagner and Sternberg (1986) and more comprehensively in a recent and admirably balanced but entirely noncritical book by Gardner, Kornhaber, and Wake (1996). Although recognizing the existence of g, Howard Gardner (1993) minimized its importance and believed that human abilities can best be described in terms of at least seven different multiple intelligences, a view that appears to have gained greater acceptance among educators than among students of psychometrics and differential psychology.

Individual differences in the functions represented by g are strongly rooted in biology. This is demonstrated by two classes of evidence.

The first line of evidence is the fact that hereditary or genetic factors are involved in individual differences in test scores, as shown by the methods of quantitative genetic analysis applied to mental test data from various kinships, such as measuring the degrees of resemblance in IQ between identical twins reared apart in different environments as compared with identical twins reared together in the same family environment, or between genetically unrelated children reared together in the same family environment. These methods have been used to estimate statistically the proportion of genetic variance in a trait (based on individual differences in the population). This proportion of genetic variance is called the *heritability* of the trait (Plomin, 1990).

The heritability of IQ increases with age, going from about .40 in early childhood to about .80 in later maturity (McGue, Bouchard, Iacona, & Lykken, 1993; Fulker, Cherny, & Cardon, 1993). By adolescence, genetic factors contribute a larger part of the variance in IQ than is contributed by nongenetic or environmental factors. It is psychometric g, rather than other components of test score variance, that reflects most of the genetic variance (Thompson, Detterman, & Plomin, 1991).

The best single predictor of the heritability of individual differences in the scores on a given cognitive test is that test's g loading as determined when the test is entered into a factor analysis among a wide variety of other tests (Jensen, 1987; Pedersen, Plomin, & McClearn, 1994). It is noteworthy that, by late adolescence, the nongenetic or environmental component of variance in IQ, at least in industrialized societies, is not attributable to differences in family background (parent's occupation, socioeconomic status, number of books in the home, and the like) but consists of a multitude of small, largely random microenvironmental causes that make for differences among siblings reared in the same family (Jensen, 1997a; Rowe, 1994). Some of these nongenetic sources of variance are of a biological nature, both prenatal and postnatal, that are related to health, nutrition, and other physical variables that can affect brain development.

The second line of evidence is that certain purely physical measurements are correlated with individual differences in mental test scores and that the relative sizes of these correlations are best predicted by the tests' *g* loadings (Jensen, 1987, 1993b). The more *g*-loaded tests generally show the stronger correlations with the physical measurements. One such physical variable is brain size, or measurements related to brain size, such as head size, internal cranial capacity, and the total volume of the brain (Rushton & Ankney, 1996). Brain volume can be determined precisely by means of magnetic resonance imaging (MRI). It shows correlations with IQ averaging close to +. 4. Another physical variable that is correlated with IQ (and with *g*) is the latency and amplitude of the average evoked potential, which measure the speed and strength of the "spike" of electrical activity that occurs in the brain in response to a single auditory or visual stimulus, such as a click or a flash of light (Deary & Caryl, 1993).

Yet another physical correlate of IQ (which also varies for different tests according to their *g* loadings), is the brain's glucose metabolic rate, as measured by the positron emission tomography (PET) scan, when the individual is engaged in an information processing task, such as taking a mental test or playing a video game (Haier, 1993).

The level of all mental abilities represented by *g* gradually increase with age from infancy to maturity, and, to the degree that they are *g*-loaded, they slowly decline with age in later maturity and, more rapidly, in old age. Brain size, reaction time, nerve conduction velocity, and brain metabolism all show a similar trajectory across the life span (Baltes & Kliegl, 1985; Birren, 1974; Cattell, 1971).

Individual differences in rates of learning are also correlated with *g* and are surprisingly large. Research in the armed forces, for example, shows that the fastest learners among recruits in the training programs are able to attain a satisfactory criterion of performance in the learning of various kinds of subject matter and technical skills some 5 to 10 times faster than the slowest learners. And on measures of *g* obtained in the public school population it has been found that the upper 10% of pupils at 7. 5 years of age are equal to the lower 10% of pupils at 15. 5 years of age in general knowledge and level of scholastic achievement. While some high school juniors and seniors are learning calculus, some others are still struggling with fractions and long division, and still others have simply given up completely on learning math. Individual differences in the ability to learn any specific cognitive skills, for example, skills and knowledge of the kind that schooling is intended to inculcate, are largely a matter of *g*. In fact, the general factor measured in cognitive learning tasks is the same *g* factor as found in psychometric tests (Jensen, 1989a; Snow & Lohman, 1989; Snow & Yalow, 1982).

To the extent that IQ tests measure specific learned cognitive skills, the test scores can be raised by special coaching or training in those specific skills. A gain in retest scores (or scores on highly similar tests) then largely reflects merely narrow transfer of training rather than an increased level of g, which is not a skill at all. I have found no bona fide evidence that the general ability represented by g is itself enhanced by such training (Jensen, 1993a). The prolonged and intensive effort experimentally to "train up" the level of g in children results in improved scores on IQ tests, but apparently what has been trained up in these cases is not g, but some of the specific learnable skills involved in conventional tests. Although the IQ scores of the tutored children are tested to be somewhat higher, these children, on average seldom perform significantly better scholastically than do age-matched control groups that were not so trained (Clarke & Clarke, 1976; Jensen, 1989b; Spitz, 1986). Moreover, the training effect rapidly fades within a year or so and the rates of mental growth of the groups of treated children and their scholastic progress merge with the same growth-curve trajectory as that of the untreated control group. In the range of human environments, the individual's growth curve for g is largely autonomous and hardly is deflected by external psychological or educational manipulations. This is probably because the main source of individual differences represented by g does not consist of a learned skill or set of specific skills but is a developmental aspect of the brain's structural capacity for information processing in general. In the Abecedarian Study (Ramey, 1992), one of the most methodologically rigorous interventions, disadvantaged children at high risk for low IQ and school failure were given intensive educational treatment from infancy to school age. At age 12, they showed a gain of 5. 1 IQ points over an untreated control group (Ramey, 1994). At the last reported testing, when the children were 15 years of age, the difference between the treatment group and the control group was 4. 6 IQ points (Campbell & Ramey 1994, 1995). The validity of even these modest findings and their interpretation, however, have been the subject of quite vehement debate (Ramey, 1993; Spitz, 1992, 1993a, 1993b).

As for social class and racial differences in g, the hypothesis that these group differences have the same causal basis as individual differences regardless of group membership is, I believe, at present most consistent with the preponderance of the empirical evidence related to this question (Rowe & Cleveland, 1997; Rowe, Vazsonyi, & Flannery, 1994, 1995). Mean differences among various population groups are viewed most reasonably simply as individual differences that have been aggregated in certain ways by a number of causal factors—evolutionary, cultural, religious, historical, political, and economic. Hence, I believe that the hypothesis for which there is the strongest evidence at present is that group differences in g (and its many correlates) are as real as individual differences, as variance in both individual and group differences are constituted of the same genetic and environmental sources of variance to about the same degree.

There are, of course, other views of the causes of racial and ethnic group differences, but those that I have examined either are contradicted by direct empirical evidence (Jensen, 1973, 1994), are philosophic opinions and historical speculation put forth in terms that would hardly be subject to empirically testable hypotheses (Gordon & Bhattacharyya, 1994), or are unsupported by relevant psychometric or statistical evidence (Ogbu, 1978; Sowell, 1994). The issue and its relevant evidence are complex, and involve a number of fields in the behavioral and biological sciences; therefore a proper discussion of it would be well beyond the scope of this chapter. Fairly comprehensive and scientifically respectable treatments of the topic are presented elsewhere (Herrnstein & Murray, 1994; Jensen, 1998; Rushton, 1995).

Mental abilities and other psychological traits range widely in every major population group. Therefore, identifying an individual in terms of race, sex, social class, or any other social group membership, affords no justifiable basis for differential educational prescription. This must depend on each pupil's own capabilities, not on group membership.

Finally, as important as *g* is in accounting for variance in scholastic performance, the sum total of educational attainments, occupational level, or career success, it is certainly not the only factor on which these outcomes depend (Shurkin, 1992). This becomes especially apparent when the life histories of the successful and the unsuccessful and of high achievers and ne'er-do-wells are contrasted in all these spheres of performance. Their *g* distributions markedly overlap. It is clear, however, that for any given type of achievement, depending on the degree of complexity of the demands it makes on information processing, the level of *g* required must exceed a certain threshold, or minimum level, to predict any realistic probability of success. This minimum level is inferred from the lowest level of IQ found in testing a large and representative sample of individuals in any given occupation. These minimum IQ levels for over 500 different occupations range from about 40 to 115 (Jensen, 1980,). For example, no one among persons employed as mathematicians was found by the U. S. Employment Service to have an IQ below 115. The probability, therefore, that anyone with an IQ truly less than 115 would become a professor of mathematics at Harvard or Berkeley, for example, is practically nil. Similarly, almost every occupation has its minimum IQ level, which is determined largely by the occupation's demands for information processing and knowledge acquisition. The probability of success in any given pursuit, to the extent that it makes such demands, increases with an increasing level of *g*.

But here is the important point: At every level of g above the requisite minimum threshold for a particular activity, the level of g itself is only a necessary but never a sufficient condition for success in any given educational or occupational pursuit. Other criteria for success, such as a successful marriage or a successful social life are much less related, if at all, to the individual's level of g. In fact, biographies of some of the greatest intellects in history, for example, Newton, Wagner, and Einstein, indicate that these geniuses were personally even less than mediocre in many respects, including what might be called social intelligence. A level of g greater than the threshold is only one of the variables among a number of other individual-difference variables necessary for outstanding performance, even in mainly intellectual pursuits. Personality variables, such as conscientiousness, dependability, emotional stability, energy level, motivation, zeal, and persistence of effort in the face of difficulty or hardship, as well as social skills and interpersonal sensitivity also play a part. For certain types of achievement, some special talent is an essential element in the equation (for example, musical, artistic, literary, mathematical, athletic, or aesthetic sensitivity). It is now believed that, in determining success, all these kinds of personal variables (including g) do not work in an additive way but rather in a multiplicative way, so that no one of the several variables needed for a particular type and level of achievement can be lacking (or be below some critical threshold). Thus an above-threshold level of any one of the several variables required for a particular accomplishment is said to be a necessary but not sufficient condition for achievement. This is as true for educational attainments as it is for occupational attainments.

On the strictly personal side in human relationships, of course, there are obviously many different reasons for one's appreciating and valuing a person regardless of his or her endowments in g or other traits associated with worldly achievements.

EDUCATIONAL IMPLICATIONS OF INDIVIDUAL DIFFERENCES IN g

The American educational system is having trouble living with the consequences of g, which is essentially the problem of unyielding individual differences in the basic information processes on which educability depends (Jensen, 1991). The egalitarian notion that equal educational opportunity should lead to equal outcome, however, is of recent origin. The origins of schooling, in Europe (and later in America), were mainly concerned with educating an intellectual elite, to become the society's professional, managerial, and governing classes. The idea of universal public education came much later. Schools had traditionally expected many children to fail in school or to drop out when their rate of progress lagged markedly behind that of their peers in the lock-step advancement through the grades governed by pupils' chronological age. In the 1920s, for example, fewer than 30% of schoolchildren graduated from high school, as compared with more than 70% in 1960 (Herrnstein & Murray, 1994). Elementary school through 8th grade was in large part a means of screening pupils and selecting the academically talented (Chapman, 1988). This practice considerably reduced the problems associated with the increasingly wide range of individual differences in academic aptitude as students entered high school.

In the early industrial and still largely agrarian society of the 19th century, the most prevalent types of employment available to the majority of the population made comparatively small demands for scholastic skills and types of knowledge much beyond the rudiments of the "three Rs", which could be rather easily acquired by a majority of pupils in 5 or 6 years in the classroom. It was not expected, nor was it even essential, at the time, that a majority would or should continue on to more advanced levels of education. The lifetime consequences of failing school or dropping out at an early age were much less serious then than they are now in our technological and information-intensive society. The traditional system of education, unfortunately, has not changed nearly as radically as the society has changed in its technological employment demands for a more highly educated populace.

The traditional method of schooling is based on one teacher in a classroom of some 30 pupils, all at about the same chronological age, all progressing through standardized lessons and grade levels in a lock-step fashion. The real trouble began when the educational system insisted on universal school attendance from kindergarten through high school without fundamentally altering the conventional lock-step system, and then even tried to do away with ability grouping or tracking. The old system clearly is not set up to do the job that is needed to prepare the vast majority of the school population for productive participation in the nation's workforce in the years ahead.

The major changes that I consider necessary for updating the educational system and materially improving its effectiveness for the whole population, rather than for just the upper half of the bell curve, are so radical, as compared to what has been tried so far, that it cannot possibly consist merely of recommending practices to be carried out by the individual classroom teacher working in the constraints of the present methods of instruction. I suspect that most teachers are doing about as good a job as they possibly can under the present conditions. Any suggestions for them to do something a little different from what they are already doing, I think, will scarcely make a dent in the main problem of today's schools.

The root problem is that the schools are not taking adequate account of individual differences in *g*, and every segment of the bell curve is neglected as a result, especially the upper and the lower quartiles of the *g* distribution. Not until this shortcoming is dealt with effectively will achievements relevant to the employment needs of modern society be materially raised for students at every level of *g*.

It has been found, however, that successful attempts to raise the level of scholastic achievement with computer assisted instruction throughout every segment of the bell curve increases the overall mean level of achievement and individual levels of achievement, but also increases the spread of individual differences (Atkinson, 1974). Despite the inevitable increase in variance, which runs against egalitarian notions, because achievement gains can occur at every level of *g*, a larger number of students will come out above the critical thresholds on educational knowledge and skills required for gainful employment in our modern society. The net result is a positive gain, both for individuals and for society as a whole.

Besides the essential facts of *g* that I have outlined, the recognition of six fundamental principles govern suggestions for educational practice. They are based not on anyone's sentiments or what we might wish for but on what is actually known empirically:

1. *All* children can learn. And all healthy children initially want to learn and like to learn, unless their keenness for learning has been "turned off" by repeated failure and frustration.

2. Some children learn more quickly than others, and these differences in the general school population are greater than most people, including many educators, seem aware.

3. A child learns certain things faster and more easily than other things, and children differ in the things that, for them, are easier or harder to learn.

4. Individual differences in intrinsic motivation for cognitive learning appear to be at least as great as individual differences in *g* and are to some extent related to *g*, although we as yet have little understanding of the causes of differences in intrinsic motivation for cognitive activity.

5. Not every individual will attain a useful mastery of concepts and skills beyond a certain level of complexity and abstraction. That is, there are marked individual differences in the points at which different persons "top out" along the trajectory toward mastery of an intellectual subject matter or skill of a type that has virtually no ceiling on its most advanced level of complexity, regardless of the method of instruction and the amount of time and effort applied. In writing skill, mathematics, or musical composition, for example, not everyone can become a Shakespeare, a Newton, or a Beethoven. Most everyone who tries nevertheless

"tops out" far below such towering levels of achievement, however strong may be their ambition and effort.

6. The best learning environment is like a good cafeteria. It not only affords the essential staples but also offers a large variety of choices to satisfy individual tastes. This allows children to discover their natural interests, proclivities, and special talents. It does not try to force round pegs into square holes. But pupils must also make some effort to learn enough about a variety of subjects and skills to enable the discovery of their areas of strongest potential for mastery. The motivation for such effort initially may have to be instigated and stimulated by parents and teachers. The father of the three Beethoven brothers had to make them practice their piano lessons; two of them discovered they were musical duds and quit taking music lessons; one of them, however, discovered he was a musical genius, but even he at first had to be made to practice, and, of course, the rest of his story is history. Psychologists now know that, at the higher levels of achievement, success is attained by individuals' trying and selecting those pursuits that best suit their particular aptitudes and interests.

In accord with these guiding principles, what sort of educational practices would probably be most effective for a system of universal public education designed to meet the future needs of our technological society?

In the most general terms, it would take into account ability differences, not by trying to eliminate variance, but by designing programs of educational input that can maximize the acquisition of the knowledge and skills most apt to benefit students (and society) after they leave school.

From the beginning of schooling, this would require a highly branching educational program, going from the same initial instruction in "basics" for all children, and thereafter branching frequently and extensively but never in a uniform or lock-step fashion for any particular group of children, whether by chronological age, or mental age, or by any other group classification. Progress through the instructional program would be geared entirely to each individual's performance at each point in time.

The kind of program I envision is impossible in the present-day classroom. If it were to be conducted under such conditions, it would require much more than a feasible extent of homogeneous ability grouping, much more testing than anyone would want, far too much continual shifting of children from one learning track to another, and way more instructional diversity than any one classroom teacher could possibly manage.

The model I have in mind can be likened more to private tutoring than to classroom instruction. It would take some 2 to 4 hours of the school day, for each pupil, with a detailed record kept of every phase of the pupil's progress, recorded during each tutorial session. Continual analyses of these records of a pupil's progress during the course of instruction, with periodic extraction of certain key summary information, would obviate any need for giving children tests as such. Measures of achievement would be a product of the learning program itself.

To accomplish this task entirely with school personnel, of course, would be wholly unfeasible. But we now have the technical capability of doing it with the aid of computer hardware and software. Further research and development is needed, however, to advance the computer software applications of the proposed technology beyond the present state of the art. Now that future educators are being recruited from the generation of youths who have grown up with computers, the time seems ripe for the developments I propose.

To use what now seems to me a rather old-fashioned term, I am referring to the development of computer-assisted instruction, (CAI), with computerized testing as a built-in and practically indistinguishable feature of the instructional program. The child's "summary key" of performance at any given point in time would be informative of the child's actual criterion-referenced achievement in the specific instructional program. It would also assess the extent of the generalizability, or breadth of transfer, of what had been learned, and would indicate the pupil's probable readiness for succeeding in the next step in the instructional program. Program branching to more advanced lessons or to remedial lessons would depend on whether certain criterion levels of performance were either attained or consistently not attained by varied instruction.

Pupils in the classroom would not be tracked or grouped in the early grades. Certain periods of the school day would be spent in small-group activities with the teacher. This is important because computers, of course, cannot be role models or potent sources of enthusiasm for learning a given subject. They cannot inculcate a love of learning, which good teachers are able to instill in their students. (In personal retrospect, I now realize that I got the most from those few teachers who evinced some genuine enthusiasm for the subject they were teaching, and in a few cases their effects on my interests and values are still evident some 50 or 60 years later; they were the few teachers who aroused in me what seemed at the time to be a spontaneous and autonomous interest in the subjects they taught.) One would not want a school that is so automated by computer-assisted instruction (CAI) that this kind of teacher influence would be lessened. Teachers' personal influence must work hand in hand with CAI. Also, in addition to instruction in academic subjects, pupils would need time to explore and develop their potential talents in writing, art, music, dance, and athletics.

I see no need in this picture for ability or achievement testing as such. The proper automatic recording and assessment of pupil performance during each instructional CAI period would supply all the information needed for the branching of the program and for the teacher's guidance of pupils. There would be no external gatekeepers who would exclude a student from entering a particular path for which he or she has demonstrated readiness through performance in prerequisites to the particular path. There would be no need for test scores per se or for tracking of pupils but only close monitoring of students' computer-recorded progress at every step of the way.

As pupils advance, the branching would become more and more extensive. Not all children would be expected to enter every branch or the same branches. Past performance would be the sole guide to future performance, and it would be tracked on a day-to-day basis. Backtracking and alternate branching at a later developmental age also would be possible. In math, for example, some students might branch into advanced algebra or calculus while some of their age peers topped out (at least temporarily) at, say, mixed fractions. They would branch into programs on applied math useful in common everyday activities—weighing and measuring things accurately, balancing a checkbook, verifying a bank statement, computing compound interest, and the like. Not measures of *g* per se, but actual performance and achievement level would be the basis for evaluation of the student's progress and advancement.

Also, by high-school age, ideally, real work apprenticeship programs would be available for students who wished to learn specific job skills that are best learned under supervision on the job. Many jobs, such as sailing a boat, cooking a dinner, or playing a musical instrument, require the automatization of many subskills and are not all that interesting or learnable without "hands on" experience and the informative feedback that comes only from trying to perform the task itself. Imagine trying to learn how to swim by listening to a lecture or reading a book on swimming!

A universal benefit of the CAI approach is that nearly all young people leaving school and entering this information-intensive and computer-dominated technological would be computer literate as if by second nature, because they would have worked with computers and learned through computers throughout their schooling. CAI would be a postgraduate mode of learning that would present no problems to those who must continue learning in order to advance in their jobs or keep up with new developments in their fields.

One can easily envision a large-scale industry growing up in the educational applications of computers. What is available to the schools in this line today, compared to what is technically feasible, given the development of a full-fledged educational research specialty in the design of instructional and evaluative computer software, could be like comparing the first airplanes with the modern jets.

Testing the efficacy of my proposal probably could be accomplished most effectively if it were instituted in schools with children whose age range from 5 to 18 years and who represent the typical range of individual differences. It would seem most feasible if this proposal were conducted under the auspices of a long-term university-based research project, in which a large team of specialists could coordinate their expertise in an all-out effort that would be the equivalent of the Human Genome Project for education.

REFERENCES

Alliger, G. M. (1988). Do zero correlations really exist among measures of different intellectual abilities? *Educational and Psychological Measurement, 48*, 275–280.

Atkinson, R. C. (1974). Teaching children to read using a computer. *American Psychologist, 29*, 169–178.

Baltes, P. B., & Kliegl, R. (1985). On the dynamics between growth and decline in the aging of intelligence and memory. In K. Poeck, H-J Freund, & H. Gänshirt (Eds.), *Neurology* (pp. 1–17). Heidelberg: Springer-Verlag.

Birren, J. E. (1974). Translations in gerontology—from lab to life: Psychology and speed of response. *American Psychologist, 29*, 808–815.

Campbell, F. A., & Ramey, C. T. (1994). Effects of early intervention on intellectual and academic achievement: A follow-up study of children from low-income families. *Child Development, 65*, 684–698.

Campbell, F. A., & Ramey, C. T. (1995). Cognitive and school outcomes for high-risk African-American students at middle-adolescence: Positive effects of early intervention. *American Educational Research Journal, 32*, 743–772.

Carroll, J. B. (1993). *Human cognitive abilities: A survey of factor-analytic studies.* Cambridge, England: Cambridge University Press.

Cattell, R. B. (1971). *Abilities: Their structure, growth, and action.* Boston: Houghton Mifflin.

Chapman, P. D. (1988). *Schools as sorters: Lewis M. Terman, applied psychology, and the intelligence testing movement, 1890–1930.* New York: N. Y. University Press.

Clarke, A. M., & Clarke, A. D. B. (1976). *Early experience: Myth and evidence.* New York: Free Press.

Cronbach, L. J., & Snow, R. E. (1977). *Aptitudes and instructional methods: A handbook for research on interactions.* New York: Irvington.

Deary, I. J., & Caryl, P. G. (1993). Intelligence, EEG, and evoked potentials. In P. A. Vernon (Ed.), *Biological approaches to the study of human intelligence* (pp. 259–315). Norwood, NJ: Ablex.

Fulker, D. W., Cherny, S. S., & Cardon, L. R. (1993). Continuity and change in cognitive development. In R. Plomin & G. E. McClearn (Eds.), *Nature, nurture, & psychology* (pp. 77–97). Washington, D. C.: American Psychological Association.

Gardner, H. (1993). *Frames of mind.* New York: Basic Books.

Gardner, H., Kornhaber, M. L., & Wake, W. K. (1996). *Intelligence: Multiple perspectives.* Fort Worth, TX: Harcourt Brace.

Gedye, C. A. (1981). *Longitudinal study (grades 1 through 10) of school achievement, self-confidence, and selected parental characteristics.* Doctoral dissertation, University of California, Berkeley.

Gordon, E. W., & Bhattacharyya, M. (1994). Race and intelligence. In R. J. Sternberg (Ed.), *Encyclopedia of human intelligence,* Vol. 2 (pp. 889–899). New York: Macmillan.

Gordon, R. A. (1997). Everyday life as an intelligence test: Effects of intelligence and intelligence context. *Intelligence, 24,* 203–320.

Gottfredson, L. S. (1997). Why *g* matters: The complexity of everyday life. *Intelligence, 24,* 79–132.

Haier, R. J. (1993). Cerebral glucose metabolism and intelligence. In P. A. Vernon (Ed.), *Biological approaches to the study of human intelligence* (pp. 317–373). Norwood, NJ: Ablex.

Herrnstein, R. J., & Murray, C. (1994). *The bell curve: Intelligence and class structure in American life.* New York: Free Press.

Jensen, A. R. (1973). *Educability and group differences.* New York: Harper & Row.

Jensen, A. R. (1980). *Bias in mental testing.* New York: Free Press.

Jensen, A. R. (1987). The *g* beyond factor analysis. In R. R. Ronning, J. A. Glover, J. C. Conoley, & J. C. Witt (Eds.), *The influence of cognitive psychology on testing* (pp. 87–142). Hillsdale, NJ: Lawrence Erlbaum Associates.

Jensen, A. R. (1989a). The relationship between learning and intelligence. *Learning and Individual Differences, 1,* 37–62.

Jensen, A. R. (1989b). Raising IQ without increasing *g*? A review of *The Milwaukee Project: Preventing mental retardation in children at risk* by H. L. Garber. *Developmental Review, 9,* 234–258.

Jensen, A. R. (1991). Spearman's *g* and the problem of educational equality. *Oxford Review of Education, 17,* 169–187.

Jensen, A. R. (1992). Understanding *g* in terms of information processing. *Educational Psychology Review, 4,* 271–308.

Jensen, A. R. (1993a). Psychometric *g* and achievement. In B. R. Gifford (Ed.), *Policy perspectives on educational testing* (pp. 117–227). Boston: Kluwer Academic Publishers.

Jensen, A. R. (1993b). Spearman's *g*: Links between psychometrics and biology. *Annals of the New York Academy of Sciences, 702,* 103–131.

Jensen, A. R. (1994). Race and IQ scores. In R. J. Sternberg (Ed.), *Encyclopedia of human intelligence,* Vol. 2 (pp. 899–907). New York: Macmillan.

Jensen, A. R. (1997a). The puzzle of nongenetic variance. In R. J. Sternberg & E. L. Grigorenko (Eds.) *Intelligence, heredity and environment* (pp. 42–88). Cambridge: Cambridge University Press.

Jensen, A. R. (1997b). The neurophysiology of *g*. In C. Cooper & V. Varma (Eds.), *Processes in individual differences* (pp. 107–124). London: Rouledge.

Jensen, A. R. (1998). *The g factor.* Westport, CT: Praeger, Kaufman, A. S., & Kaufman, N. L. (1983). *K-ABC: Interpretive manual.* Circle Pines:, MN: American Guidance Service.

Kaufman, A. S., & Kaufman, N. L. (1983). *Kaufman assessment battery for children: Interpretive manual.* Circle Pines, MN: American Guidance Service.

Matarazzo, J. D. (1972). *Wechsler's measurement and appraisal of adult intelligence.* 5th ed. Baltimore: Williams & Wilkins.

McGue, M., Bouchard, T. J., Jr., Iacono, W. G., & Lykken, D. T. (1993). Behavioral genetics of cognitive ability: A life-span perspective. In R. Plomin & G. E. McClearn (Eds.), *Nature, nurture, and psychology* (pp. 59–76). Washington, D.C.: American Psychological Association.

Ogbu, J. U. (1978). *Minority education and caste: The American system in cross-cultural perspective.* New York: Academic Press.

Pedersen, N. L., Plomin, R. & McClearn, G. E. (1994). Is there G beyond *g*? (Is there genetic influence on specific cognitive abilities independent of genetic influence on general cognitive ability?). *Intelligence, 18,* 133–143.

Plomin, R. (1990). *Nature and nurture: An introduction to human behavioral genetics.* Pacific Grove, CA: Brooks/Cole.

Ramey, C. T. (1992). High-risk children and IQ: Altering intergenerational patterns. *Intelligence, 16,* 239–256.

Ramey, C. T. (1993). A rejoinder to Spitz's critique of the Abecedarian experiment. *Intelligence, 17,* 25–30.

Ramey, C. T. (1994). Abecedarian Project. In R. J. Sternberg (Ed.) *Encyclopedia of human intelligence* (Vol. 1, pp. 1–3). New York: Macmillan.

Rowe, D. C. (1994). *The limits of family influence: Genes, experience, and behavior.* New York: Guilford Press.

Rowe, D. C., & Cleveland, H. H. (1997). Academic achievement in African Americans and whites: Are the developmental processes similar? *Intelligence, 23,* 205–228.

Rowe, D. C., Vazsonyi, A. T., & Flannery, D. J. (1994). No more than skin deep: Ethnic and racial similarity in developmental process. *Psychological Review, 101,* 396–413.

Rowe, D. C., Vazsonyi, A. T., & Flannery, D. J. (1995). Ethnic and racial similarity in developmental process: A study of academic achievement. *Psychological Science, 6,* 33–38.

Rushton, J. P. (1995). *Race, evolution, and behavior: A life history perspective.* New Brunswick, NJ: Transaction.

Rushton, J. P., & Ankney, C. D. (1996). Brain size and cognitive ability: Correlations with age, sex, social class, and race. *Psychonomic Bulletin and Review, 3,* 21–36.

Shurkin, J. N. (1992). *Terman's kids.* Boston: Little, Brown & Co. Snow, R. E. & Lohman, D. F. (1989). Implications of cognitive psychology for educational measurement. In R. L. Linn (Ed.), *Educational measurement* (3rd ed., pp. 263–331).

Snow, R. E., & Lohman, D. F. (1989). Implications of cognitive psychology for educational measurement. In R. L. Linn (Ed.), *Educational measurement* (3rd ed., pp. 263–331. New York: Macmillan.

Snow, R. E. & Yalow, E. (1982). *Education and intelligence.* In R. J. Sternberg (Ed.), *Handbook of human intelligence* (pp. 493–585). Cambridge: Cambridge University Press.

Sowell, T. (1994). *Race and culture: A world view.* New York: Basic Books.

Spearman, C. (1927). *The abilities of man: Their nature and measurement.* New York: Macmillan.

Spitz, H. H. (1986). *The raising of intelligence: A selected history of attempts to raise retarded intelligence.* Hillsdale, NJ: Lawrence Erlbaum Associates.

Spitz, H. H. (1992). Does the Carolina Abecedarian early intervention project prevent sociocultural mental retardation? *Intelligence, 16,* 225–237.

Spitz, H. H. (1993a). When prophecy fails: On Ramey's response to Spitz's critique of the Abecedarian Project. *Intelligence, 17,* 17–23.

Spitz, H. H. (1993b). Spitz's reply to Ramey's response to Spitz'z first reply to Ramey's first response to Spitz's critique of the Abecedarian Project. *Intelligence, 17,* 31–35.

Sternberg, R. J., & Gardner, M. K. (1982). A componential interpretation of the general factor in human intelligence. In H. J. Eysenck (Ed.), *A model for intelligence* (pp. 231–254). New York: Springer-Verlag.

Thompson, L. A., Detterman, D. K., & Plomin, R. (1991). Associations between cognitive abilities and scholastic achievement: Genetic overlap but environmental differences. *Psychological Science, 2,* 158–165.

Thorndike, R. L., Hagen, E., & Sattler, J. (1986). *The Stanford-Binet Intelligence Scale: Fourth edition, Technical manual.* Chicago: Riverside.

Wagner, R. K., & Sternberg, R. J. (1986). Alternative conceptions of intelligence and their implications for education. In T. M. Tomlinson & H. J. Walberg (Eds.), *Academic work and educational excellence: Rasing student productivity* (pp. 223–283). Berkeley, CA: McCutchan.

CHAPTER 7

Intelligent Thinking
and the Reflective Essay

Jonathan Baron
University of Pennsylvania

Those in schools and colleges can improve students' thinking and thus make them more intelligent. We may be able to do this more effectively if we have a better idea of what we are doing. "We" means students and faculty: Students apply standards of thinking to each other, just as faculty apply them to students and to other faculty. In early universities, the standards came from Aristotle. Logic was an essential part of the curriculum. We still sometimes criticize each other for begging the question, introducing *non sequiturs*, and stumbling into other Aristotelian fallacies. Recent scholarship has given us a clearer idea of what good thinking is, where thinking goes wrong, and how education can help.

I argue here that the most important standards are those that concern active open-mindedness in consideration of arguments on all sides of a question. We can support these standards by making them explicit and by taking them seriously when we assign grades, especially for essays and essay examinations. We should not give high grades to papers that ignore obvious arguments that fly in the face of the point being made.

To make this argument, I first present my view of thinking and then discuss the essay itself.

WHAT IS THINKING?

Thinking concerns the resolution of doubt about what to do, what to believe, or what to value. It consists of search and inference. (Logic concerns inference only.) When we think, we search for possibilities, which are ways of resolving the doubt; for evidence, which bears on the merit of the possibilities; and for relevant values, which allow us to evaluate the possibilities in the light of the evidence. For buying a car, the possibilities are cars (and perhaps other options such as not buying the car and taking the train instead), the bits of evidence are about quality, safety, price, price of alternatives, and so on, and the values are what we care about, from avoiding hassle to minimizing pollution. During and after our search, we make inferences from what we have found. Possibilities strengthen and weaken and sometimes are rejected from the set under consideration or adopted as our provisional or final choice.

This is an example of thinking about a decision, but we also think about beliefs and values. We think about beliefs by gathering evidence from both our own pre-existing beliefs and from other sources. For example, we may recall things we have heard about the effects of gasoline combustion on the environment and the economy, and we may read more or ask others. Thinking about values relies more heavily on pre-existing values rather than external ones. We can, for example, think about how our choice of cars bears up in the light of our deepest values about what is important in life, including such things as enjoying the experience of life and protecting the environment. Here, the evidence consists of these other values, brought to bear on the values we form for a particular kind of decision. See Keeney's (1992) book for an excellent discussion of how to think about values.

The examples so far involve mostly search. We also make inferences from what our search has found, increasingly as we go along and find more and more. Many of the inferences are simple matters of weighing arguments against one another in the light of our values that are relevant to the case at hand. In other cases, we follow rules, principles, or schemas of inference. These range from heuristic methods of problem solving, to rules of moral or religious behavior, to social conventions. These rules themselves are often the results of prior decisions to adopt or try to follow them. Thinking well or badly about our rules can affect how good they are.

For example, some people follow a rule that says, "Do not cause harm," meaning, "Do not cause harm through action (but causing harm through inaction may be OK, especially when you don't think about it but in other cases too)." In general, this is a good rule that is consistent with people's personal and moral values. Sometimes, however, it causes trouble, as when people resist beneficial reforms because they harm some people (even though failing to pass the reforms would hurt more people to a greater extent), or when they resist risky actions that are expected to be beneficial, such as vaccinating a child (when the vaccine might itself cause the disease it more often prevents; Baron, 1994a). If people reflected on this rule, they might realize that it is the consequences they really care about, and they might modify it.

MODELS OF THINKING: NORMATIVE, DESCRIPTIVE, AND PRESCRIPTIVE

I have suggested that thinking may be evaluated as better or worse, but I have not said how or how such evaluation may be justified. Table 7.1 shows three ways of describing thinking. *Normative models* describe the standard we use to evaluate thinking. *Descriptive models* tell us how thinking usually is done, in terms that we can compare to the normative models. *Prescriptive models* tell us which way we need to push one another to make our thinking better according to the normative standard.

The normative standard is derived from the goals of thinking itself. We think because we want to reach the best decision or conclusion, given our other values. We also do not want to take too much time or effort. In other words, we have values for things we want to do other than think, and the more we think the less time and energy we have for everything else.

Thus, the normative standard for the *duration* of thinking is that it should achieve the optimal balance between costs and benefits of thinking. As we think more and more about something, the benefits of further thinking decline, but the costs of further thinking do not decline. Each minute is one minute less for everything else. So, ideally, we should stop thinking when the costs of further thinking exceed the benefits. Descriptively, people are somewhat insensitive to these costs and benefits. They think too much about trivia and not enough about things that are really important, or they

TABLE 7.1

Models of Thinking in General

	Normative	Descriptive	Prescriptive
Search			
duration	optimal	too moderate	more responsive
direction	fair	my side*	self-critical
	appropriate	high when extreme	less extreme
Confidence			
inference			
direction	fair	my side*	self-critical
rules	optimal	too general	specific or purposive

*Perkins (1983) calls a person's favor for what he or she already likes *my side* bias.

do not focus their thinking efforts on areas in which the benefits of further thought are particularly great, such as schoolwork. Thus, we need to teach people to be more sensitive to these costs and benefits. For example, many tedious meetings often concern decisions about which of two options is better when the outcome of each seem equally good or bad, especially in the light of our uncertainty about the outcomes. It often does not occur to people that further thinking about the options is not going to make one of them leap above the other and that, in fact, flipping a coin would answer the question equally well. On the other hand, decisions that are collectively very important, such as voting and other political behavior, are often made on the basis of very little thought. Likewise, people rush into impulsive personal and financial decisions that bring them to ruin.

By *direction* I mean toward or away from possibilities that are initially strong. Ideally, thinking should be unbiased, giving both old and new possibilities an equal chance. If we are going to think only by looking for reasons why we were right all along in our initial opinion, we are just wasting time. We have no reason to think at all, for such reasons can surely be found. Here is where the simplest, most pervasive, and most easily corrected biases are found in the descriptive model. People are biased in favor of what they already favor, for whatever reason. This happens in both search and inference. We search for evidence that supports these favored possibilities, and when we find evidence against them we give it too little weight (Baron, 1994b). Perkins aptly named this *myside bias* (Perkins, Allen, & Hafner, 1983). This does not mean that there is an adversary who favors the other side. Often nobody holds the opposing opinion, but it still deserves fair consideration.

For example, pertussis vaccination (the P in *DPT*) often causes the disease it prevents, and some parents resist having their children vaccinated with this vaccine in particular, because they are afraid of the harm it might cause. When mothers were shown government statistics about the effects of the vaccine, they became even more opposed to it (Meszaros et al., 1996). They focus on the evidence of harm. Mothers who favored vaccination initially favored it even more after reading exactly the same statistics. They focused on the (greater) risks of the disease that were avoided. It seems that the initial choice of the vaccination resisters was based on a rule of inference, a rule of avoiding active harm, but then, once the decision was made, evidence against it was ignored.

Prescriptively, to avoid this bias, we must learn to consider the other side. Later, I discuss a simple way to do this. For now, let me just mention one cause of myside bias: some people believe that thinking is better when it proceeds this way (Baron, 1995; Kuhn, 1991; Stanovich & West, 1996). These people, in questionnaires and open-ended responses, seem to feel that it is bad to be wishy-washy, to be disloyal to one's beliefs, and that its good to be firm and unyielding. They think that a good argument is one sided. They seem to adopt principles that might be appropriate to some people in some situations, for example, a lawyer in a courtroom, but not when someone is trying to think about something that is truly unknown or undecided. Again, if one is going to *think* in a one-sided way, why bother to think at all? It is just a waste of time. It might be said that they take a lawyer's view toward their prior beliefs, as if they are obliged to defend them. People with these beliefs do tend to follow them in a variety of tasks, thinking as they think they should think, in a one-sided way. They also have more difficulty than others in logical reasoning, and they show more of the kinds of inferential biases that I mentioned earlier (Stanovich & West, 1996).

It is encouraging to think that poor thinking results from mistaken beliefs about what good thinking is. If it resulted from some sort of biological limitation, we would have less reason to think we could change it. It is possible, however, to convince people to honor a certain standard. This is the basic function of acculturation, as it happens in schools and elsewhere. I have called this standard *actively open-minded thinking*. See Nickerson's (1989) work for a similar view.

Myside bias is related to, but not the same as, wishful thinking. In wishful thinking, we try to bolster beliefs that we would like to be true, as if we could make them true through our efforts to convince ourselves (which we cannot do). Most people favor beliefs of this sort. Exceptions to this rule are people living with depression, whose myside bias favors beliefs that they are responsible for everything bad that happens and for nothing good (Beck, 1976). Another exception appears to be those of typical Japanese culture, and perhaps those of typical East Asian culture in general (Heine & Lehman, 1995).

Table 7.1 has two other rows. The story about *confidence* is somewhat interesting. It is often thought that confidence is an unalloyed good. People who are confident take risks for the sake of achievement, and, as a result, they achieve more. Note, however, that the confidence involved here is in the results of what one does in the future. Confidence in the result of past efforts, especially past thinking, can have exactly the opposite effect, making people reluctant to think further, because the results of their past thinking are sufficient. Overconfidence in the results of past thinking is thus one cause of both insufficient thinking and of myside bias in inference. (If I have the right answer, then the evidence must favor it, so any evidence against it must be incorrect.) Much evidence indicates that extremely high confidence is typically unwarranted (Baron, 1994b). For example, when people judge that they are 100% correct on a difficult test item, they are typically correct less than 80% of the items on which they say this. Asking people to think of reasons why they might be wrong reduces this bias (Koriat, Lichtenstein, & Fischhoff, 1980). Gilovich (1991) described the effects of this bias in real life.

I have already mentioned the fact that people follow *rules* that are appropriate in many cases but are overapplied to cases in which they are not appropriate, such as the "do no harm" rule. *Appropriate* means most consistent with the values that motivate the thinking in the first place. Another example is the rule that people have against wasting money. They try not to spend money on things they will not use. But they then apply this rule in reverse, as a rule against 'not using" what they have already spent money on. Thus, on a beautiful day in April, when plenty of outdoor tennis courts are available at the local YMCA, we see people trudging inside to play on the indoor court that they have paid for through the end of the month, so that they don't "waste" the money they spent on it, even though they would prefer the outdoor court. If they thought about the rules of behavior they follow, in an actively open-minded way, they might play outside and enjoy themselves more.

Examples of the effects of myside bias are easy to find. Janis, for example, showed how just this sort of thinking led to such fiascos as the Bay of Pigs invasion (Janis, 1972/1982). Herek, Janis, and Huth (1987) found that such bias is correlated with bad outcomes in major foreign policy decision made by the U.S. government.

THINKING AND INTELLIGENCE

This book is about intelligence, so I need to say why good thinking is part of intelligence. I spelled this argument out at great length in a book (Baron, 1995). In a nutshell, the concept of intelligence is supposed to represent something good, something that we all want. It refers to those abilities that help us live well according to our values whatever those values might be. Moreover, the abilities in question ought to be somewhat general. We often distinguish between intelligence and expertise, with the latter referring to abilities in a specific field. This is not important except in dividing up scholarly territory. A concept of intelligence as general abilities that help us live up to our values is like certain concepts in social science such as national well-being or standard of living. Measures of such things, although necessarily imperfect, are useful in measuring effects of various social inventions, from education to capitalism.

Such abilities surely can include those that are acquired through culture. Arguably, the success of some cultures and the failure of others to give people good lives (by their own standards) is partly the result of "intellectual capital," and such capital is not just specific knowledge but also general ways of thinking and approaching the world. Of course, parts of intelligence are biologically determined, not only by inheritance but also by nutrition and general health. For other purposes, of course, we might want measures that are more specific to these biological determinants. In that small part of the world where adequate nutrition and sanitation are widespread, scores on IQ tests are heavily affected by genetic inheritance. But, in much of the world, test scores are heavily affected by experience, such as number of years of basic schooling (see Baron, 1985).

IQ tests may not be very sensitive to the kind of good thinking that I am advocating here (although some evidence suggests that they are somewhat sensitive, e.g., Baron, Badgio, & Gaskins, 1986). But this does not mean that it is any less important. IQ tests do not define intelligence, despite E.G. Boring's (1923) sarcastic comment that intelligence is what the tests test. If teaching people better thinking can help them, then it does not even matter whether it is called "improving intelligence" or not.

HOW EDUCATION CAN HELP

Education can help by insisting on thorough and fair search, fair inference, and appropriate confidence. I call this *actively open-minded thinking* because we must work actively against wishful thinking and bias toward pet possibilities. Because good thinking involves competition among possibilities, evidence, and values, it is almost always quantitative, in the sense of weighing things against each other. When we pit safety against price, we must ask how much safety for how much price, and how much we care about each. Sometimes it may help to make the quantitative aspects explicit.

More generally, actively open-minded thinking is fundamental to academic inquiry. When I submit a paper to a journal, the criticisms I get concern my failure to search, for example, for opposing views in the literature or for alternative interpretations of my result, and they concern biased inference, such as dismissing discrepant results. We criticize students this way, too. Colleges are thus well situated to teach actively open-minded thinking. Tenure and promotion of faculty are based to a large extent on upholding these scholarly values in their own work.

In some of my classes, I explicitly try to encourage actively open-minded thinking. For example, I assign a reflective essay with the following suggested outline:

1. Explain your question and why it is important.
2. Present the most obvious answer or answers.
3. Consider less obvious alternatives, or objections to the obvious answers.

4. Rebut the criticisms, or explain how the original answers can be modified to deal with them.

Many students have trouble with this, although some, not otherwise the best students, take to it easily. Those who fail usually err on the side of "making a case" for one side, like a lawyer, but neglecting the other side. In the 1970s, when students were more rebellious, I used to get essays that erred by making a one-sided attack on, for example, me. It was particularly easy in these cases to point out the students' failures to consider arguments on the other side.

Good thinking is encouraged in other ways, such as by encouraging discussion in which alternative points of view are requested and debated. Even in grading exams, we can give credit for bringing up an alternative or a criticism. Most importantly, we can help students learn to think by telling them explicitly what our standards are and then acting consistently with these standards both in the classroom and when assigning grades.

The essay is still a very useful tool because it is a kind of set exercise. It has no real purpose, although it may be good enough to serve some purpose.

Of course, essays are practice for writing and speaking in the real world. Just as essays can be actively open-minded or not, so can public expressions. Consider the two following excerpts from public writings about the slavery debate in the United States between 1844 and 1860 (from Tetlock, Armor, & Peterson, 1994):

1. I deny the right of Congress to look at the existence of slavery in the States, that shall be formed with these territories, because I deny that there can be Constitutional slavery in any of the States of the American Union—future States, or present States—new or old. I hold that the Constitution not only authorizes no slavery, but permits no slavery; not only creates no slavery in any part of the land, but abolishes slavery in every part of the land. In other words, I hold that there is no law for American slavery.

2. It may be asked, then, are the people of the States without regress against the tyranny and oppression of the federal government? By no means. The right of resistance on the part of the governed against the oppression of their government cannot be denied. It exists independently of all constitutions, and has been exercised at all periods of the world's history. Under it, old governments have been destroyed and new ones have taken their place. It is embodied in strong and express language in our own Declaration of Independence. But the distinction must ever be observed that this is a revolution against an established government, and not a voluntary secession from it by virtue of an inherent Constitutional right. In short, let us look the danger

> fairly in the face: secession is neither more nor less than revolution.
> It may or may not be a justifiable revolution; but it is still a revolution.

The first excerpt is a clear example of myside bias, to the point of making assertions about the U.S. Constitution that went well beyond the text and well beyond the standard interpretations of judges and scholars before or since—the Constitution is usually understood to be ambiguous about slavery because of the existence of slavery in many of the home states of the people who wrote it. The writer thus makes biased inferences from evidence, as well as fails to consider the other side of the immediate debate. The second example is just as clear an example of actively open-minded thinking about the question of secession. Of course, such thinking is more likely when the thinker is truly conflicted, as this person appears to be.

Here are two other examples from the current debate about euthanasia, both excerpts from editorials in the *St. Louis Post-Dispatch*. The first (Dec. 12, 1992) is by Ellie Dillon, representing Missouri Right to Life, Brentwood. The second (June 14, 1990) is by John E. Morley, professor of gerontology at St. Louis University.

1. The Dec. 3 article describing an international conference on the debate over maintaining the lives of severely brain-damaged people like Nancy Cruzan and Christine Busalacchi makes a serious yet common error. During the symposium, participants heard the personal accounts of Joe and Joyce Cruzan, Pete Busalacchi and the parents of Marc Kerness, a California child left severely brain damaged at 14 months of age. ...

   The error the article makes is in equating what these parents sought with what is sought by advocates of assisted suicide. When life support is removed from a person in a persistent vegetative state, as in the case of Nancy Cruzan, the cause of death is the underlying fatal condition that necessitated the use of the life support. Assisted suicide is quite a different thing. Suicide is a voluntary act by which one intends and causes one's own death. Assisted suicide implies that the person cannot accomplish the intention or action to bring death about alone. Assistance in the suicide of another can be accomplished by acts of commission. Assistance also can be rendered in a less active way through persuasion and encouragement. But in either case, the person who contributes to the death-dealing effort shares in the intention to bring death about through the introduction of a causative agent. Thus there is a clear distinction between the ethically acceptable act of removing life support and allowing death to come and assisted suicide where death is both intended and directly caused.

   Jean deBlois. ... compares the case of an 11-year-old boy who died after being detached from his life-support machines with Christine Busalacchi, who receives food through a tube. There is a very distinct difference between these two cases. The boy's body could not function on its own, and he could not breathe without a ventilator. He died within minutes of removing the machines. Busalacchi is not on any machines; her body functions on its own, and she is aware of her surroundings. In fact, she is higher functioning than many of the students I taught when I was a special education teacher! However, she does receive her food through a tube because it is the faster, more efficient way for the nurses to feed her. There are millions of disabled Americans who cannot feed themselves. Busalacchi is not dying. She is a disabled woman due to injuries she incurred from a car accident. Her father wants the feeding tube removed so she can starve to death. It would take between seven to 14 days for her to die. She would die from starvation, not from injuries from the accident. Not only is this deliberate killing, but it is discrimination against the disabled of the highest degree. When we check into a hospital now, we have confidence that the doctors will do all they can to help us. But soon, we will lose that confidence for fear that the doctors will be judging our "quality of life," rather than the fact that we are human beings deserving of their best care. ...

2. The dramatic experiment in the laboratory of life whereby a physician assisted Janet Adkins in taking her own life has forced all Americans to reflect on the ethics of the good death (euthanasia). We are all born to die, and as such it is not surprising that the concept that sometimes death may be preferable to life is not new. Seneca stated, "I will not escape by death from disease so long as it may be healed and leaves my mind unimpaired; I will not raise my hand against myself. ... but if I know I must suffer without hope or relief, I will depart." Physicians daily practice passive euthanasia by withholding or even withdrawing life-sustaining treatments on the grounds that these are extraordinary means that prolong suffering to the detriment of life. On the other hand, in some cases, such as the withdrawal of a feeding tube, the conscious patient may be consigned to a lingering death from malnutrition associated with bed sores and with infection. A picture of a malnourished Ethiopian child angers us all, but for some reason many people do not have the same abhorrence when consigning an 80-year-old to a similar fate.

However, before we consider the individual's position on physician-assisted suicide, societal concerns need to be addressed. America is an aging nation. Already ethicists such as Dan Callahan at the Hastings Institute have called for setting limits on medical treatment using age as the deciding factor, the ultimate example of economic needs dictating ethical principles. Should we condone doctor-assisted suicide, this brings closer the possibility of state-mandated suicide at an age when the individual is no longer deemed useful or is seen as too costly a liability. Unbelievable? Remember that physician-assisted "suicide" was a part of the Holocaust, an event in our all-too-recent past.

At the individual level I have often had elderly patients who have requested that their lives be ended or that they be allowed to starve themselves to death, who after appropriate diagnosis and treatment of their depression, have returned to a vibrant, happy life. Finally, it should be stressed that many services are available to alleviate the suffering of the terminally ill and the Alzheimer's patient. Referral to hospice care or to the Alzheimer's Association is an essential part of the care of these patients. Clearly, should physician-assisted suicide ever become acceptable in America, it is not a decision that should be left to a single, possibly paternalistic physician; rather, it should be the decision of an ethics panel including presentation of a diverse section of society.

Physician-assisted suicide may be no greater crime than the slow death of selling cigarettes to millions of Americans and those in Third World countries, but this certainly does not make it right. The time has come for a thoughtful and logical debate on the pros and cons of this issue. However, the time has not come for physicians to give a deadly drug for any reason.

Again, the first editorial is one sided and acknowledges no arguments on the other side, such as those arguments made in the second editorial about the difficulty of drawing a line between active euthanasia (which the editorial opposes) and passive euthanasia (which it favors). Other arguments about the moral relevance of this distinction are also ignored (e.g., Singer, 1993). The second editorial clearly considers both sides and arrives at a moderate conclusion. (The moderation of the conclusion is not a necessary result of actively open-minded thinking, however.) Otherwise, both editorials are well written and well argued.

Which would get the higher grade if it were submitted as an assignment for a writing class? Quite possibly, both would get high grades. Some teachers might even give the first a higher grade because it is not "wishy washy" and does not contradict itself. Yet, insofar as grades express the standards we want to convey, the first deserves a lower grade. If we, as teachers, mean business about encouraging good thinking, we must grade this way. If we give low grades at all, we must consider the willingness of students to show that they are actively open minded.

Note that the second editorial would have been one-sided on the other side if it had not acknowledged the dangers of legalizing assisted suicide without restriction. These arguments are public. Many have made them. To neglect them without either taking them into account (as this editorial did) or answering them is irresponsible. A teacher can recognize such omissions while still agreeing with the writers conclusion. The point to remember is that we want students to reach correct conclusions (those we agree with) for the right reasons. If they reach these conclusions out of loyalty, conformity, political correctness, or even rebellion, they will be likely to reach incorrect conclusions in the same ways in the future. The only insurance against error is to question everything.

COUNTERARGUMENTS

Let me try to be a little actively open-minded myself, not too much, but enough to keep up appearances. Tetlock argued that the emphasis on seeing the other side is misplaced for two reasons. First, it is not so much a matter of individual predispositions but, rather, of what one is thinking about. Although Tetlock did find significant individual differences, he found large effects of value conflict (Tetlock, 1986). For example, American liberals are often caught in the conflict between individual liberty and social justice, so they tend to agonize about government regulation for the sake of social justice, such as regulations that favor affirmative action. Conservatives care more about individual liberty, so their thinking appears simpler about such issues, which make up much of American political debate. However, conservatives appear more open minded when they think about such issues as the military draft, which pits the need for a strong defense (one of their traditional concerns) against individual liberty. Thus, people are more likely to see both sides when they are themselves truly conflicted. Second, acknowledging the other side is wrong when the other side has nothing to be said for it (Tetlock, 1993). To take the extreme case, should we be open minded about the ideology of Nazis? Perhaps, too, the one-sided abolitionist quoted above would have failed a course in critical thinking but was ultimately on the side of the angels.

Let me answer these objections. On the first point, Tetlock is simply correct. When we are truly conflicted, we consider both sides (see also Perkins et al., 1983). But the real test of our open-mindedness comes when we are not initially conflicted or when we have some motive to favor a particular side, such as if we were slave owners. Individual differences exist too, and differences in education may affect them.

The second point hinges on the particular measure of thinking that Tetlock uses, which is relevant because it is, like a student's essay, public, or at least not completely private. He scores speeches, interviews, and any other archival records that he can think of. These are not the same as thinking. And, as I argue later, public expressions sometimes should be one sided even when the thinking that went into them was open to both sides. The fact that a one-sided speech against Nazism or slavery might be more morally praiseworthy than a more agonized one is not to say that private thinking should be similarly one sided.

The point here is this: In hindsight, it is easy to see that the Nazis were completely wrong. Even at the time, it should not have taken a thoughtful person very long to grasp this. However, that is one case. If we think we always "know" that certain views are unworthy of a hearing, we reject the good along with the bad. Those who rejected Nazi ideology without a *moment's* thought might also reject more reasonable ideologies in the same way. How would they know which is which unless they spend a little time search for reasons? In fact, we see such rejections all the time in various polarized debates, such as in the conflict between Arabs and Israelis, or between those favoring and opposing legal prohibition of abortion or euthanasia. Each side "knows" without thinking that their side is right, but they both cannot be right. The wisdom of hindsight is great, but, until the time machine is invented, we cannot depend on it at the moment of decision.

The other point I need to make is that public expression is indeed different from private thinking. Psychologists have carried out many studies of whether one-sided or two-sided arguments are more persuasive (Sorrentino, Bobocel, Gitta, & Olson, 1988, and others that they cite). The answer is sometimes one and sometimes two. It depends on factors such as the previous knowledge of the listeners (more knowledge makes two-sided arguments more effective), the amount of attention they are paying to the persuasive message (more attention makes two-sided arguments more effective), and whether the listener is disposed to prefer uncertainty or certainty (a dimension that might be related to actively open-minded thinking). In many situations, however, one-sided arguments are more effective, and not necessarily inappropriate either. Under some conditions, it is necessary to rally the troops rather than inspire a reflective search for truth and good. At such times, it is good to have come to know the arguments on the other side—in the past—but we must suppress this knowledge in the present. So Tetlock is right for expression, but not for thinking.

This issue bears directly on the grading of essays. They are not pure expressions of thought. Students may see them as part of a debating game in which their role is to make as many points as possible on one side. The same students may habitually engage in actively open-minded thinking but suppress it for the task at hand. The reader, however, cannot distinguish such students from those who just don't do it and who think it is a bad idea.

If students are to be graded down for failing to consider the other side, like the speaker mentioned earlier who neglected the usual interpretations of the Constitution, they should be told this in advance. Some students will get the point immediately. Others will have difficulty because it is a new way of thinking for them. These are the ones who need the most help.

In other cases, of course, students might benefit from specific instruction how to write a persuasive one-sided essay when that is appropriate. Even in such cases, however, it is usually most effective to be aware of the arguments on the other side, so that one does not say things that fly in their face, so that opponents will easily rebut the arguments provided. And, sometimes, it is most effective, and certainly most responsible, to raise them and rebut them specifically.

CONCLUSION

Asking students to write reflective essays is a natural way to convey standards that favor actively open-minded thinking. When we assign essays, we should explain clearly that we expect careful consideration of arguments on both sides in a fair-minded search for truth or rightness and that it is not acceptable to ignore obvious arguments against the position being advocated (including arguments presented in the course in question). Such essays are best assigned in courses in which essays are assigned anyway. I am not suggesting here an add-on to the curriculum in either high school or college, just a way of thinking about a type of assignment that is given anyway. The same standards can, of course, be applied to essay examinations. I am sure that many professors and teachers are already doing exactly what I am suggesting, although perhaps not as explicitly as they might do it.

I cannot promise that reflective essays will improve thinking or increase intelligence. However, if we do not express our standards for thinking in our assignments and our grading, we have little hope of maintaining them from one generation to the next.

REFERENCES

Baron, J. (1985). *Rationality and intelligence.* New York: Cambridge University Press.

Baron, J. (1994a). Nonconsequentialist decisions (with commentary and reply). *Behavioral and Brain Sciences, 17,* 1—42.

Baron, J. (1994b). *Thinking and deciding* (2nd ed.). New York: Cambridge University Press.

Baron, J. (1995). Myside bias in thinking about abortion. *Thinking and Reasoning, 1,* 221—235.

Baron, J., Badgio, P., & Gaskins, I. W. (1986). Cognitive style and its improvement: A normative approach. In R. J. Sternberg (Ed.), *Advances in the psychology of human intelligence, Vol. 3* (pp. 173–220). Hillsdale, NJ: Lawrence Erlbaum Associates.

Beck, A. T. (1976). *Cognitive therapy and the emotional disorders.* New York: International Universities Press.

Boring, E. G. (1923). Intelligence as the tests test it. *New Republic, 35,* 35–37.

Dillon, E. (1992, Dec. 12). Missouri right to life [Editorial]. *St. Louis Post Dispatch.*

Gilovich, T. (1991). *How we know what isn't so: The fallibility of human reason in everyday life.* New York: Free Press.

Heine, S. J., Lehman, D. R. (1995). Cultural variation in unrealistic optimism: Does the West feel more vulnerable than the East? *Journal of Personality and Social Psychology, 68,* 595—607.

Herek, G. M., Janis, I. L., & Huth, P. (1987). Decision making during international crises. Is quality of process related to outcome? *Journal of Conflict Resolution, 31*, 203—226.

Janis, I. L. (1982). *Groupthink: Psychological studies of policy decisions and fiascoes.* Boston: Houghton Mifflin. (Original work published 1972) Keeney, R. L. (1992). *Value-focused thinking: A path to creative decision making.* Cambridge, MA: Harvard University Press.

Keeney, R. L. (1992). *Value-focused thinking: A path to creative decision making.* Cambridge, MA: Harvard University Press.

Koriat, A., Lichtenstein, S., & Fischhoff, B. (1980). Reasons for confidence. *Journal of Experimental Psychology: Human Learning and Memory, 6*, 107—118.

Kuhn, D. (1991). *The skills of argument.* Cambridge University Press.

Meszaros, J. R., Asch, D. A., Baron, J., Hershey, J. C., Kunreuther, H., & Schwartz-Buzaglo, J. (1996). Cognitive processes and the decisions of some parents to forego pertussis vaccination for their children. *Journal of Clinical Epidemiology, 49*, 697—703.

Morley, J. E. (1990, June 14). Missouri right to life [Editorial] *St. Louis Post Dispatch.*

Nickerson, R. S. (1989). On improving thinking through instruction. *Review of Research in Education, 15*, 3—57.

Perkins, D. N., Allen, R., & Hafner, J. (1983). Difficulties in everyday reasoning. In W. Maxwell (Ed.), *Thinking: The expanding frontier* (pp. 177—189). Philadelphia: Franklin Institute.

Singer, P. (1993). *Practical ethics* (2nd ed.). Cambridge, England: Cambridge University Press.

Sorrentino, R. M., Bobocel, D. R., Gitta, M. Z., & Olson, J. M.(1988). Uncertainty orientation and persuasion: Individual differences in the effects of personal relevance on social judgments. *Journal of Personality and Social Psychology, 55*, 357—371.

Stanovich, K. E., & West, R. F. (1996). *Which responses are correct in reasoning tasks? Normative models meet individual differences.* Unpublished manuscript, University of Toronto.

Tetlock, P. E. (1986). A value pluralism model of ideological reasoning. *Journal of Personality and Social Psychology, 50*, 819—827.

Tetlock, P. E. (1993). Flattering and unflattering personality portraits of integratively simple and complex managers. *Journal of Personality and Social Psychology, 50*, 819—827.

Tetlock, P. E., Armor, D., & Peterson, R. S. (1994). The slavery debate in antebellum America: Cognitive style, value conflict, and the limits of compromise. *Journal of Personality and Social Psychology, 66*, 115—126.

CHAPTER 8

A Three-Level Theory
of the Developing Mind:
Basic Principles and Implications
For Instruction and Assessment

Andreas Demetriou

Nicos Valanides
University of Cyprus

In the beginning, there was Piaget, and since publication of his theory, the psychology of cognitive development has contributed significantly to educational theory and practice. There are good theoretical and practical reasons for this affinity between education and the psychology of cognitive development.

First, the psychology of cognitive development defines human cognitive competence at successive phases of development. That is, it specifies what aspects of the world can be understood at different ages, what kinds of concepts can be constructed, and what types of problems can be solved. Education aims to help students acquire knowledge and develop skills that are compatible with their understanding and problem-solving capabilities at different ages. Thus, knowing the students' level on a developmental sequence provides information about the kind and level of knowledge they can assimilate, which, in turn, can be used as a frame for organizing the subject matter to be taught at different school grades.

Second, the psychology of cognitive development involves understanding how cognitive change takes place and recognizing the factors and processes that enable cognitive competence to develop. Education also capitalizes on cognitive change. The transmission of information and the construction of knowledge presupposes effective teaching methods. "Effective teaching methods have to enable the student to move from a lower to a higher level of understanding or abandon less efficient skills for more efficient ones" (Demetriou, 1996, p. 63). Therefore, knowledge of change mechanisms can be used as a basis for designing instructional interventions that will be both subject- and age-appropriate.

Finally, the psychology of cognitive development is concerned with individual differences in the organization of cognitive processes and abilities, in their rate of change, and in their mechanisms of change. Understanding the principles underlying intra- and interindividual differences could be useful educationally, because it might highlight why the same student is not an equally good learner in different domains and why different students in the same classroom react differently to the same instructional materials. Identifying individual differences with regard to the various aspects of cognitive development could be the basis for the development of programs of individualized instruction that might focus on the gifted student or be of a remedial nature.

This chapter elaborates on these issues from the perspective of a theory of cognitive development (Demetriou, 1993, 1996, 1998, in press; Demetriou & Efklides, 1994; Demetriou, Efklides, & Platsidou, 1993). This theory originated in the Piagetian tradition, and over the years it has evolved with the aim to transcend the limitations of Piaget's theory, which theoretical and empirical scrutiny of the theory had revealed. The theory should be regarded as an another attempt to enhance understanding of cognitive developmental phenomena that Piaget's theory neither fully described nor adequately explained, such as the organization of cognitive processes underlying different domains of knowledge, the mechanisms of cognitive change, and individual differences in cognitive development.

To avoid the problems encountered by Piaget's theory, our theory is based on methods and concepts from different fields of psychology, mainly psychometric, cognitive, and developmental psychology. Thus, this theory integrates various psychology traditions and involves assumptions and hypotheses related to the architecture and development of mind. Space limitations do not permit the discussion of the relationships among this and other theories. The interested reader may, however, refer to a number of other sources (Demetriou, Pachaury, Metallidou, & Kazi, 1996; Demetriou,

Efklides, Papadaki, Papantoniou, & Economou, 1993; Demetriou, Efklides, & Platsidou, 1993). In the following sections, the theory is presented and its main implications on instruction and assessment are delineated.

THE ARCHITECTURE OF MIND

According to this theory, the mind is conceived as a hierarchical edifice composed of three main levels: an environment-oriented level, a self-oriented level, and a third level which involves processes related to information-processing as such. Each level involves several systems, which also might be hierarchically organized. The environment-oriented level involves systems that both represent and process information from different domains in the environment. That is, each system involves mental operations, processes, and skills specific to a particular reality domain, and each system makes use of symbols, such as mental images, numbers, or language, that are also domain-appropriate. Information related to space, for example, is best represented through mental images, whereas information on quantitative relations is best represented through mathematical notation. At the environment oriented level, input consists of information coming from the environment; output refers to actions, actual or mental, directed to the environment.

The self-oriented level involves processes and knowledge that guide self-understanding, understanding of other minds, and self-regulation. This level involves functions that are responsible for (a) monitoring one's own and others' cognitive activity; (b) recording this activity in mental "maps" that can be used as a basis for self-definition and categorization of other individuals; and (c) regulating one's own and others' mental activity on the basis of these maps, when decisions need to be made and problems solved, where no ready-made solutions exist.

The last level involves structures and functions that determine the capability of the mind, at a given age, to process information. The structures and functions at this level are largely content-free, but they constrain the complexity of the problems (whether environment- or self-oriented) that can be solved by persons at a given age. The structures and functions of each system of mind are described fully and analyzed in subsequent sections. Figure 8.1 presents an overview of the general architecture of mind and of the relations between the various levels and systems.

Environment-Oriented Systems of Thought

Our research has identified and delineated seven environment-oriented systems, that is, the categorical, the quantitative, the causal, the spatial, the propositional, the social, and the pictographic system (Bonoti, 1997; Demetriou & Efklides, 1985, 1989; Demetriou, Kazi, Platsidou, Sirmali, & Kiosseoglou, 1997; Loizos, 1992; Shayer, Demetriou, & Prevez, 1988). Each system involves many different processes that are themselves organized hierarchically. Specifically, each system involves (a) core processes, (b) rules, mental operations, and processing skills, and (c) knowledge and beliefs. Table 8.1 summarizes the main characteristics and processes involved in the various systems.

Core processes are special kinds of mental processes in each system. That is, they are very fundamental processes that date back millions of years into our evolution as a species and somehow might characterize the cognitive functioning of other species, mammals in particular. During development, core processes are the first manifestations of the systems, and these are predominantly perceptual. If a minimum set of conditions are present in the input, they will be activated and provide an interpretation of the input, which is consistent with their organization. In other words, core processes constitute a particular kind of structure in a system that evolved to cope with particular patterns in the environment and are adaptively important to the organism. Each system of thought involves thought processes that match relations in the environment typical of the reality domain to which each system is affiliated. An example of core processes in the social system is the ability of the human infant to differentiate the human face from other stimuli from the very first days of life and to respond accordingly (Butter-worth, 1998). For instance, infants smile if they are shown a sketch of the human face. Another example is the "flee or attack" behavior many animals demonstrate in response to an aggressive face. Examples of core processes for each system are presented in the respective sections.

Admittedly, core processes may not be very important in cognitive functioning when the operations and knowledge structures (described later) are in place. They are, however, important in that they constitute the starting points for the construction of these structures, and, therefore, individual differences in these core processes are reflected subsequently in these operations and knowledge structures. Moreover, whenever these operations and knowledge structures need to change, the core processes may function as guides that direct the process of change.

The second kind of integral components involved in the various systems comprises the processes that enable an individual to cope with problems for which no ready-made core processes are available. Specifically, these processes arise through interactions between the core processes and the corresponding domain of the environment, because both the organism and the environment are not stable across occasions. For instance, the infant encounters many different faces from the very first day of life and even the face of the infant's mother may somehow vary from occasion to occasion. This makes face recognition strategies necessary on top of the core processes that enable differentiation of human faces from other figures in the first place.

TABLE 8.1

The Levels and Systems of Mind and their Basic Processes and Components

Levels and Systems	Core Processes	Operations and Rules	Knowledge and Beliefs
Environment oriented systems			
1. Qualitative-analytic	Categorical perception	Classification strategies concept formation strategies	Descriptive and declarative, knowledge, attributions about persons and things.
2. Quantitative-relational	Subsidization	Counting, arithmetic operations, proportional reasoning	Time reading, money knowledge, multiplication tables.
3. Causal-experimental	Perception of causality	Trial and error, experimentation, hypothesis formation	Knowledge and attributions about the causal structure of the world.
4. Spatial-imaginal	Perception of depth, size, and orientation	Processes for scanning and transformation of mental images, mental rotation	All imaginal representations and knowledge out the world.
5. Verbal-propositional	Primary reasoning, i.e., automatic inference based on the structure of language.	Secondary reasoning, i.e., reasoning based on considerations of truth and validity.	Explicit knowledge about reasoning and logic.
Hypercognitive system			
1. Working Hypercognition	Differential sensitivity to various cognitive experiences, feelings of knowing.	Self-monitoring and self-regulation strategies	
2. Long-term Hypercognition			Models about the mind, intelligence, and the self
Processing system			
1. Encoding	Perceptual registering	Stimulus identification	
2. Control	Inhibition mechanisms	Selective attention	
3. Storage	Primary representation of information	Rehearsal, chunking, and other organization strategies.	

153

That is, core processes are gradually differentiated into systems of mental actions that provide rules, strategies, and skills that can be used to solve complex problems in each domain. The processes and strategies in each system and the mechanisms that lead from core processes to representations, rules, and problem-solving skills are explained in detail later.

Finally, each system involves knowledge of the reality domain to which it is affiliated, a knowledge that accrues over the years as a result of the interactions between a particular system and its respective domain of reality. Conceptual and belief systems pertaining to the physical, the biological, psychological, and the social world are found at this level of the organization of the various systems. Prejudices about particular groups of people, for example, involve both categorizations resulting from the functions of the categorical thought and causal attributions resulting from the functions of causal thought. Only five of the seven systems are described here as our research is still in progress for the last two.

The System of Categorical Thought

This system has two important functions. The first is to identify and abstract from all the information in the environment these properties and characteristics which are important to the organism; the second is to reduce unnecessary complexity. This system is, thus, the basic mechanism underlying the construction, representation, and use of categorical structures. Processes related to the recognition of conspecifics (i.e., recognition of the members of the same species), such as the infant's preference for the human face compared to other objects, or categorical perception according to color are examples of the kernel elements involved in this system.

There are many examples of the operations and strategies belonging to the second level of the organization of this system. Browsing, scanning, and selection strategies enabling an individual to identify the properties related to a categorization task are examples of abstraction processes. Classification strategies, primarily involving organization skills, are examples of processes aimed at reducing complexity. Finally, the categorizations and attributions for persons and things we all hold, such as that some people are friendly and some hostile, are examples of the third layer of the categorical system (Shayer et al.,1988).

The System of Quantitative Thought

All elements of reality potentially can undergo quantitative transformations. Things aggregate or separate so that they increase, decrease, split, or multiply in space or time and for many different reasons. Some of these aspects of reality are of adaptational value and many living organisms are sensitive to some quantitative variations in the environment considered important for their species (Gallistel, 1993). In humans, subitization is an example of the core processes involved in this system. *Subitization* refers to our ability to specify the numerosity of small sets (smaller than 3 or 4 elements) by simply looking at them.

At the second level of organization, this system involves abilities and skills of quantitative specification, for example, counting, pointing, bringing in or removing, and sharing. Internalizing these skills into coordinated mental actions results in the four basic arithmetic operations, which provide understanding of the basic quantitative functions of increase, decrease, redistribution, and so on. This level also involves rules and operations for identification of various types of quantitative relations. Understanding fractions or decimal numbers are examples of these processes. The ability to conceptualize dimensions, such as height, weight, and volume in the physical world, or ambition, beauty, and passion in the social world, are other examples, as are the skills and operations required to indicate relations between different dimensions, for example, the relation between changes in height and weight in nature or the relation between beauty and passion. These processes constitute the basis of complex mathematical thinking, such as proportional reasoning.

The third level of the organization of this system involves all kinds of factual knowledge about the quantitative aspects of the world. Examples include knowledge about time reading; money values, and rules underlying everyday transactions; numerical knowledge, such as the multiplication tables, the meaning of mathematical symbols (i.e., the symbols which stand for the four arithmetic operations); and content knowledge of the various branches of mathematics (i.e., algebra or geometry; Demetriou et al., 1993, Demetriou et al., 1996; Demetriou, Platsidou, Efklides, Metallidou, & Shayer, 1991).

The System of Causal Thought

Objects and people very often are related dynamically, sometimes functioning as the cause of changes and other times as the recipients of effects. Cause–effect relationships are rarely clear or directly available to the senses; often they are hidden due to the presence of unrelated elements and frequently may be so concealed that they never strike the senses. In the physical world, all kinds of counterintuitive phenomena, such as electromagnetic, nuclear, or astronomical phenomena, are examples of causal interactions. The immaterial effects exerted on human behavior by desires, ambitions, and feelings are examples of masked causal relationships in the psychological and the social world. That is, this system comprises all kinds of interactive reality structures. Perception of fundamental causal relationships, such as when there is direct transfer of energy from one object to another (e.g., we push something to move it), are examples of the core processes involved in this system.

At the second level of organization, this system involves processes that enable the thinker to manipulate and represent causal relations. Specifically, it involves hypothesis formation, experimentation, and model construction. *Hypothesis formation* enables one to take a "what-if" stance to reality and imagine alternative cause–effect connections involved in a given situation which can then be tested by experimentation. For instance, one may test the hypothesis that the combination of sunny weather and high altitude increases the productivity of a given crop, whereas the combination of cloudy weather and low altitude results in decreased productivity. *Experimentation* enables the person to test hypotheses by designing appropriate experiments. Trial and error is a rather weak method of experimentation, whereas isolation of variables, which Piaget considered an indication of formal thought, is a more advanced method of experimentation. The isolation-of-variables strategy enables one to vary systematically a factor which is supposed to cause an effect and keep all other factors constant. Finally, *model construction* enables the individual to synthesize the results of experimentation with the original hypotheses in order to arrive at an acceptable interpretative framework or theory. Model construction is a double-sided process. On the one hand, it involves the rejection or modification of the hypotheses not confirmed by the results of experimentation, and, on the other hand, it raises the confirmed hypotheses to the level of an explanatory model. Model construction also involves an understanding that the credibility of any model depends on future evidence so that, in principle, any model can be rejected if there is evidence contrary to its premises.

Knowledge related to the "why" and "how" of things pertains to the third level of the organization of this system. Our understanding of the reasons underlying physical and social events as well as their procedural aspects come from the functioning of the operations mentioned above and constitute our ready-made attributions about the dynamic aspects of the world (Demetriou, Efklides, Papadaki, et al., 1993; Demetriou, Efklides, & Platsidou, 1993).

The System of Spatial Thought

This system is directed to the representation and processing of two aspects of reality: orientation and movement in space, and situations or scenes that can be visualized mentally as integral wholes and processed as such. Therefore, anything that can be perceived and then somehow preserved as a mental image can become the object of the activity of this system. Formation of mental images and processes, such as perception of size, depth, and orientation of objects, are examples of this system's core processes.

The second level of organization involves processes and operations that enable the individual to apply to mental images actions that can be applied to their real-world counterparts. Thus, this level involves processes whereby the individual can transform an image, for example, through various mental actions such as removal, addition, rotation, and transposition of the elements involved in the image.

All images that can be drawn from memory belong to the third level of the organization of this system (Shayer et al., 1988). Moreover, memories of locations where things can be found, mental maps, scripts about how to move, and so on, constitute one's knowledge about the imaginable and spatial aspects of one's environment.

The System of Propositional Thought

This system serves two main functions. First, it enables one to abstract information from verbal interaction in a meaningful way. Thus, it facilitates interaction between persons, and it is used as a guide to action. Imagine, for instance, a conversation such as the following: "Mom, can I play outside?" "Yes, but only if you finish your homework."; or "Mom, can I have them both?" "No, you can't; you can either have the green or the red one." From a very young age children understand that they have to do their homework before they go out to play, in the first case, or that they have to choose, in the second case. The propositional system comprises the ability to understand the relations among various actions mentioned in the conversation. Core processes in this system underlie the ability, which is present from infancy, to use the grammatical and syntactical structures of language (e.g., "*if* this *then* that," "*either* this *or* that") to infer the relations among the events or situations mentioned in a sequence of sentences (Bernicot, 1998; Demetriou, 1998).

At the second level of organization, this system enables the individual to check whether a series of statements are connected in a valid way, often independently of their content. Imagine, for instance, two statements such as the following: (a) "The hand is red *and* is not red;" (b) "The thing that I have in my hand is red *or* not red" (Osherson & Markman, 1975). The first of these statements is not valid because nothing can, at one and the same time, have and not have a given attribute. The second, however, is valid because an object can have a given attribute or a different one. This system enables the person to grasp if a statement is consistent and therefore valid, or inconsistent and therefore invalid.

Two types of skills are involved in this system. First, there are skills that enable the individual to interpret and interrelate the components in verbal statements so that information may be abstracted in goal-relevant, meaningful, and coherent ways. Interpretation of words or strings of words are examples of these skills. Second, there are skills that enable one to differentiate the contextual from the formal elements in a series of statements and operate on the latter. For example, focusing on such verbs as "is" or "belongs to," or connectives such as "and," "if," and "or" directs thinking to the relations between the statements, rather than simply the statements themselves. These processes, the second in particular, enable one to grasp the basic logical relations of conjunction (... and ... and ...), disjunction (either ... or), implication (if ... then), and so on. (Efklides, Demetriou, & Metallidou, 1994).

Explicit knowledge about grammar and syntax and explicit knowledge about logical reasoning belong to the third level of the organization of this system. Actually, schools provide this kind of knowledge to the students with the hope that it will affect their reasoning capabilities.

Validation of the Environment-Oriented Systems

These systems of thought were induced on the basis of evidence generated by a large number of studies. In these studies, participants were examined by means of a wide array of tasks addressing different modules or subsystems involved in each system (e.g., hypothesis formation, experimentation, and model construction in the causal system, or arithmetic operations, algebraic reasoning, and proportional reasoning in the quantitative system). The participants were found to treat tasks addressed to the same module in very similar ways. Tasks representing different modules of the same system were found to be less closely related than tasks representing the same module, because, although the modules share common processes such as the core processes, they each activate certain unique processes. For instance, although both mental rotation and orientation in space require mental visualization, each requires something specific. For example, mental rotation means to see the different parts of an object in different relations to other objects (imagine rotating a suitcase mentally to see how it is fixed in the trunk of your car); orientation in space means to place oneself in relation to the three dimensions of Euclidean space (imagine trying to figure out if you have to turn right or left at a crossroad). Tasks addressing different systems also might share common constraints imposed from the two domain-general systems (i.e., the processing system and the hypercognitive system). They do not, however, share much in common in regard to computational processes and operations. A model representing the organization of performance attained in these experiments is shown in panel A of Figure 8.1. This model was found to accommodate the evidence obtained by a large number of studies (Demetriou, Efklides, & Platsidou, 1993; Demetriou et al., 1996; Demetriou et al, 1991; Demetriou, Efklides, Papadaki, 1993; Efklides et al., 1994; Loizos, 1992). Figure 8.1 presents an

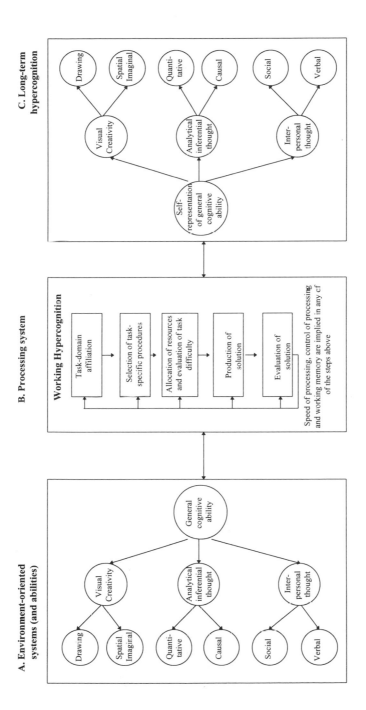

Fig. 8.1. The three levels of mind and their internal structure. *Note*: Attention is drawn to the equivalence between the structure of abilities in the environment-oriented level and their representation in the hypercognitive system. Attention is also drawn to the assumption that the processing system is occupied by the self-monitoring and self-regulation processes involved in working hypercognition.

overview of the general architecture of mind and of the relations between the various levels and systems.

A series of training studies was also conducted to verify the assumptions about the relations among environment-oriented systems. We provided learning experiences directed to one component of a particular system and we examined whether the experience was transferable to other components both within the same system or in other systems. These studies showed that the positive effects of training generalize within the same system, but they do not generalize across different systems. These findings indicate that the processes involved in one system are not directly affected by the learning experiences directed to another system. These results indicate that each system has a unique structure (Demetriou, Efklides, & Platsidou, 1993, Study 2; Efklides, Demetriou, & Gustafsson, 1992). Evidence consistent with these findings recently has been provided by other researchers (Case et al., 1996).

Educational Relevance of the Environment-Oriented Systems

All five systems involve the processes and concepts that students bring to bear on the different types of subject matter. For example, the level of a child's quantitative system relates directly to the kind of mathematical concepts the child can process. If students cannot represent the relations among different dimensions, which are required for understanding proportional relations, teaching them mathematical proportions in all likelihood will fail. The condition of the causal system, to a certain extent, determines which science concepts can be understood. If the child does not possess the isolation-of- variables strategy, it is rather improbable that the child is able to conceptualize science as a process of inquiry as opposed to a process of description. If a student cannot mentally visualize the changes and transformations that objects can undergo, it is unlikely that the student can draw them or form concepts that require visualization. Determination of an individual's developmental status with regard to each system can provide guidelines specifying level- and subject-appropriate curricula.

The evidence for the structural differences among the various systems suggests that topics related to all systems must be included in the school curriculum. The evidence also indicates that instruction should be differentiated so that it is suitable for the level of each particular system. This is necessary because teaching interventions that benefit one system do not necessarily apply to another.

Real-life problems usually require the application of more than one system to be satisfactorily understood and solved. For example, some concepts of natural sciences involving causal relations also draw on the quantitative system. Mathematics frequently requires other systems in addition to the quantitative one. For example, geometry requires spatial processes whereas algebra requires propositional and general symbolization abilities. Of course, application of the present theory for instructional purposes presupposes a satisfactory cognitive science analysis of both the specific composition of the systems and the curriculum requirements. Demetriou, Gustafsson, Efklides, and Platsidou (1992) presented a first attempt in this direction.

The Hypercognitive System

Any cognitive system that involves specialized processing modules, such as the systems described above, does not necessarily involve mind. Animals and computers, for example, possess system-specific skills or programs that enable them to solve various problems with varying degrees of complexity, but we do not credit them with mind. To have mind, a cognitive system must be aware of itself; it must somehow be able to record both its own activity and that of other minds; it must be aware of doing so, and must use this knowledge for the purpose of understanding and regulating both its own activity and that of other cognitive systems (such as other persons, animals, and computers). In other words, a cognitive system must involve a higher-order system of knowing, or a hypercognitive system, in order to be mindful. The adverb *hyper* in Greek means "higher than," or "on top of," or "going beyond," and when added to the word *cognitive* indicates the supervising and coordinating functions of the hypercognitive system (Demetriou, Efklides, & Platsidou, 1993).

The input to this system are those experiences generated by the functioning of the environment-oriented systems. Mental effort and ensuing feelings of difficulty can provide information on the cost of having the various systems activated. We all have had the experience of working on one type of problem that is easy and pleasant, and working on another type that is hard and frequently unsuccessful. Searching for strategies for the sake of solving problems gives us information on similarities and differences in the processes involved in the various systems. These differential experiences contribute to the creation of mental "maps" that reflect the organization of the environment-oriented systems. These maps are used to guide the functioning of the environment-oriented level. Thus, the hypercognitive system is the interface between (a) mind and reality, which of course involves other minds as well; (b) any of the environment-oriented systems or any other cognitive functions, such as memory and attention; and (c) the processing system and the environment-oriented systems (Demetriou & Efklides, 1989; Demetriou, Efklides, & Platsidou, 1993).

The hypercognitive system functions by employing working hypercognition and long-term hypercognition (see Table 8.1). *Working hypercogni-*

tion involves a number of mind-reading and mind-steering processes and skills that are used during on-line problem solving (see panel B of Figure 8.1). When directed to one's own cognitive functioning, working hypercognition monitors ongoing cognitive activity and makes three kinds of decisions when there is a problem to be solved. First, it determines the appropriate cognitive functions or the relevant system to be activated. Second, it makes evaluative decisions to ensure that working on a problem is worth the attempt. Third, it evaluates the attained outcomes in terms of the goal and the effort exerted. These decisions feed back to the hypercognitive system, and this makes it more efficient (Demetriou & Efklides, 1988, 1989).

When directed to the functioning of other minds, these processes ensure that the individual understands how and why others embark on particular activities, which are of interest to them or to the thinker himself. Attending to verbal and nonverbal cues indicative of cognitive and emotional states are examples of these processes.

The products of working hypercognition are integrated in long-term hypercognition. *Long-term hypercognition* comprises knowledge and rules related to the nature of mind, the functions it can serve, and the ways in which it can serve the needs of the person. Our theory posits that the contents of long-term hypercognition are organized into three distinct but interrelated models, namely, a model of cognition, a model of intelligence, and a model of the cognitive self. The basic attributes of these models are subsequently summarized.

The Model of Cognition

This model contains rules, knowledge, and beliefs related to the structure and functioning of the cognitive system. First, the model specifies the specific cognitive functions that exist, for example, that there is memory that is distinct from thought, or that there are different types of mental operations, such as those performed by each environment-oriented system. According to the theory, this model involves mental maps that reflect how the mind is actually organized. This reflection of the actual organization of the mind at the level of the hypercognitive system is shown in panel C of Figure 8.1. It can be seen that this panel, which stands for one's model of cognition involves the same constructs and it is organized in the same way as panel A, which stands for performance. Second, it specifies how the functions and processes can be used most efficiently in relation to the task requirements. For example, it comprises rules suggesting the best ways that memory can store or recall different types of information. Rehearsal, for example, is an efficient strategy for memorizing a short list of digits, but organization according to meaning is preferable for remembering a long shopping list involving many categories of products. This part of the model is related to earlier work on metacognition, carried out in the 1970s and 1980s (Demetriou & Efklides, 1989; Demetriou, Efklides, & Platsidou, 1993; Fabricius & Schwanenflugel, 1994).

The model of cognition also involves the realization that the mind is capable of influencing behavior and human interaction. Representations that individuals have about others or about the physical world can affect others' behavior and interaction. For instance, people act aggressively when they want to undermine another's interests. This part of the model of cognition is related to what has come to be known in recent years as the theory of mind (Wellman, 1990).

The Model of Intelligence

This model involves an individual's knowledge and beliefs in relation to what constitutes intelligent behavior in a given environment and time. For example, we must learn quickly, speak fluently and accurately, be socially flexible and considerate, must control our behavior, and so on. This model specifies how we must regulate our behavior to achieve personal goals and avoid unnecessary conflicts with our particular social or cultural group. Thus, our theory of intelligence may be viewed as value-guided system, in which an individual's knowledge and expertise is emphasized to maximize the gains of action based on his interpretation of the specific situation (Demetriou et al., 1997; Sternberg, Conway, Ketron, & Bernstein, 1981).

The Model of Cognitive Self

This model resides at the intersection of one's model of cognition and model of intelligence. It involves how individuals view themselves as intelligent thinking beings and answers questions such as the following: How flexible or intelligent or wise am I? Which kinds of problems am I, or am I not, good at solving? How efficient am I in using different cognitive functions such as memory, imagery, problem solving, and others? The cognitive self-image involves all the implicit and explicit attributes that individuals ascribe to themselves in regard to different mental functions, abilities, strategies, and skills (Demetriou, Efklides, & Platsidou, 1993, Demetriou et al., 1997).

Validation of the Hypercognitive System

Our assumptions related to the model of cognition and the cognitive self were tested and verified in a series of studies that investigated the various "hypercognitive maps" that persons hold about their own minds. In these studies, participants were first asked to solve tasks addressing the different environment-oriented systems. They were then given descriptions of various processes (which, according to the theory, are employed in the processing of each type of tasks) and were asked to specify which processes and to what degree were used to solve each task. Overall, participants associated the processes in accordance with the theory. In fact, a recent study has shown that even 5-year-olds are able to differentiate between different tasks, such as mathematical and classification tasks, on the basis of the thought activity that is required for each task. It must be noted, however, that the various environment-oriented systems are differentially amenable to awareness. The spatial system seems to generate experiences that are rather easily self-monitored, and, accordingly, this system is more easily differentiated from the others. Mathematical operations also seem to be more clearly visible to awareness than are operations of the causal system (Demetriou, Efklides, & Platsidou, 1993, study 3; Demetriou et al., 1997; Makris, 1995; Kazi, 1998).

Educational Relevance of the Hypercognitive System

The models and processes involved in the hypercognitive system specify how an individual is self-defined and self-regulated in relation to various types of knowledge and activities. In other words, individuals' conceptions of intelligence and themselves constrain the strategies that they will employ to solve problems under different conditions and channel their preferences and activities, overt or mental. For example, we are frequently able to circumvent, to a certain extent, the limitations of our processing systems by employing strategies we consider appropriate. We may reorganize information (e.g., break it down into smaller bits or group it into larger units) to fit the current capacity of our processing system. These strategies seem to be as important as the processing capacity itself for the semantic integration of information into one's current conceptual structures, and are frequently very personal and idiosyncratic. Some individuals, for example, use visualization strategies, whereas others use integration strategies that depend on verbal analysis of meaning. Recognizing students' strategies for managing information load and semantic integration might help the teacher to accommodate the varying needs of different students.

The students' cognitive self-image might have more far-reaching implications, insofar as it might affect their attitudes toward learning, study habits, and long-term orientations and planning. For instance, students who believe that their mathematical potential is limited might be reluctant to get involved in activities requiring mathematics, even despite positive feedback. The more they abstain from these activities, the less likely it becomes that their mathematical potential, whatever it is, will be actualized. Eventually, their chosen life paths will implicate mathematics as little as possible. This orientation may be justified if their self-images accurately represent their actual capabilities; however, they might have selected a less suitable life course. Therefore, helping students to acquire accurate self-monitoring and self-image building strategies may be as important as is the teaching of any particular subject at a given age (Demetriou et al., 1997).

The Processing System

Structure and Functions of the Processing System

The processing system receives information from both the environment-oriented and the self-oriented level. At any moment, the inputs to the processing system are environment-relevant information, skills, and processes that pertain to one or more of the environment-oriented systems, and monitoring, management, and evaluation processes that pertain to the hypercognitive system. Specifically, our research indicates that working hypercognition is the management system which is responsible for regulating the processing system (Demetriou, Efklides, & Platsidou, 1993). The theory presented here ascribes three fundamental functions to the processing system, that is, an *encoding function*, a *control function,* and a *storage function* (see Table 8.1).

Encoding refers to the processes that make the recording and recognition of stimuli possible. Encoding efficiency is traditionally measured in terms of the time needed to identify a simple unit of information (a letter, a word, or a one-digit number) under conditions of maximum facilitation. The individual is asked, for example, to recognize if two letters presented side by side (e.g., Aa or AB) are identical with respect to a particular attribute, such as meaning or appearance (Sternberg, 1975). In another experimental paradigm, the individual is asked to read as quickly as possible words denoting colors printed in the same ink color (i.e., the word *red* written in red ink; Stroop, 1935). Under these conditions, speed of processing indicates the time needed by the system to record and give meaning to information. Traditionally, the faster an individual is, the more efficient his processing system.

The information which is of value or interest at one particular moment seldom appears alone—it usually coexists along side other information that must be distinguished and ignored. The control function refers to the processes that identify and register goal-relevant information and block out dominant or appealing but actually irrelevant information. Control comprises simultaneously a dual function: It comprises a matching function that looks at the input for goal-relevant information; at the same time, it comprises an inhibition function that discards goal-irrelevant information or activities. Control of processing determines the system's efficiency in selecting the appropriate mental act. This function is usually tested under conditions which can generate conflicting interpretations. A well known example is the Stroop phenomenon (Stroop, 1935), in which words denoting color but written with a different ink color are presented, and the individual is asked to name the ink color as quickly as possible (i.e., the word *red* written with blue color). These conditions accurately test control of processing, because the subject is required to inhibit a dominant but irrelevant response (to read the word) in order to select and emit a weaker but relevant response (name the ink color; DemetriouEfklides, Platsidou, 1993; Spanoudis, Demetriou, Platsidou, Kiosseoglou, & Sirmali, 1996).

Finally, once information is selected and encoded, it must be actively represented in relation to the present problem. *Storage* refers to the processes that enable a person to hold information in an active state while integrating it with other information until the problem is solved. A common measure of the storage function is the maximum amount of information and mental acts that the mind can activate efficiently and simultaneously.

It must be noted that there seem to be two types of storage, specifically, storage for auditory information and storage for visual information. Although largely independent of one another, these kinds of storage share common processes, and they are also interconnected by the encoding and the control functions which seem to be common to both (Demetriou, Efklides, & Platsidou, 1993). Our conception of the processing system builds on and integrates the work of a number of other scholars in the neo-Piagetian and the information processing tradition (Baddeley, 1991; Case, 1985; Halford, 1993; Kail, 1988; Pascual-Leone, 1970).

The interdependence among the three main levels of the mental architecture was demonstrated in a number of studies (Demetriou, Efklides, & Platsidou, 1993). Only one study (Demetriou et al., 1997) is summarized here, because it shows neatly how the processing system and the environment-oriented systems together affect self-image, which belongs to the hypercognitive system. Specifically, participants were tested for their performance on tasks measuring the encoding function or speed of processing and their performance on a number of deductive and inductive reasoning tasks. The first set of tasks tests the processing system and the second tests the environment-oriented knowing systems. Based on preliminary tests, four participant groups were formed: slow processors and low reasoners, slow processors and high reasoners, fast processors and low reasoners, and fast processors and high reasoners. How participants viewed themselves in regard to logical reasoning and learning ability, which represent the hypercognitive level, was also investigated. That is, participants were asked to rate themselves in regard to various processes involved in learning and reasoning (e.g., "I learn very fast," "I never forget something I learned," "When I hear somebody speaking, I check systematically if what he says is logically consistent," etc.) Findings are illustrated in Figure 8.2, in which the state of

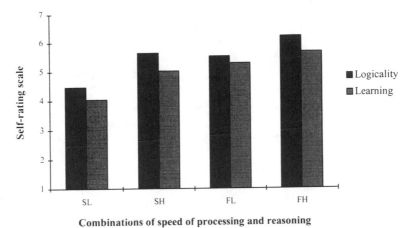

Combinations of speed of processing and reasoning

Fig 8.2. Self-attribution of learning and logically scores according to the combination of performance on the speed of processing—slow (S) and fast (F) individuals—and the verbal analogies tasks—low (L) and high (H) individuals.

the processing system and reasoning are taken as the independent variables and self-representation in regard to reasoning and learning as the dependent variable. It is clear that the faster in processing and the more proficient on the reasoning tasks the participants were, the better they considered themselves to be in reasoning and learning ability. This finding suggests that the hypercognitive system directly registers and represents the condition of the processing system and the environment-oriented reasoning processes (Demetriou et al., 1997).

Educational Relevance of the Processing System

The condition of the processing system sets the limits of what can and what cannot be processed at a given age. Specifying individuals' conditions in regard to the three dimensions of the processing system delineates the range of their potential learning capability, and this, in turn, would guide the classroom teacher toward appropriate teaching strategies.

For example, presenting information at a rate higher than that at which it can be encoded by the students' processing system would jeopardize the learning process, even if the concepts are within the assimilatory capabilities of a given group. Knowing the limits of information processing capacity possessed by a target group would enable the teacher to make decisions about the rate at which teaching may proceed.

Control of processing determines the students' ability to focus attention on the most relevant aspects of teaching and learning and to resist stimuli that might be dominant but irrelevant to the instructional goals. Therefore, this dimension of the processing system is related to the students' ability to ignore environmental distractions and use their mental energies in the most profitable way from the point of view of the teaching–learning process. Thus, knowing the students' ability to control information processing would enable the teacher to present subject matter so that information does not exceed student understanding.

Finally, working memory capacity determines the degree of complexity of the concepts or instructional events that can be processed at a given age. Concepts that demand more working memory than the individual's working memory cannot be processed. For example, to multiply 2 one-digit numbers—if no ready-made answer is available to be retrieved from long-term memory—students need a working memory that can sustain three units of information: the two digits to be multiplied and the mathematical operation to be applied. If one is unable to keep this information active for the time needed to make calculations, the task is impossible. Multiplication of 2 two-digit numbers mentally (for instance 36 x 24) demands a larger working memory capacity, because the results of the intermediate steps of the computation in addition to the two numbers and the appropriate mathematical operation all must be retained. Knowing the students' limits of working memory capacity would help the teacher to keep the instructional demands within the limits of students' potentials.

The dimensions of the processing system are, thus, related to important instructional variables. Specifically, some aspects of instructional time, such as "allocated time," "engaged time," and "academic learning time" are highly relevant to the condition of the processing system and instructional effectiveness (Berliner, 1979). As a rule of thumb, students always should be provided the optimum time they need for each phase in the instructional process, if they are to figure out satisfactorily what a problem is about and work out their solutions.

THE DEVELOPMENT AND DYNAMICS OF MIND

This section describes the development of the systems previously outlined and elaborates on why and how they develop and interact. Specifically, we first attempt to show that the architecture of mind as specified by this theory is a necessary precondition for cognitive change. We then argue that the peculiarities of the different levels and systems of mind yield different types of developmental change and different mechanisms of cognitive change that are responsible for the development of the various systems. These mechanisms also are outlined.

Developmental Sequences

The Development of the Processing System

There is ample evidence that the three functions of the processing system improve systematically from birth to early adulthood, when they remain stable until early middle age, at which time they start to decline. Figure 8.3 summarizes the results of our research on the development of these three functions for the age span of 8 to 70 years. It can be seen that, although there are changes in all three functions, at some ages these changes occur more rapidly. For example, the greatest improvement in encoding and control functions occurs between the ages of 9 and 11 (Demetriou, Efklides, & Platsidou, 1993; Spanoudis et al., 1996).

As age increases, the mind becomes more efficient in encoding, controlling, and storing information. That is, it becomes faster in recognizing and making meaning of information, more able to focus on goal-relevant information and ignore irrelevant information, and better able to process more chunks of information simultaneously. Further, the changes in the three dimensions of the processing system occur during the same age range when there are major changes in the other two systems of mind, that is, the environment-oriented systems and the hypercognitive system. However, there is no one-to-one correspondence in the degree or type of change from one level of mind to the other. Interrelationships among these changes will be clarified in the section on dynamics of development.

The Development of the Environment-Oriented Systems

Space limitations do not allow a complete presentation on the development of each environment-oriented system, but a summary of the basic characteristics of all these systems from 2 to 20 years of age is found appended in Table 8.2. One can examine the information in Table 8.2 from several perspectives: From one perspective, the similarities in the development of different environment-oriented systems are impressive, yet viewed from another, their differences look equally impressive.

With regard to the similarities, at some phases of development there are representational changes across all systems. Specifically, representations tend to become more inclusive, abstract, and arbitrary with age. At about the age of 2 years, representation becomes detached or arbitrary, that is, rather than using symbols directly related to the objects or events to be represented, it uses symbols with no direct correspondence to the properties of the objects or events. Most words of language, for example, have no physical resemblance to the objects they represent. Even accurate mental images and photographs are on a different scale from the thing they represent. This representational shift immensely increases the flexibility of

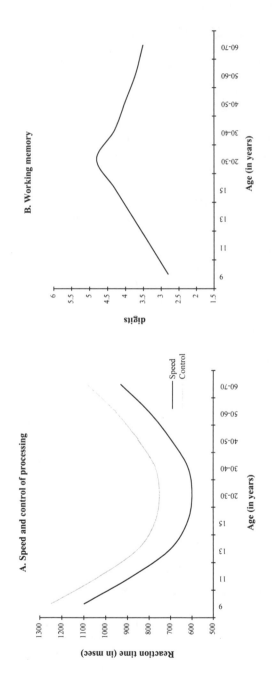

Fig. 8.3. The general patterns of developmental changes in speed of processing, control of processing, and working memory. Note: These patterns describe changes in different symbolic modes such as the verbal, the numerical, and the figural mode.

TABLE 8.2

Modal Characteristics of the Five Environment-Oriented Systems and the Hypercognitive System During Development

Age	Qualitative-Analytical	Quantitative-Relational	Causal-Experimental	Spatial-Imaginal	Verbal-Propositional	Hypercognition
3	Protocategories. Classifications are based on phen-omenal criteria. Categorical inference is based on the transformation of observed characteristics into a conclusion (i.e., "He is a 'doctor' because he has a stethoscope").	Protoquantitative schemes. Understating of the effects of fundamental quantitative acts, such as addition or removal of elements from a set of things. Understanding of the basic principles of counting, e.g., that each number name corresponds to one set only.	Protocausal schemes. Causal sequences can be differentiated from random sequences on the basis of the structure of events in space and time. Experimentation is based on "trial and error" because no preconceived hypothesis is present	· Global mental images. These may be very accurate but their different parts cannot be mentally manipulated independently of each other.	Primary reasoning, i.e., automatic use or understanding of propositions in everyday speech.	Differentiation between the real and the mental. Self-image depends on physical characteristics and action.
5	A criterion may be preselected and applied in order to specify the identity of objects and their similarity relations (e.g., color, shape etc.). This criterion may be used to classify things on the basis of having or not having this attribute. Class inclusion relations based on natural kinds may be understood.	Co-ordination of proto-quantitative schemes. The "increase–decrease scheme" is, for example, coordinated with the basic principles of counting. This generates a first understanding of number conservation.	Coordination of protocausal schemes. This enables accurate descriptions of causal sequences. The child may search for the cause of an event (e.g., why does a toy not work?) by testing (usually persistently and inflexibly) some idea directly suggested by the apparent aspects of the event.	Pictures can now be analyzed in their parts. Spatial dimensions are constructed and spatial operations, such as mental rotation can be effected.	Propositions can be distinguished from each other and organized in order to suggest a given conclusion. Permission rules are now understood (If you do X, then you can do Y).	Differentiation between basic cognitive functions, such as thought, from noncognitive functions, such as perception.

(Table 8.2 continues)

7	Analytical strategies are intentionally and systematically applied. As a result, logical multiplication is possible. This yields novel categories and classes.	Appearance of proper mathematical concepts, such as cardinal and ordinal number, which integrate different proto-quantitative schemes. This enables the child to dimensionalize reality, and, thus, conceive of properties, such as, quantity, length, weight, area, volume, etc.	Prototheories, i.e., integrated views about the phenomena of the social and physical world. These are geared in personal experience and they are not taken as models to be tested.	Fluent mental imagery, that is spatial and imaginal operations can skillfully be applied in order to analyze and transform mental images or representations of space	Inference is explicitly applied. A series of premises can be connected and the conclusion can be deduced, if the logical relations suggested by the premises are real.	Differentiation between different cognitive functions, such as thought, memory, and attention. Self-image starts to include behavioral properties.
9	Analysis and logical multiplication can be applied on unfamiliar material.	Simple mathematical relations can be processed even when they are symbolically represented (e.g., equations, such as $8 - 3 = 5$ or $a + 5 = 8$, can be solved).	Prototheories become theories in action, i.e., it is understood that they may not be valid and may be falsified by reality. The testing of these theories is, however, occasional and fragmentary and is guided by each next happening rather than by a preconstructed plan.	Representation of very complex realities. The new and the unfamiliar cannot yet be imaginally constructed.	Logical necessity appears as a functional aspect of reasoning.	Understanding that different actions are needed to attain different mental effects.

(Table 8.2 continues)

11					
Analysis and logical multiplication is first applied on the goals of analysis as such rather than on the objects of analysis. As a result, children become able to differentiate between goal-relevant and goal-irrelevant information, focus on the first, and ignore the latter.	Quantitative reality is represented as a complex set of relations. Proportional reasoning (understanding of relations between relations) appears. Simple symbolic representations can, moreover, be coordinated in order to specify a general quantity (e.g., equations, such as $x = y + 3$, can be solved when y is specified.	Suppositions, i.e., alternative conceptions about causal relations begin to appear. This generates systematic combinatorial thought. The isolation-of-variables strategy can now be applied, when a hypothesis to be tested is presented. Under this condition, the supposed causal factor is systematically varied and one or two other factors are held constant.	The imaginal representation of the nonreal starts to become possible.	Premises are conceived as expressions of the possible. Thus, reasoning can be applied to test the logical validity of the formal relations between propositions independently of their content. This approach is now applied to easy relations, such as conjunction and disjunction.	Understanding of the mind as the interface between self and realty and between persons. Understanding that one's reality depends on one's representations about it. Self-image starts to include dispositions and personality attributes.

the child's thought for two reasons. First, the child is now able both to represent the same thing by more than one representations (e.g., we use more than one word to refer to the same thing or we use images, words, or numbers to denote the same entity) and also to signify different things by the same representation (e.g., the same number can refer to an endless variety of things or an outline of the human figure can stand for any person). Second, the child also becomes capable of representing invisible and immaterial things, such as mental states, which enable him to think about and explore entities and relations that were not accessible earlier. The abilities to classify, build number concepts, grasp causal interactions, orient things in space, and have a theory of mind now become possible, because this representational shift generates multiple representations that can or must be interconnected. This is true for all environment-oriented systems, although the needs of the moment determine which of the systems are activated.

An equally important representational shift occurs at the beginning of adolescence. At this phase, representation becomes transcendent, that is, it takes the representations of the previous phase as inputs and develops them into new, more sophisticated representations. Transcendent representations provide thought with two main advantages over those of the previous phase. First, thought becomes suppositional; it can now take a "what-if" stance to problems that enables it to propose alternative solutions and then select the most appropriate. Second, individuals at this stage can conceive of the counterintuitive—however unreal it might appear—because processing operates on representations that themselves go beyond reality. These representational changes enable thought processes to categorize the unseen or untouchable; deal with "beyond reality mathematics," such as algebra; manipulate variables and build theories about reality; visualize the very small, such as the atom, or the very big, such as the universe; and reason interpropositionally, and so construct a differentiated theory of the mind and a more accurate self-image.

There are still other changes that affect the functioning of all domain-specific systems—generally changes that enable the individual to deal with the new type of representations. Each representational change carries two concomitant changes. First, there are structural changes that allow the person to deal simultaneously with increasingly more representations; that is, more complex knowledge structures or problem-solving strategies are constructed during each phase of representation. For instance, when children can mentally retain two representations, they become able to have a theory of mind, because they can understand that the same thing can be represented differently by two persons. Second, there are refinement and expansional changes. As a result of repeated use, representations become more accurate with respect to what and how they represent things. For example, young children initially use words to denote either more objects (e.g., the word "dad" is used to denote men in general) or fewer objects (e.g., a category word such as "dog" is used only for a particular dog) than in their standard adult usage, but they gradually focus on their standard referents.

The preceding analysis indicates that there are certain representational changes that affect all environment-oriented systems. There are also important differences in the development of the various systems of mind, most of which relate to the number of representations involved in the problems that can be solved at corresponding levels of development of the environment-oriented systems. It proved, for example, to be very difficult to find fully equivalent formations for the concepts or problems that can be represented and addressed across the various environment-oriented systems at the same age. For the sake of comparison, the development of two environment-oriented systems, the quantitative-relational and the causal-experimental, is summarized here.

Between the ages of 3 and 5, quantitative thought functions on the basis of what has been called *protoquantitative schemes* (Resnick, Bill, & Lesgold, 1992). These schemes, which are based on quantitative core processes such as subitization, are used to solve simple mathematical tasks that require judgment on the basis of absolute criteria (e.g., "few," "many," "a lot") or comparisons on the basis of a single dimension (e.g., "less," "more," etc; see Gelman & Gallistel, 1992). Overt quantifying acts such as pointing, adding, or removing objects are very powerful means of quantifying the world until as late as age 7.

Both protoquantitative schemes and quantifying acts are gradually integrated and refined to produce mathematical operations, rules, and skills. The ability to execute basic arithmetic operations mentally is, for example, established during the primary school years. This ability is initially limited to the application of only one operation on two single-digit numbers. It expands gradually to encompass problems requiring the application of a combination of operations. For instance, at the age of 9, children can specify the operations represented by the two symbols in the equation 8 ♣ 3 ♠ = 10, where the first stands for subtraction and the second for multiplication. By the age of about 12, they are able to solve problems that require them to specify four operations. This reflects an increased capacity to hold representations in an active state and combine them in order to solve a problem.

Proportional reasoning appears at age 11 to 12 initially as an ability to intuitively grasp proportional relations that appear obvious (e.g., problems involving numbers that are multiples of one another, such as 2/4 and 4/8). It gradually evolves through a number of levels until, at age 14 to 15, individuals are able to grasp complex and counter-intuitive relationships (e.g., they can specify which of the two ratios, 4/5 or 7/8, is bigger).

Interestingly enough, the development of algebraic reasoning spans the entire period from about age 8 to 15. Algebraic reasoning allows individuals initially to specify quantitative relations on the basis of well-defined elements (for example, eight-year-old children can solve the problem: $8 - x = 5$). By middle adolescence, individuals become able to coordinate symbolic structures on the basis of their logical relationships to specify complex quantitative relations (for example, specify x, if $x + y + z = 30$ and $x = y + z$; to solve this problem one has to realize that 30 involves two equal parts and that x is the one of them; therefore x can be specified by dividing 30 by 2, which gives 15).

Development of these three mathematical capabilities, (i.e., handling of arithmetic operations, proportional reasoning, and algebraic reasoning) evolves along partially overlapping developmental trajectories. When one capability reaches a certain level, it opens the way for the second ability to develop further on its own trajectory, and when this second ability reaches a certain level, it provides, in turn, the necessary bases for the first one to develop further. When both of them attain a certain level of development, they make the emergence of the third one possible, which, once developed, facilitates the further development of the other two and so on and so forth. For instance, some versatility in applying arithmetic operations in combination with one another paves the way for the ability to deal with simple problems in algebra and this, when in place, provides the integrative processes needed to deal with problems of ratio and proportionality.

The development of the causal system proceeds in a similar fashion. Up to the age of 5 to 6 there is a kind of protocausal understanding that provides descriptions of observable reality. That is, the child forms representations that preserve the order of events in time. Although this implies that children can grasp causal relationships, in fact they have no systematic method to dissociate and manipulate different parts of these sequences to distinguish causal from apparent relationships. Instead, children at this age primarily use trial-and-error for studying cause–effect relationships. For children between the ages of 7 to 10, causal thought begins to change from descriptive to theory-guided. At this phase, however, theories are only implicit: Children are not aware of them nor can they generate explicit predictions based on them. For these children theories simply generate ideas which they randomly test (see Karmiloff-Smith & Inhelder, 1974).

For children at approximately age 11 to 12, causal thought becomes suppositional, and implicit theories now become explicit. The young adolescent now possesses a true experimental orientation to questions regarding causal relationships. This becomes evident through a number of component processes. Specifically, combinatorial thought is the first manifestation of this suppositional orientation to causal reality. It appears at about age 11 as an ability to randomly conceive combinations between different elements, and is consolidated at about age 15 as an ability to systematically and exhaustively generate all possible combinations between many different elements. Simple experimentation and hypothesis formation abilities appear simultaneously at approximately 12 to 13 years of age, and continually undergo expansion and refinement until late adolescence. At first, preadolescents can formulate only simple hypotheses that match a possible cause with an expected outcome, and they also can grasp the idea of the control of variables (that is, in order to test the possible effect of one given factor, the other factors must be constant). At this initial phase, however, controls are clumsy and simplistic. Preadolescents might vary the factor to be controlled instead of the hypothesized causal factor. By age 15, adolescents can formulate complex chains of hypotheses and design experiments involving multiple controls. Model construction ability, that is, the ability to integrate hypotheses with experimental data into a unified theory, appears at the age of about 15, and may not be well refined even at postuniversity level. Signs of an explicit personal epistemology regarding the causal structure of the world appear during late adolescence or early adulthood. This involves a grasp of the limits of both the mechanisms an experimenter employs to produce empirical evidence and the models to which experimentation may eventuate, which are not achieved earlier. Individuals begin to understand that their models are, to a large extent, nothing more than heuristic tools which, in principle, are always refutable. Our theory posits that this sequencing of developmental trajectories is part of the process of development:

> Combinatorial abilities of the lower levels serve to set up the mental space in which the first hypotheses can be formulated. At a subsequent phase, hypothesis formation abilities enable the young adolescent to fix the combinations he or she conceives in structures that can function as frames that can direct his or her manipulations of reality. Thus, systematic experimentation begins to be possible. Once it is acquired, experimentation acts in two directions. On the one hand, it provides strategies that can be put into the service of the combinatorial ability itself. As a result, the construction of the higher level combinatorial abilities is facilitated. On the other hand, it generates a data space that has to be understood. Evidently, a good way to gain an understanding is to map this data space onto the space of the hypotheses that served as the starting point of experimentation. This is the beginning of model construction. In turn, when model construction advances to a certain level, it functions as a frame for the conception of more complex hypotheses and consequently for the design of more sophisticated experiments. These then may loop

back by providing the material, external or mental, for the construction of more complex model, and so on and so forth. (Demetriou, & Efklides, & Platsidou, 1993, p. 495)

The Development of the Hypercognitive System

All components of the hypercognitive system also change extensively. In this section we will summarize research on the development of the individuals' understanding of the mind's organization and functioning and the development of self awareness as such.

Understanding the Organization and Functioning of the Mind

Research on the child's understanding of the mind highlights how various cognitive functions and processes are understood at different ages. According to Flavell, Green, and Flavell (1995), preschoolers differentiate thinking from other cognitive (i.e., perception) and noncognitive activities (e.g., movement), but they do not yet understand how thinking is activated or how it works. For example, 3-year-olds understand that people who are blindfolded and have their ears covered cannot see the object nor hear the noise from the object, but they can think about it. Young preschoolers also understand that a person can have knowledge of things about which they are not currently thinking; however, they do not realize that perception may determine the content of thought (e.g., one is thinking about what one is looking at), and they are unaware of the basic properties of thinking. Specifically, they do not understand the associative nature of thinking. They do not realize that one idea or thought triggers another, which subsequently triggers another and so on. Neither do preschoolers seem able to understand that thought is partly controllable and partly uncontrollable (i.e., you can start thinking about something if you decide to, but you cannot always avoid thinking about something just because you want to).

All these difficulties diminish considerably by age 7 to 8, when children begin to understand the interpretative nature of thought. Carpendale and Chandler (1996) showed, for example, that at this age children can understand that the phrase *wait for a ring* (a phone call or a diamond ring) can be interpreted differently depending on the available information. Also, at this age, children begin to differentiate among various cognitive functions, such as memory and inference, but they cannot differentiate between different aspects of the same cognitive function. Fabricius and Schwanenflugel (1994) conducted a study in which simple descriptions of cognitive functions, such as a list memory (e.g., getting all the things at the store that your mother asked for), prospective memory (e.g., saying "happy birthday" on the right day to your friend who told you her birthday a long time ago), comprehension (e.g., learning a new board game from the instructions on the box), attention (e.g., listening to what your friend is saying to you in a noisy classroom), and inference (e.g., figuring out what your friend wants when she says, "boy, that cookie looks good!") were given to the participants. The participants were then asked to compare each sentence with all other sentences and indicate the degree of similarity among the processes referred to in each pair of sentences. Eight-year-olds were able to differentiate memory from other functions, but they were unable to differentiate the various kinds of memory. They were unable to identify any other functions.

Awareness of cognitive processes and operations develops gradually in adolescence. Our research focused on understanding the similarities and differences between the processes required for solving different types of problems, such as mathematical and spatial problems, and problems requiring the design of an experiment to test a hypothesis. Our results showed that no differentiation between different problem-solving or reasoning strategies—such as those stated earlier—is possible before approximately age 13. At age 14, adolescents begin to differentiate between spatial thought and experimental or mathematical thought, although they cannot differentiate between experimental and mathematical thought. Some differentiation appears initially at about age 16 culminating during the college years (Demetriou, Efklides, & Platsidou, 1993; Demetriou et al., 1997).

Understanding Ability and Intelligence. Understanding the mind as a combination of traits, tendencies, and abilities that determine both what and how problems can be solved and how they can be solved also develops gradually, becoming more objective and norm-referenced with age. Preschool children do not differentiate intellectual ability as an innate quality; they tend to use it in relation to various characteristics, such as work habits and conduct, and therefore believe that it may be increased by practice and hard work. The differentiation of these dimensions appears gradually during the elementary school years, and the child does not grasp the difference between effort and ability nor can the child recognize how these are related to intelligence until adolescence. Only in middle adolescence, for example, do individuals understand that hard work can compensate for low ability only to a certain degree, or that high ability is an advantage in general, although there are tasks for which high ability must be complemented by hard and systematic effort (Demetriou et al., 1997; Nicholls, 1990; Phillips & Zimmerman, 1990; Stipek & MacIver, 1989).

Changes in Cognitive Self-Image. Similarly, the self-image becomes differentiated and better articulated with increasing age. Harter (1990), for example, showed that throughout progressive stages—childhood, middle to late childhood, adolescence, college, and adult years—individuals described themselves in reference to 4, 5, 8, 12, and 13 domains, respectively. These domains evolve from a self-concept involving global representations of the physical, social, and intellectual self to a more differentiated one, in which each of these domains is analyzed into different dimensions. As a result of the changes related to the understanding of mind and intelligence, self-evaluations of intellectual competence and academic achievement become more accurate and more modest with increasing age. A standard finding supportive of this notion is a clear decline in self-evaluation and academic self-esteem scores from late childhood to early adolescence (Demetriou et al., 1997; Harter, 1998).

In conclusion, all systems and subsystems of mind appear to change systematically from birth to maturity, and certain changes are more visible at specific age phases. For example, the changes occurring in the first two years of life culminate in the child's ability to use conventional symbolic systems (i.e., language). The changes occurring throughout childhood culminate in the young adolescent's ability to think about her models of the world as opposed to the real world. It seems that from one point of view, development appears to be a recycling process; that is, the major representational changes may be taken as the end of one developmental cycle and the beginning of another (Case, 1992). The sequence of levels within each cycle may be viewed as a progression toward increasingly more complex, elaborate, and efficiently applied structures of understanding and problem solving. Each subsequent level in each cycle involves, by definition, more and better organized cycle-specific representations than its preceding levels. However, levels corresponding sequentially across the various environment-oriented systems do not necessarily involve the same number of representations nor are they structurally fully identical. Our theory argues that this is due to the fact that the mental actions involved in the representations particular to each environment-oriented system are themselves different. For example, the evaluation of a hypothesis based on the results of experimentation, which belongs to the causal system, and the grasp of numerical proportions, which belongs to the quantitative system, are both acquired at about 12 to 13 years of age. It is difficult, however, to see how operations in one of these abilities (e.g., comparison of evidence with a hypothesis) can be considered equivalent to operations in the other ability (e.g., computation of the relations between the two numbers involved in each pair). In the following section, we attempt to explain how the changes in individual components are orchestrated to boost each other and result in the grand macroscopic changes capturing the attention of both the developmentalists and the laymen.

Explaining Cognitive Development

Although the levels and systems of the mental architecture might be distinct from one another, this does not imply that they are totally independent. We already have explained how the levels and systems of mind are functionally interrelated. The processing system constrains the functioning of both the environment-oriented systems and the hypercognitive system, setting limits to what cannot be processed. The various environment-oriented systems actualize the potentials inherent in the processing system and the self-regulation strategies inherent in the hypercognitive system into representations and actions that are relevant to different domains of the environment. The hypercognitive system involves "maps" of the other systems and rules for their functioning as well. It is believed that a change anywhere in the mind would disturb the existing relations between the various systems. Our theory posits that developmental causality is a synergetic force and thus assumes that cognitive changes occurring anywhere cause changes to other systems in the mind, which may then loop back and cause further changes to the first system, and so on. Our theory also provides a typology of the dynamics of change based on where a change starts and how it moves on to other systems. This typology, which is summarized in Table 8.3, involves bottom–up, horizontal, and top–down changes.

Bottom–Up Changes

These changes begin at the more basic levels of the mental architecture and spread to the hierarchically more advanced levels. The most characteristic example of this type of change can be seen in the encoding function, which represents the most basic function of the processing system. Changes in this function spread upward to affect the structures at the environment-oriented level and the hypercognitive level. Therefore, changes at a lower level modify the functioning of the systems that reside at the higher levels of the mental architecture. The changes in higher levels become necessary to cope with the consequences of a major change at a lower level. Changes in the flow of information that result from improvements in the efficiency of the encoding function, for example, necessitate improvements in the control of incoming information, because an increase in encoding speed increases the likelihood that irrelevant information may pass into the system. As a result, the mind must work to improve its control of processing. Improvements in handling the flow of information in the system contribute to more efficient utilization of the available storage space or capabilities. One reason is that the storage space is protected from the intrusion of irrelevant information, and, thus, more space is left free for the storage of relevant information (Demetriou, Efklides, & Platsidou, 1993). These changes enhance the

TABLE 8.3

Mechanisms of Change

Systems/Mechanisms	Type and Direction of Change
Processing system	**Bottom–up**
Information search	Formation of skills enabling search of goal-relevant information.
Selective attention	Formation of skills for active filtering and deactivation of representations.
SCSs	**Horizontal**
Refinement and elimination	Abandonment of unwanted mental units.
Differentiation	Increasing focusing of mental units.
Fusion	Construction of new mental units by integrating available units in the same submodule.
Interweaving	Construction of new mental units by integrating available units in the same systems.
Bridging	Construction of new mental units by integrating available units from different systems.
Hypercognitive system	**Top–down**
Metarepresentation	Construction of new inference patterns and new strategies for the manipulation of representations as a result of self-monitoring and self-regulatory experiences.
Individuation	Association of the new units with symbols—available or constructed

likelihood of constructing new specific skills that affect the functioning of the hypercognitive system. It should be remembered that improvements in the lower levels of the mental architecture affect the individual's cognitive self-image as well. The faster individuals become at processing and the more powerful the reasoning strategies they acquire, the more able they are to learn and the more logical they see themselves (Demetriou et al., 1997). In fact, we have recently showed that this aspect of one's self-image is involved in one's personality dispositions. That is, we found that persons who view themselves as fast and powerful in reasoning are more open to experience from those who do not feel as fast and strong in reasoning (Demetriou & Kazi, in press).

Bottom–up changes affect the flow of information in the mind and necessitate better information management strategies. These changes require mechanisms related to information handling and management, such as information search and selective attention. These mechanisms enable the individual to selectively process information relevant to the desired goal and ignore irrelevant information.

Horizontal Changes

These changes affect systems or subsystems at the same hierarchical level and basically represent changes that affect the relations among component processes either in the same or across different environment-oriented systems. The typology of changes includes bridging, interweaving, fusion, differentiation, refinement, and elimination.

Bridging, one of the mechanisms causing horizontal changes in the relations between different environment-oriented systems, refers to the construction of new mental units by establishing relations among units from different environment-oriented systems. This mechanism is activated when the thinker faces problems requiring the coordinated application of more than one environment-oriented system. One example of problems that make bridging necessary would be the need to make use of graphical representations (the spatial system) to express covariation relations (the quantitative system). Another example would be the use of algebraic functions (the quantitative system) to express causal relations (the causal system). Interrelating these abilities generates new functional units that not only link different environment-oriented systems but, in a way, go beyond them. The construction of these units does not, however, cancel the autonomy of any system, nor does it lead to the elimination of the units involved. In the previous example, algebraic reasoning and experimentation continue to operate autonomously in their respective domains after the construction of strategies for the generation of graphical representations or the construction of the graphical representations themselves. This construction, however, provides flexibility and broadens the scope of the problems which an individual can present and process.

Interweaving is similar to bridging in that it generates new mental units by integrating units already available; however, interweaving involves mental units that belong to the same environment-oriented system instead of units from two or more environment-oriented systems. We have shown above that in the quantitative system the ability to mentally execute arithmetic operations is interwoven with algebraic reasoning to make proportional reasoning possible, and in the causal system the ability to form hypotheses is linked to the ability to isolate variables to enable model construction.

Fusion is a special kind of interweaving. It refers to the mechanism that generates new mental units in environment-oriented systems that absorb their building blocks and terminate their autonomous use. An example of fusion would be the integration of the concept of number succession with verbal counting. Once this construction is established, it is improbable that thoughts related to number succession can be achieved without activation of the number name sequence, or that stating this sequence can be free from a representation of the succession of numbers.

There are two fundamental differences between bridging, on the one hand, and interweaving and fusion, on the other. First, the integration of units in the same environment-oriented system by interweaving or fusion engenders a preference for the use of the new unit and an ensuing reduction in the isolated use of the units involved in the integration. This does not occur in bridging. The model construction ability, once established, dominates the hypothesis-formation and control-of-variables abilities whenever the individual deals with a problem which requires any of them. Second, interweaving and fusion might be easier to apply, because there are common elements and schemes in an environment-oriented system that can guide the integration. All component processes involved in model construction are, however, related to causal relations, and all component processes involved in proportional reasoning are related to quantitative relations. This commonality simplifies the transfer of representations and operations from one process to the other. In the case of bridging, thinkers need to work out the relations and make the translation from one domain to the other by themselves and ad hoc. This is in itself more demanding than interweaving and fusion, which operate in the same environment-oriented system, and is directed, so to speak, by the dynamics of the domain concerned.

Differentiation. The mechanisms just mentioned are concerned with the construction of a new mental unit on the basis of other already available units either in the same or across different environment-oriented systems. However, development is frequently tantamount to an improvement in the accuracy of the functioning of an already available mental unit. This usually implies either a better focusing on target elements (environmental or mental) or a better mapping of the possible variations onto the target elements to which variation is related. The mechanism responsible for these changes is *differentiation*. An example of differentiation may be the understanding that number names cannot be used to denote increase in natural numbers in the same way as for fractions. Quite obviously, an increase in the former corresponds one-to-one to the sequence of number names whereas fraction names are more complex compositions. Hartnett and Gelman (in press) showed that time and effort are required to differentiate between the many variations of counting or measurement. Another example would be the generation of alternative concepts for the same language expression (e.g., imagine the various meanings of expressions such as *it rings a bell*). Finally, it may be noted that the conception of humor is based on this mechanism.

Refinement and Elimination.   A mechanism similar to differentiation is *refinement*, which is responsible for the abandonment of strategies or skills involved in a mental unit, when they become redundant to the unit's field of application. Such a mechanism is particularly useful at the beginning of the acquisition of a new strategy, when the tendency to continue to apply the old strategies is still very strong. This mechanism prompts the individual to avoid applying the old concepts or strategies instead of the new ones, when dealing with relevant problems. A classic example of elimination is the rejection of quantity judgments on the basis of spatial criteria once the quantity-relevant structure is established.

Top–Down Changes

These changes initiate in the hypercognitive system, and affect the functioning of the environment-oriented systems and the processing system. Metacognitive training, which aims at improving self-monitoring and self-regulation strategies, is based on this type of change, because it assumes that improving the functioning of the hypercognitive system will improve the functioning of the other levels of the mental architecture as well (Adey & Shayer, 1994). Our theory suggested that there are two top–down mechanisms, namely, metarepresentation and symbolic individuation.

Metarepresentation is a basic property of the hypercognitive system that gives meaning to the flow of mental experience by interrelating present and past representations. Past representations are activated from memory, when they seem to be related to the present situation. Moreover, by applying these mechanisms, past representations are differentiated into new ones. Metarepresentation is an inwardly directed process that looks for, codifies, and typifies similarities between mental experiences (past or present). Then, it enhances understanding and problem-solving efficiency because it generates patterns of processing that go beyond particular contents and contexts. When a child, for example, realizes that the sequencing of the *if ... then* connectives in language is associated with situations in which the event or thing introduced by *if* always comes first, and that it causes the occurrence of the event or thing accompanying *then*, the child is actually formulating an inference schema that guides predictions and interpretations of events that are specific to this schema. When abstracted over many different occasions (e.g., over causal relations in the physical and the social world), and somehow stabilized in the mind through the symbolization processes to be discussed next, this schema becomes the frame which guides reasoning by implication. Metarepresentation is, thus, the mechanism that leads from experiences and processes specific to a particular system to the construction of pragmatic reasoning schemas (Cheng & Holyoak, 1985; Cheng, Holyoak, Nisbet, & Oliver, 1986; Valanides, 1990), and from these to content-

and context-free general reasoning patterns, such as those involved in deductive reasoning.

Symbolic Individuation.   Constructing new mental units does not automatically ensure they will be available for future use. We all have had the experience of conceiving of an idea that was subsequently forgotten, because no effort was made to remember it. One reason for the loss of newly acquired ideas is the failure to pair them with symbols, which can make them identifiable and mentally useful. We propose, therefore, that the endurance of new mental units depends on the process of *symbolic individuation,* which pairs newly generated ideas with specific symbols (Demetriou, 1993). These symbols, which may be either idiosyncratic (mental images or personal scripts) or conventional (language or scientific formalisms) are considered comparable to the process of *identity ascription* to newborns. Naming newborns reduces the possibility that they will be mistaken for other newborns and ensures that they will be integrated into the family tree of their parents and relatives.

Symbolic individuation is differentially effected in each of the various environment-oriented systems, because their procedural and functional differences raise different symbolization needs. For instance, the symbolization needs of the pictographic system are quite different from those of the quantitative system. The first may need all possible shades of color to convey the beauty of a sunset by the sea, and the other needs arbitrary notations to express the relations among quantitative operations independently of the particular characteristics of the objects involved. Shaping an image to individuate a newly conceived figurative idea cannot, therefore, be the same as pairing mathematical symbols with a given reality to individuate a newly conceived quantitative relation.

Interestingly enough, children seem to realize this difference quite early in their development. Tolchinsky-Landsmann (1993), for example, asked 4-, 5-, and 6-year-old children to use written symbols to denote the identity (*what* objects are there on a card) and the quantity of concrete objects (*how many*). The results showed clearly that from the age of 4, children understand that to denote the identity or the quantity of things, different symbol systems, which obey different constraints, are needed. Specifically, they produced interlinked, handwriting-like strings of symbols to denote identity and separate, repeated symbols to denote quantity. From the age of 5, children used letters to stand for identity and ciphers to stand for quantity. Similar research in our laboratory in Thessaloniki shows that from the age of 5 children use different graphical codes to convey different types of relations, such as categorical, causal, and spatial (Bonoti, 1997).

Change Mechanisms and the Course of Development

It has been argued that different types of developmental change, namely, representational, structural, and refinement changes, occur at different phases of development. This implies that different mechanisms dominate at various points in a developmental cycle. At the beginning of a cycle, the operations, concepts, and skills involved in the various environment-oriented systems need to be reconstructed to implement the potential afforded by a change in the general systems before they can be interconnected. Thus, at the beginning of a cycle, differentiation and refinement are the mechanisms necessary for developing concepts, strategies, and skills in environment-oriented systems up to the level of the new potentials. When the environment-oriented systems are developed to a satisfactory level of functioning, interweavings and fusions may become possible or even necessary to establish new connections in existing structures. At the end of a cycle, connections that bridge concepts and skills from different environment-oriented systems might become possible when the need for them arises.

The two top–down mechanisms do not function in the same way throughout the course of development. Children at age 5, can differentiate only among gross mental functions such as perception, memory, and thought; their metarepresentational ability is not as sophisticated as that of adolescents, in whom it becomes detailed enough to include different kinds of operations in each of these functions. There is a kind of loop between the resolution of one's mental maps and the refinement of the mental units that can be constructed. The finer the present mental maps are, the finer the new units become, and the finer the present units are, the more detailed and refined the mental maps. The same arguments can be advanced in relation to symbolic individuation. The more developing people master a given symbolic medium such as writing, drawing, or mathematical symbolism, the more versatile they become at embodying ideas in symbols, which stabilizes them and makes them available for future use.

The preceding analysis suggests that change is a permanent characteristic of development. That is, at any phase, some kind of cognitive construction and reconstruction is always under way (see also Siegler, 1996). Thus, from the point of view of education, one might say that it is more important to ask what kind of changes students can undergo at a particular age rather than at what stage they are or what abilities they possess. Approaching cognitive development from the dynamic rather than from the static point of view is a better ground for designing educational interventions, because education aims to change the students' minds rather than preserve them in their current state. In the following section we discuss the educational implications of this concept in more depth.

Educational Relevance of the Dynamics of Mind

In the preceding sections, we discussed the educational relevance of each particular level and system of mind. In this section, we outline the basic implications of the overall theory insofar as it can provide a general theory of learning and instruction. We argue that the architecture of mind constrains the mind's development and that both the architecture of mind and its development constrain learning. Our evaluation is directed to the architecture and development of mind and learning and subsequently provides guidelines for the design and implementation of instruction.

Learning and Instruction

Our theory posits that learning can take place at any hierarchical level or system of the mind, which implies that there is both domain-specific and domain-general learning. *Domain-specific learning* refers to changes in the knowledge structures, processes, and skills that are activated by particular domains of the environment to cope with the demands posed by them. It springs from and affects the functioning of the domain-specific modules and involves mechanisms, such as interweaving, fusion, differentiation, and elimination, that require the newly acquired skills and concepts to be domain-specific, operationally specific, and symbolically biased. This kind of learning is called *modular learning* (ML); it does not generalize and is not transferable to other domains.

Domain-general learning refers to changes in the knowledge structures, processes, and skills which are concerned with knowing and handling the functioning of the mind itself. This kind of learning, called hyperlearning (HL), always involves the hypercognitive system in some way. Hyperlearning involves mechanisms such as metarepresentation and symbolic individuation, which generate, refine, and stabilize general patterns of mental action. Logical reasoning, one of the most important products of hyperlearning, by definition is transferable over different domains, and when it occurs it has immediate or delayed implications for the functioning of the other systems.

The transfer of learning is not, however, an all-or-none phenomenon. The very construction of the environment-oriented systems and the hypercognitive system suggests that there are possibly varying degrees of ML transfer within the environment-oriented systems and of HL across the systems.

In relation to ML, we must remember that the environment-oriented systems involve both core elements and component processes that represent and process particular types of relations from environmental input. For example, the principle of number succession and the four basic arithmetic operations are involved in most types of quantitative processing. In the same system, the range of applicability of concepts, such as ratio and proportionality, is narrower than the range of the processes mentioned earlier but wider than the range of more specialized processes, such as the principles for transposing elements from one part of an algebraic equation to the other. Thus, our theory suggests that the transfer of modular learning in an environment-oriented system is proportional to the status of the affected component in the system. In general, learning involving very basic processes would transfer more easily and expand more quickly than learning involving processes specific to a particular module or submodule. The second type of learning requires effort and practice.

Hyperlearning (HL) is by definition domain-general, but this does not imply that it automatically generalizes over different domains. Acquiring a new self-monitoring or self-regulation strategy related to the organization of information that can be stored in memory might be useful for all kinds of information processing. The efficient application of this strategy in different domains presupposes that the thinkers take into account the semantic constraints underlying meaning in each domain. Thus, it would be more efficient to organize a list of words in groups according to their meaning rather than according to their length, and more efficient to arrange a list of objects of ascending length according to their size rather than according to their possible conceptual similarity. Even general inferential processes, such as analogical or deductive reasoning, are affected by the individual's familiarity with the domain in which they are applied. Domains, due to their very organization, provide hints that direct the tuning of a general rule or strategy to the particularities of the domain.

These assumptions related to the nature of learning bear a number of implications for instruction concerned with ML and HL or with their interaction. Specifically, content and context are extremely crucial to ML, that is, the more specific the content and context of learning are, the easier and faster the learning process. Therefore, if teachers wish to produce ML, they must provide experiences and practice specific to the module of interest. For instance, when teachers teach quantitative skills, easily quantifiable concepts, such as time or money, are more appropriate than concepts that seem resistant to quantification, such as human emotions. In this way, the requisite operations can easily be activated and also specific intuitive rules may also be invoked. Moreover, care should be taken to ensure that unwanted or unnecessary elements are filtered out from the constructed skill (drawing attention to cases in which the skill does not apply). Finally, the learned skill should be stabilized by interlinking it with appropriate symbols.

Once learning has reached a certain level of efficiency in its primary domain, examples involving contents belonging to an environment-oriented system other than the target one may be used. For instance, after a core mathematical skill has been constructed, it might then be used to specify and express the causal relations between two variables that had been manipulated through experimentation especially for this purpose. This approach requires bridging and metarepresentation, and it may help consolidate the target skill and activate the self-mapping and self-regulation processes of the hypercognitive system, and this leads to HL.

Certain constraints limit and channel learning, and these vary according to the kind of learning. Modular learning is constrained by the existing condition of the activated module and by the two domain-general systems, which means that a new operation, concept, or skill can be constructed only when the building blocks of this new unit are somehow already available to be integrated into the new unit (for instance, by mechanisms such as bridging or fusion). Even then, however, these processes of integration have to take place in the current limitations of the processing system. That is, these processes (a) cannot evolve faster than the current processing speed; (b) they must be protected from the intrusion of not directly relevant elements that cannot be filtered by the available control capabilities of the system; and (c) the constituent elements of the new capability cannot exceed the existing representational capacity of the system. Moreover, if the learning process is to make use of the hypercognitive system, it has to be directed to the level of the monitoring and regulating capabilities of this system. For instance, we cannot design learning experiences for 5-year-olds that presuppose awareness of particular operations that are not available to children of that age. In the same example, it must be remembered that 5-year-old children do not differentiate between effort and ability, and therefore they are not inclined to try more than is needed.

Hyperlearning is constrained by the condition of the processing system, the condition of the environment-oriented system(s) involved at a given moment, and the condition of the hypercognitive system itself. For instance, many cognitive tasks need to be processed faster than a certain minimum speed; otherwise processing would fail, as when one has to operate on many numbers. If processing is slower than a certain limit the results of intervening steps might be forgotten from working memory, making the task insoluble. However, the operations involved escape reflection when processing becomes too fast. Thus, to encourage HL, the teacher should reduce the information flow so that the hypercognitive system is aware of, and can manage processing steps and their outcomes, but be careful enough not to slow processing as much as to make it inefficient. In other words, the teacher needs to be aware that the needs of processing and learning at one level may be incompatible with the needs of processing and learning at another.

Moreover, some environment-oriented systems (for example, the quantitative and the pictographic) are more amenable to awareness than others (i.e., the causal). Also, some combinations of the environment-oriented systems enable better monitoring and self-mapping (i.e., the quantitative and the spatial as opposed to the quantitative and the causal system). Therefore, to accelerate the formation of general reasoning patterns, the teacher would have to rely on examples from environment-oriented systems and their combinations that facilitate metarepresentation. Finally, because the hypercognitive system is the basis and origin of HL, its condition limits the kind and scope of HL. Our research and other studies on reflectivity's impact on cognitive development clearly suggest that the higher and more accurate self-monitoring is the faster learning and integration of learning proceeds (Demetriou et al., 1997).

Assessment

Our theory describes the mind as a hierarchical, multidimensional, and multisystem universe. A complete test of assessing the functional capabilities of the developing mind still needs to be developed, and should address all levels, systems, and dynamic functions of the developing mind. Specifically, such a test would have to involve the following modules:

1. *The processing-system module.* This module should provide information on the condition of the three major functions of the processing system (i.e., the encoding function, the control of processing, and storage). Examples of tasks addressing each of these functions were provided previously. Furthermore, each of these functions should be addressed via different symbol systems (e.g., verbal, iconic, arithmetic) and different modalities (e.g., visual and acoustic). The reader is reminded of the tasks requiring that the subject reads as quickly as possible words denoting color (i.e., the word *red*) written in the same ink color (speed of processing), or to recognize the ink color (e.g., blue) of words denoting different colors (e.g., the word *red* written in blue ink; control of processing). Corresponding tasks addressing the iconic system could involve recognition of geometric figures (e.g., circles or squares) which are composed of the same figure (e.g., large square made up of small squares; speed of processing) or a different figure (e.g., large square made up of small triangles; control of processing). Participants also could be asked to recognize a given word which is presented in the context of other words having similar meaning (speed of processing) or clearly different meaning (control of processing). A variety of contexts and items that test the functioning capabilities can provide information on the effects that symbolic biases and modality preferences may have on the processing potentials at a given age (see Demetriou, Efklides, & Platsidou, 1993; Spanoudis et al., 1996).

Admittedly, we do not fully understand how each of the three functions is related to everyday school learning and performance, but such a test would be a first step in the direction of deciphering and mapping the relationships between a students' processing capabilities and their school performance.

Information collected through this module designates learners' capabilities in relation to the efficiency of their processing system. To a certain degree, this corresponds to the concept of aptitude (Carroll, 1977). From this perspective, aptitude is defined as the time it takes to learn any given material rather than the ability to master it. Aptitude is thus at the core of mastery learning (Bloom, 1971), which is directly related to the time one needs to work on a task. This part of the test would be the most difficult to administer and interpret. To design and administer tasks directed to the three dimensions of the processing system requires special training, instrumentation, and individual testing.

2. *The environment-oriented-systems module.* This module of the test should be the most complex and diversified, because, ideally, tests would address each of the three hierarchical levels comprised in each environment-oriented system. This should involve items addressing the core processes, the processing rules and operations, and the knowledge relevant to various aspects of the reality domain to which each environment-oriented system is affiliated.

Items addressing the core processes of each environment-oriented system were not tested systematically until very recently. Examples of the tasks that can be used to address these processes can be found in research conducted on infants to determine the very early status of cognitive processes, such as spatial, quantitative, or categorical thought. Research on perceptual processes directly involved in these environment-oriented systems also involves examples of the items that may be included in this submodule of the test. One may refer here to tasks addressed to spatial perception, perception of causality, categorical perception, and so on. Very little is known about how core processes are involved in the construction of higher level specific constructs and knowledge, or about how they affect the functioning of each environment-oriented system at any stage beyond infancy. Therefore, developing such a test might clarify the role of local processing constraints, although there might be considerable difficulties to be removed, because this type of testing requires special testing conditions, instrumentation, and training.

The second submodule of the test would be easier to construct, because there is a long tradition of cognitive developmental research on which to draw. Specifically, this sub-module would comprise tests addressing the various functions of each environment-oriented system—for example, hypothesis formation, experimentation, and model construction tasks in the causal system; arithmetic operations, proportionality, and algebraic reasoning tasks in the quantitative system; or picture recognition, picture assembly, and mental rotation in the spatial system. Our research involved tasks which could be included in this submodule of the test, for example, those tasks that aimed to map each of the various environment-oriented systems and specify their relationships during development. Many of Piaget's classical tasks or variants of them, such as those used by cognitive acceleration researchers (Adey & Shayer 1994; Kuhn, Amsel, & O'Loughlin, 1988; Tobin & Capie, 1981; Valanides, 1996, 1997) would also be relevant. This submodule is highly relevant to everyday classroom practice, and it is well documented that performance on these tests shows the students' potential to construct new thinking skills and acquire knowledge in the domain of interest. For instance, specifying the students experimentation and hypothesis formation skills shows what aspects of science can be understood and how. The research showing the positive relationship between performance on these tests and school achievement is documented very well.

The third submodule should test knowledge and skills in particular conceptual domains such as human relations, biology, physics, economy, and so forth. This part of the test resembles the information items involved in traditional tests of intelligence and the knowledge tests which are used in schools. These modules may be designed for individual, group, or even computerized testing.

3. *The hypercognitive system module.* This module should be designed to provide information about an individual's attitudes, preferences, and awareness of different aspects of intellectual functioning. Thus, it should involve a submodule addressing three elements. First, it should address ideas about learning and intelligence (the functions it involves, whether it is caused by effort or ability, whether it is modifiable, etc.), Second, the model of the mind (its composition and organization, its causative role in individual behavior and interpersonal interaction, etc.); and third, self-representation with respect to all functions and processes involved in the two previous submodules. This module may involve a combination of tasks such as those used by theory of mind researchers and inventories involving self-definition items (e.g., I am a fast learner, I am very good at remembering faces, etc.) that the participants would specify in relation to themselves. Examples of these tests can be found in Bandura's (1989) work on self-efficacy, in Harter's (1998), and in our own (Demetriou & Kazi, in press; Demetriou et al., 1997) on self-representation and self-concept.

4. *The change dynamics module.* This module should address flexibility to change. It can employ short-term training tasks that show how efficiently an individual can reorganize rules, operations, procedures, and knowl-

edge in each of the environment-oriented systems and the hypercognitive system. Ideally, this module should involve tasks such as those suggested for the previous submodules, and also include additional instructions and prompts aimed to produce reorganizations that would elevate the thinker to higher levels of functioning. Furthermore, this module would test for versatility in using the various mechanisms of change. For example, identifying metarepresentation strategies might indicate not only how students learn but also how they organize the products of learning for future use. *Metarepresentation* is defined as the mechanism that advances simple inference patterns into reasoning schematas. Thus, students who are more proficient in metarepresentation activity might have an advantage because they are able to use domain-specific learning to produce domain-general—and thus transferable—problem-solving skills. Specifying symbolization strategies would indicate one's efficiency to integrate the present results of learning with what is already known so that they can be readily and properly used in the future.

CONCLUSIONS

In this chapter we outlined our model on the organization and development of mind, and we tried to specify the implications of this model for instruction and assessment. The ideas advanced in this chapter can be summarized in terms of the following postulates (see Demetriou, in press).

Postulate 1: The mind is a hierarchical, multisystem, and multidimensional universe. It involves two knowledge levels, one oriented toward the environment and one oriented toward itself. Each level involves several systems, each representing and processing different aspects of the world. At the intersection of these two levels there is a processing system which constrains both the kind and amount of information that can be processed and the efficiency with which it can be processed (see Table 8.1).

Postulate 2. Due to its multilevel and multisystem nature, the mind develops along multiple paths. It evolves (a) from fewer to more representations (the processing system); (b) from global, less integrated, and reality referenced mental operations to differentiated but better integrated and reciprocally referenced ones (the environment-oriented systems); and (c) from being reality-driven and action-bound to self-guided, reflective and self-aware (the hypercognitive system; see Table 8.2).

Postulate 3: Development at different levels or in different systems of mind takes place through different developmental mechanisms. This is due to the structural and functional differences of the various levels and systems. Therefore, to change, each system uses mechanisms suitable for its own particular structures that ensure the adaptive organization of these structures is not jeopardized (see Table 8.3).

Postulate 4: Learning varies across hierarchical levels or systems. Learning in the environment-oriented systems is modular and thus not easily transferable to other environment-oriented systems. Learning in the hypercognitive system is transmodular and, in principle, generalizes across the levels and systems of mind, although even this type of learning requires special effort and special change mechanisms to be generalized efficiently and stably.

Postulate 5: Intra- and interindividual variability is the rule in development. That is, the rate and forms of change—more often than not—vary across the levels and systems of the individual mind, and the rate and forms of change in the development of the same level or system vary across individuals. When applied to classrooms in schools, we see that the kind and quality of understanding at any moment involves much more than interaction between teacher and students. When students ask questions or make and provoke comments, they employ particular organizational and developmental dynamics that intervene in subtle ways with both other students' dynamics and the teaching environment. In short, classrooms are developmental mixers in which each student's developmental dynamics constrain and are constrained by the developmental dynamics of many other students and of the classroom as a whole. To highlight the complexities of these dynamics, we need an assessment device that is able to reveal the condition of all systems and functions involved at each level of mind. We are far from having such a device; however, we hope that the ideas advanced in this chapter can point a way to this end.

Postulate 6: There is no one-to-one correspondence between the architecture of mind and the structure of knowledge or the curriculum. Although our theory suggests that there may be a rough correspondence between the systems and levels of mind and different knowledge domains represented in the curriculum (such as the *causal system—science* correspondence or the *quantitative system—mathematics* correspondence), the various fields of study in education are usually complex domains that require the coordinated application of various systems. Moreover, the hypercognitive system is variously involved in school performance across different subject areas (Demetriou et al., 1992).

Educators need to specify the exact composition of different fields of study in a systematic way. Specifically, school curricula need to be analyzed from three different points of view: cognitive science, developmental science, and instructional science. Analysis from the point of view of cognitive science would highlight the cognitive composition of the modules of interest in the curriculum (*what* is required to grasp the various concepts). Analysis from the point of view of developmental science would highlight the developmental dimensions of the various concepts and skills to be taught in the curriculum (*when* each of the various concepts can be taught). Analysis from the point of view of instructional science would highlight how to organize and deploy teaching in the daily classroom, and would remind us of Gagne's (1970) learning hierarchies and sequence of instruction or curriculum (*how* each of the various concepts is to be presented and exemplified). Such an analysis could inform the design of powerful learning environments that would foster cognitive growth (De Corte, Greer, & Verschaffel, 1996) and increase the efficiency of education by capitalizing as much as possible on the mind's differential capabilities, preferences, and proclivities at the ages of interest.

REFERENCES

Adey, P., & Shayer, M. (1994). *Really raising standards: Cognitive intervention and academic achievement.* London: Routledge.

Baddeley, A. (1991). *Working memory.* Oxford: Oxford University Press.

Bandura, A. (1989). Regulation of cognitive processes through perceived self-efficacy. *Developmental Psychology, 25,* 729–735.

Berliner, D. C. (1979). Tempus educare. In P. Peterson & H. Walberg (Eds.), *Research on teaching: Concepts, findings and implications* (pp. 120–135) Berkley, CA: McCutcham.

Bernicot, J. (1998). Communication and language development. In A. Demetriou, W. Doise, & K. F. M. van Lieshout, (Eds.), *Developmental psychology.* (137–177). London: Wiley.

Bloom, B. S. (1976). *Human characteristics and school learning.* New York: McGraw-Hill.

Bonoti, P. (1997). *Drawing relations in different domains: A study of the relations between drawing and domain-specificity in cognitive development.* Thessalonika: Aristotle University of Thessaloniki.

Butterworth, G. (1998). Perceptual and motor development. In A. Demetriou, W. Doise, & K. F. M. van Lieshout, (Eds), *Developmental psychology* (101–135). London: Wiley.

Carpendale, J. I., & Chandler, M. J. (1996). On the distinction of between false belief understanding and subscribing to an interpretive theory of mind. *Child Development, 67,* 1686–1706.

Carroll, J. B. (1977). A revisionist model of school learning. *Review of Education, 3,* 155–167.

Case, R. (1985). *Intellectual development: Birth to adulthood.* New York: Academic Press.

Case, R. (1992). *The mind's staircase.* Hillsdale, NJ: Lawrence Erlbaum Associates.

Case, R., Okamoto, Y., Griffin, S., McKeough, A., Bleiker, C., Henderson, B., & Stephenson, K. M. (1996). The role of central conceptual structures in the development of children's thought. *Monographs of the Society for Research in Child Development, 61* (1–2, Serial No. 246).

Changeux, J. P., & Connes, A. (1995). *La materielle de la pense.* [The material of thought]. Athens: Katoptro.

Cheng, P., & Holyoak, K. (1985). Pragmatic reasoning schemas. *Cognitive Psychology, 17,* 391–416.

Cheng, P., & Holyoak, K., Nisbet, R. E., & Oliver, L. M. (1986). Pragmatic versus syntactic approaches to training deductive reasoning. *Cognitive Psychology, 18,* 293–328.

De Corte, E., Greer, B., & Verschaffel, L. (1996). Mathematics teaching and learning. In D. Berliner & R. Caffe (Eds.), *Handbook of educational psychology* (pp. 491–549). New York: MacMillan.

Demetriou, A. (1993). *Cognitive development: Models, methods, and applications.* Thessaloniki: Art of Text.

Demetriou, A. (1996). Outline for a developmental theory of cognitive change: General principles and educational implications. *The School Field, 7,* 7–41.

Demetriou, A. (in press). 10 + 1 postulates about the formation of mind. *Learning and Instruction: The Journal of the European Association for Research on Learning and Instruction.*

Demetriou, A. (1998). Cognitive development. In A. Demetriou, W. Doise, & K. F. M. van Lieshout, (Eds.), *Developmental psychology* (179–269). London: Wiley.

Demetriou, A., & Efklides, A. (1985). Structure and sequence of formal and postformal thought: General patterns and individual differences. *Child Development, 56,* 1062–1091.

Demetriou, A., & Efklides, A. (1988). Experiential Structuralism and neo-Piagetian theories: Toward an integrated model. In A. Demetriou (Ed.), *The neo-Piagetian theories of cognitive development: Toward an integration* (pp. 173–222). Amsterdam: North-Holland.

Demetriou A., & Efklides, A. (1989). The person's conception of the structures of developing intellect: Early adolescence to middle age. *Genetic, Social, and General Psychology Monographs, 115,* 371–423.

Demetriou, A., & Efklides, A. (1994). Structure, development, and dynamics of mind. In A. Demetriou and A. Efklides (Eds.), *Mind, intelligence, and reasoning: Structure and development* (pp. 75–109). Amsterdam: Elsevier.

Demetriou, A., Efklides, A., & Platsidou, M. (1993). The architecture and dynamics of developing mind: Experiential structuralism as a frame for unifying cognitive developmental theories. *Monographs of the Society for Research in Child Development, 58* (5, Serial No. 234).

Demetriou, A., Efklides, E., Papadaki, M., Papantoniou, A. & Economou, A. (1993). The structure and development of causal-experimental thought. *Developmental Psychology, 29,* 480–497.

Demetriou, A., Gustafsson, J. E., Efklides, A., & Platsidou, M. (1992). Structural systems in developing cognition, science, and education. In A. Demetriou, M. Shayer, & A. Efklides (Eds.), *The neo-Piagetian theories of cognitive development go to school: Implications and applications for education* (pp. 79 – 103). London: Routledge.

Demetriou, A., & Kazi, S. (in press). Mind, self, personality, and thinking styles: Levels in self-understanding and self-management. In M. Boekaerts, P. Pintrich & M. Zeidner (Eds.), *Handbook of self-regulation.* New York: Academic Press.

Demetriou, A., Kazi, S., Platsidou, M., Sirmali, K., & Kiosseoglou, G. (1997). *Self-image and cognitive development: Structure, development, and functions of self-evaluation and self-rep* Handbook of self-regulation *representation in adolescence.* Manuscript submitted for publication.

Demetriou, A., Pachaury, A., Metallidou, Y., & Kazi. S. (1996). Universal and specificities in the structure and development of quantitative-relational thought: A cross-cultural study in Greece and India. *International Journal of Behavioral Development, 19,* 255–290.

Demetriou, A., Platsidou, M., Efklides A., Metallidou, Y., & Shayer, M. (1991). Structure and sequence of the quantitative-relational abilities and processing potential from childhood and adolescence. *Learning and Instruction: The Journal of the European Association for Research on Learning and Instruction, 1,* 19–44.

Efklides, A., Demetriou, A., & Metallidou, Y. (1994). The structure and development of propositional reasoning ability: Cognitive and metacognitive aspects. In A. Demetriou & A. Efklides (Eds.), *Intelligence, mind, and reasoning: Structure and development* (pp. 151–172). Amsterdam: North-Holland.

Efklides, A., Demetriou, A., Gustafsson, J. E. (1992). Training, cognitive change, and individual differences. In A. Demetriou, M. Shayer, & A. Efklides (Eds.), *Neo-Piagetian theories of cognitive development: Implications and applications for education* (pp. 122–143). London: Routledge.

Fabricius, W. V., & Schwanenflugel, P. J. (1994). The older child's theory of mind. In A. Demetriou & A. Efklides (Eds.), *Intelligence, mind, and reasoning: Structure and development* (pp. 111–132). Amsterdam: North-Holland.

Flavell, J. H., Green, F. L., & Flavell, E. R. (1995). Young children's knowledge about thinking. *Monographs of the Society for Research in Child Development, 60* (1, Serial No. 243).

Gagne, R. M. (1970). *The conditions of learning.* New York: Holt, Rinehart, & Winston.

Gallistel, C. R. (1993). *The organization of learning.* Cambridge, MA: MIT Press.

Gelman, R., & Gallistel, C. R. (1992). Preverbal and verbal counting and computation. *Cognition, 44,* 43–74.

Halford, G. (1993). *Children's understanding: The development of mental models.* Hillsdale, NJ: Lawrence Erlbaum Associates.

Harter, S. (1990). Causes, correlates, and the functional role of global self-worth: A life-span perspective. In R. J. Sternberg & J. Kolligian, Jr. (Eds.), *Competence considered* (pp. 67–97). New Haven, CT: Yale University Press.

Harter, S. (1998). The development of self-representations. In W. Damon (Series Ed.) & E. Eisenberg (Vol. Ed.), *Handbook of child psychology: Vol. 3, Social, emotional, and personality development* (5th ed.), (553–617). New York: Wiley.

Hartnett, P., & Gelman, R. (in press). Early understanding of number: Paths or barriers to the construction of new understandings. Learning and Instruction: The Journal of the European Association for Research on Learning and Instruction, 7.

Kail, R. (1988). Developmental functions for speeds of cognitive processes. *Journal of Experimental Child Psychology, 45,* 339–364.

Karmiloff-Smith, A., & Inhelder, B. (1974). If you want to go ahead, get a theory. *Cognition, 3,* 195–212.

Kazi, S. (1998). *Awareness about the domains of mind from 3 to 5 years of age.* Manuscript in preparation.

Kuhn, D., Amsel, E., & O'Loughlin, M. (1988). *The development of scientific thinking skills.* New York: Academic Press.

Loizos, L. (1992). Structure and development of spatial and meta-spatial abilities from 10 to 18 years of age. *Psychology: The Journal of the Hellenic Psychological Society, 1,* 71–91.

Makris, N. (1995). *Personal theory of mind and its relationship with cognitive abilities.* Unpublished doctoral thesis. Department of Psychology, Aristotle University of Thessaloniki.

Nicholls, J. G. (1990). What is ability and why are we mindful of it? A developmental perspective. In R. J. Sternberg & J. Kolligian, Jr. (Eds.), *Competence considered* (pp. 11–40). New Haven, CT: Yale University Press.

Osherson, D. N., & Markman, E. (1975). Language and the ability to evaluate contradictions and tautologies. *Cognition, 3*, 213–226.

Pascual-Leone, J. (1970). A mathematical model for the transition rule in Piaget's developmental stages. *Acta Psychologica, 32*, 301–345.

Phillips, D. A., & Zimmerman, M. (1990). The developmental course of perceived competence and incompetence among competent children. In R. J. Sternberg & J. Kolligian, Jr. (Eds.), *Competence considered* (pp. 41–66). New Haven, CT: Yale University Press.

Resnick, L. B., Bill, V., & Lesgold, S. (1992). Developing thinking abilities in arithmetic class. In A. Demetriou, M. Shayer, & A. Efklides (Eds.), *Neo-Piagetian theories of cognitive development: Implications and applications for education* (pp. 210–230). London: Routledge.

Shayer, M., Demetriou, A., & Prevez, M. (1988). The structure and scaling of concrete operational thought: Three studies in four countries. *Genetic, Social, and General Psychology Monographs, 114*, 307–376.

Siegler, R. (1996). *Emerging minds: The process of change in cognitive development.* Oxford: Oxford University Press.

Spanoudis, G., Demetriou, A., Platsidou, M., Kiosseoglou, G., & Sirmali, K. (1996). A longitudinal study of speed and control of processing from childhood to adolescence. *Psychology: The Journal of the Greek Psychological Society, 3*(1), 29–70.

Sternberg, R. J., Conway, B. E., Ketron, J. I., & Bernstein, M. (1981). People's conceptions of intelligence. *Journal of Personality and Social Psychology, 41*, 37–55.

Sternberg, S. (1975). Memory scanning: New findings and controversies. *Quarterly Journal of Experimental Psychology, 27*, 1–32.

Stipek, D., & MacIver, D. (1989). Developmental change in children's assessment of intellectual competence. *Child Development, 60*, 521–538.

Stroop, J. R. (1935). Studies of interference in serial verbal reactions. *Journal of Experimental Psychology, 18*, 643–662.

Tobin, K., & Capie, W. (1981). The development and validation of a group test of logical thinking. *Educational and Psychological Measurement, 41*, 413–423.

Tolchinsky-Landsmann, L. (1993). *Preschoolers use of writing and ciphers as referential-communicative tools.* Paper presented at the fifth Conference of the European Association for Research on Learning and Instruction, Aix-en-Provence.

Valanides, N. (1990). Pragmatic versus syntactic approaches to deductive reasoning. *Dissertation Abstracts International, 51*, 1175A. (University Microfilms No. 90–24947)

Valanides, N. (1996). Formal reasoning abilities and science teaching. *School Science and Mathematics, 96*(2), 99–107.

Valanides, N. (1997). Formal reasoning abilities and school achievement. *Studies in Educational Evaluation, 23*(2), 169–185.

Wellman, H. M. (1990). *The child's theory of mind.* Cambridge, MA: MIT Press.

CHAPTER 9

Mastering Tools of the Mind in School
(Trying out Vygotsky's Ideas in Classrooms)

Elena L. Grigorenko
Yale University and Moscow State University

What makes us believe a scientific theory? What makes us interested in a particular theory? What characteristics does a theory need to have to be taken out of the laboratory or a scientific publication and noticed by the public, to be appreciated, valued, and applied? Virtually all scientists ask themselves these questions. Virtually all scientists want their theories to be verified, applied, and appreciated. As Russian psychologist Lev Vygotsky wrote, "Man proves the truth of his thoughts only by application" (Vygotsky, 1993, p. 55). Indeed, nothing can be as beneficial or as detrimental to a theory as its application to real life. This chapter considers the application of one psychological theory to real life. The theory is that of Vygotsky. Real life in this case is life in school.

Lev Vygotsky (1896–1934) was certainly one of the most influential and distinguished psychologists of the 20th century. His creativity touched many subfields of psychology, spanning a spectrum from the psychology of art to the special education of handicapped children. Throughout the many specific topics he addressed, questions of child development and education were always important. In my opinion, Vygotsky's main gift to the art of education is his theory of the tools of the mind. As part of his broader cultural-historical theory, the theory of mental tools (the tools of the mind) rightly belongs among the outstanding ideas of modern psychology.

In this chapter, I join the attempts of many scientists, both North American and Russian, to help illustrate with empirical evidence the great thinker's theoretical claims (or, at least, our interpretations of his claims) of the importance of the tools of mind for child development. This chapter presents the reader with some of Vygotsky's key ideas, discusses their relevance to education, and then illustrates some of these ideas with brief examples from various psychological and pedagogical programs derived from his work. The word *derived* is key here, because none of the programs discussed in this chapter is a direct implementation of Vygotsky's ideas; nevertheless, each is rooted in his work. Thus, the first part of the chapter is devoted to the presentation of Vygotsky's concepts that are most relevant to school settings. The second part of the chapter illustrates applications of both Vygotsky's original ideas and some derivative programs, all in educational settings.

LEARNING AND DEVELOPMENT

Vygotsky's work was concerned with questions related to learning, teaching, and children's development of mind—as well as their relations. He addressed these issues in a number of writings (Vygotsky, 1978, 1983, 1986, 1987). Vygotsky's main idea was that the development of the mind takes place in the course of social experiences. The main outcome of these social experiences is the mastering of so-called mental tools (language, concepts, symbols, reading, writing, etc.). According to Vygotsky, humans created tools to enhance their natural capacities. Just as they invented physical tools to extend their physical capacities, humans created the tools of the mind to extend their mental abilities. These mental tools help us think, remember, direct attention, understand, and so on. For example, by using mnemonic techniques, people can increase the amount of information they remember. Similarly, the essence of using computers is to make the amount of information we can access unlimited. However, the tools of mind do more than improve, extend, and enhance our natural capabilities. According to Vygotsky, they also change our mental functions: The use of tools, along with other mechanisms, builds higher mental functions (i.e., the functions that are human-specific), the very nature of which are different from our lower mental functions (i.e., the functions humans share with lower creatures).

Driven by his belief that the tools of the mind play a critical role in development, Vygotsky and his students and followers studied the pathways of tool acquisition. Most frequently, an adult or more capable peer presents mental tools to a child. The presentation of the tool takes place in the course of joint activity. Initially the tool is used by either an adult or a peer (the other) and its functions are shown to the child. Then the other slowly withdraws from the situation, giving the child a chance to use the tool independently, while still being available in case the child needs help. Finally, the other is not needed at all; as children develop they themselves become active tool users and creators (Paris & Winograd, 1990). Although, initially, the child gets the tools and uses them externally, eventually the tools are internalized and become the child's psychological property—enriching the child and altering his or her mental functions.

In this interpretation, it is obvious that mental development depends on acquiring psychological tools—that is, on learning. For Vygotsky, the relations between development and learning were very complex. Unaware of the importance of developmental prerequisites that determine a child's ability to learn new things and master new functions, Vygotsky and his followers very actively promoted the idea that learning stimulates and even causes development. This statement, however, is not absolute. To be precise, learning leads development (or learning leads to development) only under the condition of proper instruction. Learning should march ahead of, or take place in advance of, development. To achieve this, learning must be based on psychological functions that have just started forming in a child's mind. If we completely ignore a child's developmental level, we end up presenting material that is either too easy or to difficult. What is the point of teaching a child to interpret complex literature if the child cannot yet read? Or what is the point of teaching a child counting if he or she already knows how to add?

Vygotsky's theory of the tools of the mind engendered a number of educational applications. The concept central to all of these applications is learning activity. As pointed out by Kozulin and Presseisen (1995), there are two interrelated notions of learning activity. First, activity, in general, is a source and active generator of psychological functions. In essence, psychological functions are crystallized forms of activity (Kozulin, 1986, 1990a, 1990b; Wertsch, 1985). Learning activity, then, is a source of psychological functions taught at school. The second notion of learning activity is related to Vygotsky's distinction between spontaneous concepts (those that are unsystematic, highly contextual, or derived from children's own reflections on their everyday experience) and scientific concepts (those that are logical, systematic, decontextualized, or initiated in a specialized activity of classroom learning). According to this idea, learning activity is the only way to master scientific concepts.

Note that the difference between learning (everyday learning) and learning activity is not trivial (Kozulin & Presseisen, 1995). Learning, in its broader sense, is often a spontaneously emerging part of many human activities (play, work, social interaction, entertainment, etc.) but is not a goal of them. The goal of working is to obtain a product; the goal of entertainment is relaxation; the goal of social interaction is an exchange of information, companionship, emotional intimacy, and so on. The goal of learning activity, however, is learning, or more specifically, a gain (cognitive, emotional, or behavioral) obtained as a result of this activity. Unlike learning in its broader sense, learning activity does not emerge spontaneously but is a result of carefully designed and culturally constructed developmental process. In a modern industrial society, learning activity is expected to be the dominant activity at a certain stage of development, namely, in the period from elementary school to adolescence (El'konin, 1971). The educational implication of this periodization of development is that it places an emphasis on the development of learning activity in primary school. If the developmental sensitivity of this period is not capitalized on, if learning activity is not then formed, the formation of it later will be much more difficult because adolescents' interests naturally shift to the domain of interpersonal relationships.

It has been noticed (Kozulin & Presseisen, 1995) that this interpretation of the significance and content of education at elementary school is different from common educational practices in which primary classroom curricula target children's acquisition of general knowledge and social skills rather than learning skills per se. In addition, quite often, learning promoted in primary school does not differ from, or differs very little from, nonspecific everyday learning. The educational system expects implicitly that learning that is structured and targeted at mastering scientific concepts takes place much later. Moreover, often schools do not prepare their students for the transition from learning as a by-product of other activities (e.g., playing and socializing) to learning as the center of experience at school. Because they are unprepared for this transition, many children do not have the skills or motivation to cope with this change in expectations so are not able to meet the requirements of modern schooling.

Vygotsky's view of the structure of the development was that the learning dyad is instrumental in understanding some of the failures of teaching at school. The ideal, in which teaching adequately corresponds to children's developmental stage and promotes their learning, is difficult to reach. However, Vygotsky and his followers developed a vision of teaching–learning situations, described these situations' common components, and analyzed what in these instances might jeopardize the ideal match between learning and teaching. Some of these findings are discussed in this chapter.

PURPOSES OF MENTAL TOOLS

One of the major assertions made by Vygotsky is that mental tools, as well as other tools, are outcomes of human civilization. He believed that the history of human culture can be viewed as the creation, adaptation, and further development of mental tools. We started with scratches on cave walls to count cattle and have developed our arsenal so that it now includes the complex categories and concepts of modern sciences. What are the purposes of mental tools and how do we use them?

Enhancing the Capacities of the Mind

The analogy Vygotsky used in his writing on mental tools is that of mechanical, physical tools. The analogy, however, has two dimensions. Like mechanical tools, mental tools (a) enhance human natural capacities, allowing people to adapt better to their environments; and (b) are designed to remain in the culture (i.e., they are invented and then given to others to be used by and taught to new generations). Unlike mechanical tools, however, mental tools have two forms, (a) the external form, and (b) the internal form. At the early developmental stages (and here Vygotsky referred to both phylogeny, i.e., the development of *homo sapiens*, and ontogeny, the development of every distinct individual), mental tools have a concrete, external manifestation. Gradually, at more advanced stages of development, mental tools become internalized and do not require external support anymore. For example, when I ask my 4-year-old neighbor to tell me how many cars his family has, he runs across the street, counts them, and comes back with the report; he needs to see the cars to count them (external manifestation). In contrast, when I am planning a dinner at my house, I do not need to invite the guests over the day before in order to count them; I can count them mentally (internal manifestation).

Becoming an Independent Tool Owner

Teachers love to see their students' minds developing and their mental behaviors maturing. The global purpose of education is to provide students with all the necessary mental equipment so that they can continue educating themselves and develop their minds independently. According to Vygotsky, much of the development of the mind at the early stages happens "outside" of the child's mind, in the interpersonal space between the child and the other (a parent, a caregiver, a teacher, a more capable peer). The child is unable to manipulate the tool without the help of the other. As children embed the mental tool into their own thought processes, it leaves the interpersonal space and moves into the intrapersonal space—that is, it becomes individualized. Now, the child is able to manipulate the tool without the help of the other. The child became an independent tool owner.

The child does not announce the fact that he or she mastered the tool—he or she simply starts using it. For example, while walking in the forest a parent explains to a child how to observe and construct landmarks in order to remember the way back. The child is shown how to notice distinct features of the landscape, how to mark a tree, how to pile stones. Some time later, the parent is told that when the child went on a forest fieldtrip with his class, he was the one who showed the other children how to mark the way. The child has mastered the tools and now is able to manipulate them independently.

Preparing for the Future

One of the goals of education is to prepare a child to perform complex cognitive operations (e.g., solving problems, writing documents, manipulating numbers, performing sophisticated spatial operations). According to Vygotsky, the child's ability to master such complex operations depends on the appropriation of mental tools and the development of higher mental functions.

Vygotsky separated mental processes into lower mental functions (LMFs) and higher mental functions (HMFs). The development of the LMFs (including such processes as sensation, reactive attention, spontaneous memory, etc.) depends on maturation. The development of the HMFs (including focused attention, deliberate memory, logical thinking, etc) depends on learning and teaching. The LMFs are involuntary and direct, whereas the HMFs are deliberate and mediated. The HMFs are considered deliberate because they are used purposefully, that is, with a specific goal (e.g., to understand) and an object (e.g., a math problem) in mind. The HMFs are mediated in that they use signs and symbols for mental processing (e.g., the use of plus and minus to perform addition and subtraction).

The development of the HMFs (a) is dependent on lower mental functions (LMFs); (b) is moderated by cultural and societal context; (c) is linked to the internalization of mental tools; (d) occurs in a system of interrelated developing HMFs; and (e) emerges through the transition from shared to individualized functioning.

The Development of the HMFs is Dependent on the LMFs. The development of the HMFs is based on the level of the LMFs. In essence, the LMFs determine the starting point (but not the upper limit) of the HMFs. For example, the starting point for the development of the higher mental function of mediated perception (e.g., perception of music as a string of meaningful sounds) is different for a person with hearing deficit than it is for a person with normal hearing or for a person with perfect pitch. However, the LMFs do not determine the limit for the development of the HMF. On the contrary, the HMF might help a person overcome his or her deficit and remediate it. Vygotsky once worked at a boarding school for children who were both deaf and blind and observed their development. He claimed that, if correctly structured, special education targeted to the formation of HMFs could help children compensate and sometimes overcompensate for their deficits. The development of the HMF, when limited by deficient corresponding LMF, involves a creative process. Vygotsky viewed special education targeted at the development of the HMF in handicapped children with disabilities as a process of equipping these children with adaptive strategies that might be unique to each individual child.

The development of the HMF is Moderated by Cultural and Societal Contexts. Cultural and societal contexts affect both the essence of the HMF and the way they develop. A number of studies show that different cultures teach and value different higher mental functions. The most famous example of these studies is Vygotsky's colleague Luria's 1930's research on the mental operation of classification (Luria, 1976). In this research, Luria showed that people with formal education and people from indigenous cultures without any formal education differed in the ways they performed classification. People without formal education classified objects on the basis of where they had encountered the objects (e.g., putting cards with drawings of apples, with those of watermelons, pears, and plates). People with formal education were likely to recognize connections between the objects that were more than just situational; these people tended to categorize cards into fruit and nonfruit and exclude plates from the group. Moreover, ways of forming and acquiring the HMFs vary in different cultures. Different cultures (or different educational approaches, for example) might facilitate different ways of acquiring the same function. To learn the alphabet, for example, children in a Moscow Montessori classroom learn short poems about every letter, whereas children educated in a Voronezh Waldorf school are told a mythological story about every letter and then asked to draw the letter.

The Acquisition of the HMFs is Linked to Mastering and Internalizing Mental Tools. One of the most specific characteristics of the HMFs is that they are mediated, that they involve the use of signs and symbols, representing behaviors or objects in the environment. In Russian schools, when a teacher enters a classroom, students are expected to acknowledge his or her presence by standing up. This symbol of the beginning of class is a sign of the HMF of mediated attention.

In his writing, Vygotsky devoted much attention to the process of mastering such cultural tools as primary language and the use of other symbolic systems. He viewed language as a uniquely powerful cultural tool affecting not only such HMFs as higher thinking, but also will and higher emotions. Once they have mastered language and other symbolic systems (e.g., numbers), children no longer need to have objects in the immediate field of vision in order to think about them. Language is a tool for creating and manipulating new ideas and sharing them with others. For Vygotsky, the function of language is twofold: It is instrumental in the development of the other HMFs, and it is also itself a mental function, the development of which is stimulated by the other HMFs. Today, cognitive tools extend to computers and data storage devices (Donald, 1993). The appropriation and use of such cognitive tools, no doubt, leads to modification of the related HMFs. As in the case of learning language, mastery of computers is dialectical—it becomes instrumental in the development of HMFs, yet, the acquisition of computer-related knowledge depends on the unfolding of other HMFs.

The Development of the HMF Occurs in a System of Interrelated Developing HMFs. The development of each HMF does not happen independently of the development of other mental functions. Quite to the contrary, the development of various mental functions (e.g., logical thinking and mediated memory) are interdependent. The HMFs develop as a true system. This does not mean that all of a child's HMFs develop equally successfully. Every child can be characterized by an individual profile of his HMF (e.g., his or her mediated attention might be higher than logical thinking, etc.). However, Vygotsky's conceptualization of the HMFs emphasized the development of certain mental functions at certain developmental stages. In addition, although they are expected to form in childhood, the HMFs do not stop developing when the child grows up. By mastering new tools of the mind, the adult can voluntarily continue developing his or her HMFs. Adults are forced to change their mental processing and develop new HMFs when they respond to technological innovations or adapt to a new culture.

The Development of the HMF is the Development of "Intramental" Functioning Out of "Intermental" Processes. Regarding the emergence of HMFs, Vygotsky believed that "every function in the child's cultural development appears twice: first, on the social level, and later on the individual level; first, between people (*intermental*), and then inside the child (*intramental*)" (Vygotsky, 1978, p. 57). This view of child development constituted the basis for Vygotsky's views on the other individual as a mediator of learning.

Vygotsky's claim that the HMFs have their origin in social interaction is one of the central assumptions of his theory, the so-called "general ... law of cultural development" (Vygotsky, 1981, p. 163). In other words, for higher mental functions to develop, they must first exist in shared activity between two people. For example, a child and a teacher share the mental process of solving a math problem based on newly explained materials. The teacher explains the problem and involves the child in the problem-solving process, giving him or her a chance to give an answer to questions that arise at every intermediate stage of the search for the solution. The child readily gives answers, so both are participating. As the child begins to appropriate this particular HMF, he or she applies it independently.

Toward the end of his career, Vygotsky viewed psychological development in terms of the development of social systems, including two major components, activity and shared activity (also referred to as action and interaction; Das, 1995). According to Vygotsky's view, this dyadic social system (i.e., the adult–child pair) is the unit through which the translation of cultural knowledge is performed.

Developing Self-Control

Some of Vygotsky's followers (Bodrova & Leong, 1996) viewed the acquisition of mental tools as the developmental pathway for the mastery of certain behaviors. For example, children can be taught not only how to count but also how to master their emotions. If a child is taught mental tools to control anger (such as, count to ten, think of something else, or breathe), he or she, instead of hitting another person, might handle the conflict more peacefully.

The Tools of the Mind in School: Why?

Besides their overall importance for the development of the child, mental tools have an important role in organizing children's learning activity in school (Bodrova & Leong, 1996). The developmental specificity of children, especially elementary school children, means their thinking, attention, perception, and memory are mostly reactive. In other words, the object of their activity (be it playing, drawing, or learning) must attract and hold their attention. Adults overexploit this characteristic of children's minds by introducing tremendous stimulation in their everyday lives. Think about how colorful and attractive children's toys are, how overwhelmingly stimulating Disney's gala productions are, and how action-intense computer and Nintendo™ games are. Children love all of these games, tricks, and shows, and they react to them and have no difficulty paying attention. The problem is that we need to teach them not only how to react but also how to voluntarily direct and sustain their attention.

One never sees a simple children's storytelling on TV anymore. Children's programs are filled with bright colors, dressed-up characters, and dramatic actions. It is very difficult for schools to match in classroom settings the intense sensory experiences provided by TV (as well as video games). Today, children's overexposure to sensory stimulation makes it difficult for teachers to teach, especially in elementary school. There have been discussions in the educational literature (e.g., Bodrova & Leong, 1996) of teachers' complaints about the difficulty of getting children's attention in the classroom without using special tricks such as singing, dancing, or acting like a cartoon, comics, or TV show character. This is where teaching mental tools comes in handy. If children have mastered the tools of the mind, they are more capable of focusing their attention, perception, memory, reasoning, and other school-related skills on their own. The teacher's role then is to introduce the tools of the mind to the child and help him or her master these tools. The teacher's role is to provide a path from complete dependence (when the tool is just introduced) to complete independence (when the tool is internalized and mastered).

MASTERING THE TOOLS OF THE MIND: WHERE AND HOW

The process of mastering the tools of the mind takes place in the zone of proximal development by a means called scaffolding.

Zone of Proximal Development

To locate the process of mental tools acquisition within the general picture of the child's development, Vygotsky formulated his notion of the zone of proximal development (ZPD). Vygotsky defined the ZPD as the distance between the child's "actual developmental level as determined by independent problem solving" and the higher level of "potential development as determined through problem solving under adult guidance or in collaboration with more capable peers" (1978, p. 96). The specific term *zone of proximal development* deserves some explanation. The word *zone* refers to the nonlinearity of children's development. In this zone, the child might move forward or backward, to the left or to the right. By *proximal*, Vygotsky meant that this zone is limited by those behaviors that will develop in the near future. The ZPD is development on the stage of the child's maturation. For example, no adult can create the ZPD for the development of mediated perception working in a 2-year-old. *Proximal* refers not to all possible behaviors that might ever be acquired by the child but to those closest to emergence at any given time (Bodrova & Leong, 1996).

The boundaries of the ZPD are determined by two levels: the child's independent performance (i.e., what the child knows and can do alone) and the child's assisted performance (i.e., what the child can reach with help). The larger the distance is between these two levels, the bigger the discrepancy between the child's independent and assisted performance, and the wider is the ZPD.

The content of the ZPD is not constant. Quite to the contrary, the skills and behaviors represented in the ZPD are dynamic and constantly shifting. In general, the upper level of the ZPD constantly goes up—what the child needs assistance for today, he or she might do independently tomorrow—challenging the child to strive for new accomplishments. However, the dynamics of the ZPD allows both some stability and sometimes even the lowering of the upper boundary. The main characteristic of the ZPD is its sensitivity to the child's individuality—its responsiveness to the unique profile of each child's skills.

The ZPD is of tremendous importance educationally. Generally, when educators evaluate a child's skills, they focus on what the child demonstrates in his or her independent performance. For example, when my neighbor goes back to his house to count the cars, we can say that he knows how to count things when he sees them. If I, however, help him by reminding him that his parents have a large red car and a smaller blue one, he visualizes the cars and counts them without any difficulty. The function of counting mentally is in his ZPD; all I needed to do was to provide him with some assistance by reminding him about the colors of his parents' cars. Vygotsky stated that the level of independent performance is an important, but not the only, index of development. To account for the dynamic process of development, we should consider the level of the child's assisted performance.

The ZPD is a completely interactive concept. Without interaction, there is no ZPD. The interaction might consist of (a) direct assistance (giving hints and clues, rephrasing questions, suggesting alternative solutions, giving examples, questioning the child's understanding, etc.) or (b) indirect help (establishing the environment, facilitating practicing, creating situations, challenging the child with difficult tasks, etc.). For example, to teach a child how to draw a tea cup, an adult might sketch the cup first and then ask the child to repeat the exercise (direct assistance). Or, the adult might bring a cup, put it in front of the child, and ask him or her to use the cup as the model for the drawing (indirect assistance).

The essence of the ZPD is its reflection of a child's individual profile of skills and abilities. Thus, the dimensions of the zone might vary for different children (even though these children might be of similar age and have similar educational backgrounds). Two students who cannot solve a given problem correctly may not necessarily have the same level of problem-solving skills.

For example, when assisted, one of the students might solve the problem easily—say with only one hint—whereas the other student might need much more assistance and require ten hints before solving the problem. In this case, the level of the assisted performance of the first student is much higher than that of the second. Thus, by evaluating students' particular responses to assistance, we can better determine the children's true level. Moreover, the ZPDs of the same child might be different in different domains: The child might be a superb reader and a poor mathematician; correspondingly, the level of his assisted performance in reading is much higher than the level of his assisted performance in math.

Teachers should be sensitive to the child's reaction to assistance. If the child accepts the assistance and carries on, making progress, then, most likely, the teacher sensed the child's ZPD correctly. On the contrary, if the child cannot use help and still, even when offered support, cannot perform at the higher level, the teacher needs to reconsider her or his strategy, because, most likely, the assistance that has been offered so far lands outside of the child's ZPD. The concept used to describe the optimal use of a child's ZPD is called *amplification* and was suggested by the Russian psychologist Zaporozhets (1986). Essentially, amplification assists behaviors that are about to emerge but uses tools the child already has and assists performance in the child's ZPD. Therefore, amplification builds on strengths and increases development without reaching beyond the ZPD.

Ultimately, the ZPD enlarges the frame of developmentally appropriate practice (Bodrova & Leong, 1996). Traditionally, what is considered developmentally appropriate tends to be linked to a child's level of independent performance (Bredecamp, 1992). The developmentally appropriate practice does not usually take into account the level of assisted performance or the child's unfolding processes, functions, and skills. Very often, teachers wait for children to demonstrate completely formed functions; teachers think that they can lead a child to the next step only after they have seen evidence that the child has successfully acquired the function taught at the previous step. As a result, children are limited in their learning opportunities to those that correspond to their level of independent performance. In other words, teachers who follow this standard practice minimize the student's ZPD by almost closing it. On the contrary, ideally, the ZPD should be wide open, so that it can expand developmentally appropriate practices up to the level of assisted performance. According to Vygotsky, the most effective teaching is that targeted at the upper level of a child's ZPD. In other words, the aim of the teacher should be to suggest activities that are more than the child can do on his or her own but less than the child can do with assistance. Student–teacher shared activities should be slightly ahead of the child's level at any given time. In summary, the developmentally appropriate practice should really be the developmentally appropriate practices—one that the child can practice independently and the other the child can practice in the context of shared activity within the child and an adult.

Scaffolding

Vygotsky did not provide a detailed account of how exactly the adult-child interaction in the ZPD should proceed. From my point of view, one of a number of concepts that appears to be closest ideologically to Vygotsky's writing is that of *scaffolding*. Wood, Bruner, and Ross (1976) coined this term, asserting that the expert essentially provides scaffolding in the ZPD to enable the novice to perform at a higher level. When scaffolding is offered initially, the task itself is not changed, but the learner's task is made easier with assistance. The idea of scaffolding is to minimize assistance and then eventually withdraw it completely as the learner's performance improves, just as the scaffolding of a building is taken away as the walls are strong enough to stand alone (Bodrova & Leong, 1996).

Wood, Bruner, and Ross (1976) described six functions of the adult in such scaffolding of a child's performance:

- Recruiting the child's interest;
- Reducing the number of steps required to solve a problem by simplifying the task so the learner can manage its components and acknowledge achieving intermediate steps;
- Maintaining the pursuit of the goal by supporting the child's motivation and directing his or her activity;
- Marking critical characteristics of discrepancies between what a child has achieved and what he or she is expected to achieve;
- Controlling frustration and risk in the child's problem-solving;
- Setting the ideal of performance by demonstrating it.

For example, when a child is asked to write his or her first short paper, the teacher might spend time explaining the overall structure of the paper and the purpose of such different parts as the introduction, body, and conclusion. The teacher might present an exemplary short paper and go over its components. The teacher might even provide the child with typical sentences opening and closing the paper. After grading the paper, the teacher should explain what in the paper needs to be changed and should provide adequate and encouraging feedback to the child. Moreover, while going over the paper, the teacher might once again describe the ideal, stressing her or his expectations and motivating the child to improve his or her skill. When another paper is assigned, the teacher expects to be involved to a lesser degree. For example, the teacher might describe the structure of the paper again but would not go into as many details as she or he did with the first assignment. After grading the paper, the teacher provides detailed feedback. Gradually, the teacher's involvement at the preparation stage becomes minimal and, finally, the teacher provides feedback only.

In managing the learning process targeted at the mastery of a certain skill, the adult provides active intervention and significant scaffolding, directing, and orchestrating much of the child's behavior. The essence of scaffolding, however, is the continual revision of the level of assistance in response to the child's advancements. As the child learns, a shift in responsibility is expected to take place, so that the learner gradually becomes directly responsible for producing the expected behaviors. The process of gradually removing the scaffolding requires great patience—the walls might collapse if the scaffolding is removed too quickly. Bruner (1983) referred to this shift of responsibility as the hand over principle. Through this process, the child, who was initially a spectator, becomes a participant.

Scaffolding characterizes globally the types of interactions that take place between the child and the other in the ZPD. Scaffolding establishes the upper level of the ZPD and indicates not only the amount of instrumental assistance given to the child but also the location of responsibility for the behavior that has been mastered. Thus, more than any other concept used to describe the nature of the ZPD interactions, the concept of scaffolding addresses both instrumental support and the formation of the learner's sense of self-control and self-efficacy.

Currently, researchers are investigating yet another type of scaffolding: scaffolding provided by external mediators of learning. A *mediator* is defined as a tool that stands between an environmental stimulus and an individual response to that stimulus. A mediator facilitates the child's learning by making it easier for a child to perform an operation or action that has not yet been mastered. In Vygotsky's framework, mediators become mental tools as the child consciously includes them in his or her activity and then automates their use. Examples of mediators are maps, graphs, memos, and so on.

Teachers design external mediators to assist children in their mastery of certain cognitive operations. They carefully plan the mediator itself as well as the moments when it should be introduced into and removed from the child's activity. The exact moment of the removal of the mediator might not be determined in advance but rather may be discovered during the learning activity itself. Examples of external mediators used in school are boxes with various labels; when children study figures and are asked to sort a pile of figures into triangles and squares, two boxes featuring pictures of squares and triangles will facilitate the sorting. After a number of consecutive successes, the labels might than be removed.

VYGOTSKY IN SCHOOLS

Vygotsky's ideas have been used, modified, and verified in schools. Many scientists in Russia, the USA, and all over the world have invested their time and energy in developing school programs facilitating the acquisition of the tools of the mind. The goal of the second part of this chapter is to sample some of these programs and illustrate how a Vygotsky-based approach can be used in school settings. From among the many studies that have implemented the concept of the ZPD in research, I have chosen to present here only a few. As I said earlier, my goal is not to evaluate these programs. Such a formal evaluation is beyond the scope of this chapter and also not always possible due to the methodological specificities of the presented work. The following section is a set of illustrations linking Vygotsky's theory to classroom activities.

VYGOTSKY IN AMERICAN SCHOOLS

In North American psychology, the concept of Vygotsky's that has gained the most attention and appreciation is the ZPD. According to Newman and Holzman (1993), the ZPD is popular because it (a) lends itself well to contemporary interests in social cognition and classroom interaction, (b) delves into the essence of learning and development, and (c) expresses individuality in society.

The most popular interpretation of assisted performance in North America refers to activities in the ZPD using the model of expert–novice interactions. In this type of interaction, one person has more knowledge of the object of the activity than the other, and it is the responsibility of the expert to communicate relevant knowledge and skills to the novice. These interactions can be both formal (as when an expert and a novice interact in educational or training settings) or informal (as when children and parents or older siblings interact).

The Oceanside School Project

The most extensive educational use of the concept of the ZPD so far probably has been its investigation in the Oceanside School Project, conducted by Newman, Griffin, and Cole (1989). The researchers expanded the pedagogical notion of the ZPD and renamed it *the construction zone*, deeming it the zone between the thoughts of two people on a shared activity in which interpsychological (that is, shared mental) processes can take place.

Cognitive change does not occur in a closed, determined system. Rather, the child's cognitive system opens up in the construction zone, in which the shared activity of constructing new (or advancing old) cognitive functions takes place. Cognitive tasks first are constructed in the interaction between expert and novice and, later, in the novice's independent activity. Initially, the novice not only lacks the skills necessary to carry out the tasks independently but also, and more importantly, does not understand the goal toward which a given situation is directed. Thus, in their school program, Newman and colleauges ensured that teaching took place in a Vygotskian manner, whereby children were introduced to a given task in such a way that "the goal and the procedure were simultaneously internalized in the course of the interaction" (p. 55). Generalizing from their school-based experiences, the researchers suggested that the concept of the ZPD refers to an interactive system in which people work on a problem that at least one of them could not solve effectively on his or her own. Thus, in their interpretation, the ZPD is a more general phenomenon, observed when two or more people with unequal expertise are accomplishing a goal jointly.

The teacher knows the goal of the task and what specifically the child needs to learn for his or her outcome performance to meet the criteria. The child, on the contrary, does not have a full grasp of either the goal he or she is trying to accomplish or the final criteria he or she must meet. When the child and the teacher—two people with different goals, roles, and resources—interact, a certain charged tension arises. This tension allows the construction of new knowledge. The process of constructing new knowledge, the specific dynamics of this process, and the new knowledge itself all lead to cognitive change.

For example, when a new cognitive operation is introduced to a child, he or she does not have a mental representation of this operation and, correspondingly, cannot formulate its goal or even relate to it. For instance, a 6-year-old shown how to play Master Mind™ (a logical game, in which one player creates a combination from a number of colored pins and the other player decodes this combination using structured feedback from the first player) most likely has not yet formed the cognitive operations underlying the game. The child might listen to the instructions, pay attention to the colors of the pins, and try to fit them into the holes, but he or she is unable to comprehend the goal of the game. Playing with the child and explaining the rules of the game to him or her while playing eventually will enable the child to understand the goal of the game. Still, the child's first mental representation of the game might be quite different from the adult's. The child, even when able to repeat the instruction, might not completely grasp the meaning of creating different combinations of colored pins. Gradually, two representations of the goal, the adult's and the child's, will converge.

The child's understanding of the goal of the game is complete when he or she can explain the rules to someone else. Grasping the goal of Master Mind™ requires mastering the cognitive processes underlying the game. Thus, the gradual convergence of the different mental representations of the goals, together with the shared activity of playing, resulted in cognitive change in the child.

According to Newman and colleagues (1989), the most important dynamic in the construction zone is the dialogue between the child and the teacher. Internalization does not occur as a byproduct of learning; internalization simply cannot be imposed on the child and it cannot be achieved by the child in isolation. Internalization happens in the shared action between the child and the teacher, in the course of dialogue. In the construction zone, the main task of the teacher is to make the child act. By asking questions, probing the child, and making sure that the child understands what is going on and that both individuals are working at the same site of the construction zone, the teacher guides the child's existence in the zone, manipulates his or her mental processing, and provokes development. However, the action that happens in the construction zone is a two-way action: The teacher simultaneously tries to communicate the goals of her or his actions to the child and to understand the child's thinking. Meanwhile, the child tries to grasp the goals of both the task and the teacher's actions. By converging in their understanding of the situation, the teacher and the child co-construct knowledge.

The goal of the Oceanside School Project was to make a cognitive task happen several times and see how different social settings deconstruct it in different ways. There were three major social settings investigated: (a) the laboratory setting (one-to-one tutorial/assessment sessions with a researcher and a child); (b) a set of classroom activities (teacher-led large group lessons, teacher-led small group lessons, child-only small group lessons, and tutorials with teachers); and (c) club activities.

The group of researchers worked closely with teachers and social club leaders to design special curriculum units for third- and fourth-grade classes that allowed them to instantiate tasks in a variety of academic and nonacademic settings and therefore to separate (at least partially) individual and social processes. There were four curriculum units: electricity, Native Americans, household chemicals, and division. Every unit contained one or more cognitive operations, and the formation and development of each operation was monitored. As a particular function took shape and improved, a related cognitive change was registered. Consider, for example, the cognitive function of combination, a function that involves relating parts to a whole and exploring all possible combinations of the parts. The laboratory version of the task was to sort cards depicting movies stars into unique pairs.

The classroom version of the combination task included a chemistry lab, preceded by a series of general lessons and activities teaching the chemistry of related elements. The chemistry lab itself resembled the card task by requiring the children to find out as much as they could about four chemicals in the course of making combinations of two. Finally, in the club settings, the activity involved yet another version of the combination task. Here, the children were asked to figure out how many different kinds of stew could be created from a limited set of dried ingredients.

It was found that, first, all three settings had structural and functional similarities. The interpersonal systems characterized by different dyads in different settings (child—researcher, child—teacher, child—expert peer) all included the ZPD. The researchers observed that the ZPD was enormously flexible. They found that the zones can accommodate multiple ways of appropriating new knowledge and acquiring cognitive change, demonstrated by students. For example, the researchers carefully analyzed the experience of one child, "Ricardo," who, once having demonstrated an adequate performance of the task, then moved backward in his ZPD. Once they observed the failure of the interpersonal system formed by Ricardo and the researcher, the authors suggested that the problem could be resolved by introducing more resources in the system to support Ricardo's cognitive growth (in this particular case, the problem was, in part, caused by Ricardo's poor English language skills).

Second, the researchers found that cognitive change that occurs in one of the social settings is transferable to other social settings.

Third, the researchers found that at the beginning of the unit on Native Americans lower-ability students benefitted more from the ZPD-based teaching than did higher-ability students. This initial relative gain, however, was virtually lost over the course of the unit. It appears that ZPD-based teaching introduces a new type of learning, which improves overall learning right away. Presumably, the higher-ability students have most of these learning-related skills in place already at the beginning of the unit, while the lower-ability students do not. Thus, ZPD-based teaching introduces a kind of jump-start to the lower-ability students. Then, this differential impact gradually shrinks, and the balance between the two groups is restored, with both groups gaining from ZPD-based teaching.

Fourth, Newman and colleagues (1989) stressed how different the ZPD concept is from traditional notions of cognitive change. Traditionally, to allow the transfer of skills or knowledge from one task to another, a teacher specifies a sequence of activities, so that the child moves from not knowing what the task is to doing it well. Thus, the sequence of the tasks moves from simple to complex, from more specific to more general, from tasks that have been mastered to more challenging tasks. In this approach, a teacher might well be replaced by a computer, because the algorithm of the sequencing of the tasks is easy to program. The concept of the ZPD, however, allows social interaction rather than temporal sequence to determine the child's breakthrough. The ZPD also involves a sequence, but it is a sequence of a different nature. It is a sequence of shifting division of labor, beginning with significant teacher involvements and ending with the maximum involvement of the child and the minimum (if any) involvement of the teacher. Meanwhile, the task itself (the whole task that needs to be accomplished by the interaction) remains the same.

Finally, according to the authors, the ZPD and the traditional view of cognitive change result in very different ways of presenting tasks to learners. In the traditional way, there is a tendency to break the work down into pieces so that an understanding of the global goal is not necessary. There is no need to understand the ultimate end of the sequence if the learning is wholly componential. Correspondingly, traditional teaching results in an emphasis on the local goals of the lower level components of the sequence. On the contrary, a ZPD-based approach emphasizes the global goal of the sequence (the goal of interaction) from the very beginning. The teacher, from the start, incorporates the child into her or his vision of the interaction, and so, the goal is shared; however, the interaction will fail and the goal will not be accomplished if the child does not do his or her part. The teacher incorporates the child's contribution and then acts as necessary to keep the child in the interaction. In other words, it is the teacher's responsibility to ensure that the child's actions bear a meaningful relation to the ultimate goal of the interaction.

Apprenticeship in Cognitive Development

Rogoff's (1990) investigation of the ZPD went beyond the classroom to explore cognitive development in informal settings. Rogoff investigated family interactions (mother–child, older sib–younger sib) and interactions between experts and novices (weaving masters and their apprentices). Although she began her work in the United States, Rogoff also compared the nature and structure of ZPDs in different cultures.

Rogoff (1990) asserted that children's cognitive and social education throughout the world is organized around the principle of guided participation. Guided participation characterizes social arrangements and the developmental engagement of children in many, possibly all, cultures. Rogoff argued that the structure of guided participation is universal, and the most notable variations in guided participation in general stem from developmental goals reflective of particular cultural and societal peculiarities. Moreover, she pointed to important cultural differences in the clarity and amount of verbal and nonverbal communication and in the overall role of children in different societies. In summarizing her work, Rogoff suggested apprenticeship as an explanatory metaphor to stress children's active role in learning the lessons of their culture as they are played out through guided participation in activities shared with more skilled companions.

Specifically, guided participation is carried out by structuring tasks into different levels or subgoals. These subgoals are then broken down further, modified, and adjusted as the ZPD is explored in the course of interaction between the participants. By choosing the external mediators of the child's activity (toys, equipment, materials, tools, etc.), the expert designs and structures the task even before the novice engages in the guided participation. The expert's goal not only is to introduce a function to the child but also to make him or her master the function, or, in other words, to turn the novice into an expert; therefore, the expert may build redundancy and repetition into the process, modeling and remodeling the situation until the skill is mastered.

Rogoff's work is rich in meaning and complex, but here I present only one especially important issue of her research—the balance between sensitivity and challenge in guided participation. In other words, how much rapport between partners is necessary for development within the ZPD to happen? Rogoff argued that a minimal accord between the partners is needed to establish the trust and openness necessary for communication. When there is no sufficient rapport, difficulties related to a lack of familiarity between partners might occur. One example of such difficulty was discussed by Michaels and Cazden (1986). In this case, White teachers, unfamiliar with the episodic narrative style favored in some Black communities, failed to establish the rapport necessary for successful functioning in the ZPD. Rapport is especially important in a multicultural society. Differences in values and practices between the partners in an interaction might close the ZPD and prevent learning; if, on the contrary, their values are handled with respect and allowed to persist, children can and will benefit from learning new cultural systems. Thus, common ground is necessary for the interaction within the ZPD, and it is up to the teacher to find it.

Rogoff introduced another concept which, at first glance, appears to contradict those assertions to some degree. According to this concept, called cognitive stretch, although a certain degree of sensitivity is critical for a successful outcome of the interaction, the atmosphere of the ZPD should be such that it contains a sufficient challenge to allow and encourage a cognitive change in the child. What is really needed for success is both common ground and stimulating differences. Otherwise the interaction will not be interesting or necessary, and the child will feel no impetus to reach a new understanding—to perform cognitive stretches toward the other's position.

For example, fathers, who traditionally are less involved with childcare than mothers, are likely to have somewhat limited shared experiences with youngsters and, thus, experience more difficulty in establishing rapport. However, if both sides are sufficiently motivated to establish communication, this situation might, actually, stimulate children to stretch themselves in order to communicate effectively with their fathers (Tomasello, Conti-Ramsden, & Ewert, 1990). Similarly, if a child interacts with more knowledgeable partners who are somewhat unfamiliar with the child but willing to communicate, and if the novelty is not excessive, she or he might experience cognitive stretching. Hence, this particular dynamic might be very resourceful and beneficial for the child's cognitive development. Often cognitive stretch leads to the acquisition of new vocabulary and new behavioral and emotional skills.

Thus, Rogoff concluded, for children to profit from the interactions in the ZPD, the social atmosphere in the zone should be such that it allows both common ground and some variety of the partners. This variety is essential—intimate partners give children the experience of deep sharing because rapport is established easily and quickly, whereas less familiar partners might stimulate children to develop. A lack of familiar partners might lead to feelings of frustration, whereas a lack of unfamiliar partners might allow the child to take social interactions with close and familiar partners for granted.

The implications of these ideas for education are quite important. A child's interactions with a familiar teacher might lead to a deepening of acquired knowledge and skills, while interactions with a less familiar teacher might lead to cognitive stretch which, in turn, could broaden acquired knowledge and skills.

VYGOTSKY IN RUSSIAN SCHOOLS

Russians who developed Vygotsky's ideas proceeded in two main directions. One investigative trajectory (e.g., Gal'perin, 1957, 1966a, 1966b, 1966c; Gal'perin, Zaporozhets, & El'konin, 1963; Zaporozhets & El'konin, 1971) explored the hypothesis that mastery of mental tools (heuristics, concepts, formulae, etc.) involves not only the acquisition of definitions but also the ability to use mastered tools effectively. In other words, Vygotsky's emphasis on language in the mastery of mental tools has been softened. Vygotsky's followers have not questioned the important role of language but have broadened our understanding the representation of the process of the mental tool acquisition. According to this view, the mastery of a tool of the mind is the acquisition of the process underlying the functional specificity of this tool. This position led to a reformulation of Vygotsky's concept of internalization (Karpov & Bransford, 1995). What is internalized is not the tool itself but the psychological processes underlying the function of the tool. These innovations on Vygotsky's theory were developed by Gal'perin and his colleagues in the theory of systematic formation.

Another innovation developed by Russian psychologists was an elaboration of the mastery of spontaneous versus scientific concepts. Here the main credit belongs to two former students and colleagues of Vygotsky, Gal'perin and El'konin, as well as to the students of Vygotsky's students, Davydov and Talyzina (Gal'perin, 1985; Gal'perin & Talyzina, 1961; Davydov, 1986, 1988a; El'konin, 1966, 1989; Talyzina, 1981). They showed in their work that the acquisitions of spontaneous and scientific concepts result of two fundamentally different types of learning—empirical learning and theoretical learning, correspondingly (Davydov, 1986, 1988a). Empirical learning, based on comparing objects and finding a common feature among them, does not necessarily result in an adequate concept. The goal of theoretical learning, on the contrary, is to form an adequate concept; thus, teaching intended to promote theoretical learning should be organized so that the only concept that can possibly be derived from the learning experience is the adequate concept.

Based on observations made in Russian schools, researchers suggested that school instruction primarily cultivated empirical learning, at least when it came to mastering school subjects (Karpov & Bransford, 1995). Generally, empirical learning occurs when students are given only verbal definitions of the concepts. Students use empirical learning to derive their own spontaneous concepts, which then may be maintained for good. For example, even if they have learned the essential attributes of mammals, birds, and fish, students nevertheless at first continue to believe that the whale is a fish (Davydov, 1972). Theoretical learning is based on supplying the student with mental tools that reflect ways of solving problems of certain classes. When mastered, tools can be applied to concrete problems. In the course of manipulating the tool, students master and internalize the psychological processes that give that particular tool its functional role. Theoretical learning takes place when learning activity is carried out.

The Theory of Systematic Formation

One of the Russian psychological theories, inspired by Vygotsky's work, was the theory of the systematic formation of mental actions and concepts (Gal'perin, 1966a, 1966b). In the context of this theory, teaching is viewed as a psychological experiment, the goal of which is to bring the student to a new, higher level of development. By conducting teaching as an experiment—that is, by determining the dependent (outcome) and the independent (treatment) variables in teaching—the researchers view teaching as the way to influence and continually monitor systematically the child's cognitive and educational progress. The teaching is conducted in the following six steps (for details, see Haenen, 1996).

1. The motivational stage—the preliminary introduction to the learner of the action and the mobilization of the learning motive.
2. The orienting stage—the construction of the psychological map of the action.
3. The materialized stage—the mastery of the action using material or materialized objects.
4. The stage of overt speech—the mastery of the action at the level of overt speech.
5. The stage of covert speech—the mastery of the action by "speaking to oneself."
6. The mental stage—the transference of the action to the mental level.

For example, to explain addition and subtraction, the teacher first tries to motivate the student to master the action and then gives him or her a whole set of orienting elements for guidance in the execution of the action (e.g., explains what subtraction does and what components it includes). Next, using the subject matter as the basis for teaching, the instructor provides the child with a means to master the using mediating tools (e.g., objects, drawing, pictures). Then, at the fourth stage, the child is taught to execute the action without any direct use of mediating tools by verbalizing the steps of subtraction learned through the manipulation of real objects. Similarly, at the fifth step, the action is still verbalized, but the learner is encouraged to whisper to himself instead of speaking aloud. Eventually, whispering disappears, and the action "moves" entirely in the mind. The child now can add and subtract mentally; the function has been mastered.

One of many interesting aspects of Gal'perin's theory of systematic formation is his view of the nature of children's errors, or, more specifically, his strategy of error avoidance. Gal'perin considered the occurrence of students' errors in the course of learning as an indication that the systematic formation had not been adequately implemented. One of Gal'perin's teaching strategies (known as the strategy of errorless learning) was designed to prevent students from making errors. Obviously, Gal'perin did not believe in learning by trial and error. According to Gal'perin, reliance on this technique in school led to repeated errors and proved frustrating for both students and teachers.

For example, one of the typical errors second graders make is to misuse capitalization (Bodrova & Leong, 1996). To make learning errorless, the teacher, together with the students, creates a list of all situations in which capital letters are used. Then, these lists are placed at every student's desk to serve as an external mediator. Students are asked to look at the list and to repeat the list to themselves as often as they can. Using an exercise provided by the teacher, the student practices capitalization by looking at every word and trying to relate it to the list of situations in which capitalization is correct. At the end of the exercise the students are asked to discuss their results with a partner. Finally, the teacher checks their exercises to monitor the process. After a few weeks, most children do not need to use the list of situations as the external mediator.

When, however, despite organized efforts to avoid errors, they do occur, the task of the teacher is to return to the very first introduction of the concept and go, step by step, through the process of systematic formation in attempt to determine which step of the formation failed. The idea here is that the teacher is expected to deconstruct the action so that the cause of the errors might be found. Once the cause is found, the teacher's role is to provide the missing link so that the child can reform the action. For example, one of my most frequent mistakes in pronunciation is the sound corresponding to the letter w. This error occurs on a regular basis if I do not pay attention to my pronunciation, that is, when my pronunciation is automatized. According to Gal'perin's theory, to correct this error, I, along with my English teacher, should go back to the orienting stage. At that stage, led by the teacher, I should find the correct imitation of the sound, exploring analogous sounds in languages known to me, so that I can form a correct representation of the sound. After much deliberate practice, automatization should result in correct pronunciation of the sound.

The followers of this approach state that their intention is not to install in the child a developmental stage or level, but, rather, to help the child gradually move on to the next, higher stage of development (Talyzina, 1995). Gal'perin's theory has never been implemented in the form of a complete curriculum, but it has been applied in many subject-specific areas, such as reading and arithmetic (El'konin, 1960), math (Obukhova, 1972; Salmina & Kolmogorova, 1980). For a general overview, see Talyzina, 1995.

The Theory of Learning Activity

As just noted, the foundation for the theory of learning activity (Davydov, 1982; Davydov & Markova, 1983) is provided by Vygotsky's notions of psychological activity and scientific concepts. Learning activity is defined as adult-orchestrated activity organized around formalized, structured, culturally dependent specific content. Examples of such content in modern industrial societies are concepts of math, science, history, and geography, basic rules of grammar, abstract ideas in art and literature, and esthetic taste. Examples of such content in indigenous societies are knowledge of self-treatment and basics of hunting and agriculture. Learning activity includes three major components: the learning task, the action (or operation), and the method of evaluation and control (Davydov, 1988b; Kozulin & Presseisen, 1995). The developmental products of learning activity, in the context of industrial societies, are the bases of theoretical reasoning, the emergence of higher mental functions, and the development of intrinsic motivation (Bodrova & Leong, 1996; Davydov, 1988b; El'konin, 1977).

On the surface, a learning task coincides with concrete reading and writing exercises, mathematical problems, or laboratory assignments. However, its meaning is much deeper. When properly constructed, a learning task reflects the underlying principles of the subject to be learned. For example, in mathematics instruction, the goal is to form the general principle of problem-solving prior to exposing children to concrete math problems. Therefore, instead of being presented with concrete numerical material, the child first should be exposed to fundamental relationships, such as the equality or inequality of two values, the concepts of part and whole, the relationships between parts and a whole, and so on. Then, these relationships should be studied through the manipulation of their objective representations and symbolic models. Finally, the children should be challenged with concrete examples.

For example, first graders are given a learning task, intended to help them master the relations between elements of two arithmetic operations, addition and subtraction. At the first stage, children are introduced to corresponding operations and values. These concepts are given initially in their abstract form by means of letter formulas (e.g., a, b, $a - b$, $b + a$). Then, children are taught how these relationships might be represented graphically as lines of different length. By manipulating these lines, children learn the concept of whole and part. Moreover, they come to understand the relationship between a whole and its parts, and they learn that if two elements are known, the value of the third element can be determined precisely. The realization of this principle allows the teacher to return to the symbolic representation of subtraction and addition as letter formulas and introduce the idea of equation ($a + b = c$, $c - a = b$, $c - b = a$). Using these equations, children are then asked to come up with verbal illustrations of subtraction and addition (e.g., Katia has two apples and Petia has two apples. How many apples do Katia and Petia have together?). Finally, children are given numeric problems (e.g., $2 + 3 = ?$, $5 - 3 = ?$, $5 - 2 = 3$), to which they are expected to apply their newly mastered skills of addition and subtraction.

Through learning activity, children master new actions (operations). The acquisition of a new operation stems from the formation of some preliminary image of the operation or a student's opportunity to try it out. For example, an art teacher may be limited by a lack of available tools for teaching and formalizing his or her subject. Moreover, the verbalization of meanings and techniques implemented, for example, in famous paintings, is limited at the elementary school level, because most first graders have not yet developed mediated perception. These youngsters simply do not have the skill to appreciate the expressivity of colors in painting, because this skill is based on the higher mental function of mediated perception.

The first step toward forming esthetic perception is to expose children to working with colors. A teacher might ask a child to use colors in a certain manner, for example, to combine two spots of different colors on a piece of paper. This exercise creates situations in which the child can appreciate shades of different colors, observe transformations of colors, and become aware of color contrast. Then, having experienced the magic of colors, the child gradually understands that colors might express emotion and motion. When presented with a famous painting now, the child has skills related to the appreciation of the painting. A foundation of esthetic perception has been established.

The mastery of operations in learning activity is inseparable from the function of control. Control depends on comparing the action performed by a child with that shown by a teacher or presented by the object of study.

For example, in a lesson of the dynamics of motion in famous paintings, children might be asked to model the motion by manipulating movable black figures on white pieces of paper (Davydov, 1988b). For this exercise, the teacher divides the class into pairs of children. With every pair, one child is nominated to be an artist, and the other child is nominated to be a spectator (later, the children exchange roles). The spectator evaluates the performance of the artist, makes comments, and gives suggestions. In this way, control is initially externalized and performed by another child. After a number of interactions between two children, the function of control becomes internalized, and every child is able to comment on his or her own performance, evaluating both the progress and concrete results of the learning activity.

Control is tightly linked to the child's evaluation of his or her own success in accomplishing the learning task. Conceptually this component of the theory of learning activity is related to the concepts of self-regulation and self-efficacy. Having mastered the function of control over their own performance, children are taught to summarize their impressions in self-evaluations. The important point here is to help the child learn that the most important aspect of learning the target operation is the mastery of the general principle applicable to all problems of a given type, rather than of concrete instances. Thus, after completing a series of lessons devoted to the mastery of a particular operation (e.g., mastering the endings of nouns in Russian), the teacher should ask the children to evaluate their progress across a number of lessons, rather than for a specific exercise or a specific test.

The mastery of scientific concepts is not the only outcome of learning activity. Correctly structured learning activity results in the development of theoretical reasoning, the emergence of HMF, and the formation of the intrinsic motivation to learn (Bodrova & Leong, 1996; Davydov, 1988a, 1988b). Theoretical reasoning refers to the child's ability to utilize newly acquired scientific concepts (the concepts of math, science, biology, etc.). In reasoning theoretically, the child focuses on reasoning, operating on essential properties of objects or abstract ideas that often are neither present in visual field nor intuitively apparent. According to Vygotsky, the development of theoretical reasoning starts after the age of 6 and continues throughout schooling until age 18 or even later. The second outcome of learning activity is the development of higher mental functions. For example, in his follow-up study conducted during the implementation of his pedagogical program, Davydov (1988b) registered the emergence and further development of thinking, planning, self-monitoring, and intentional memory. Moreover, Gal'perin (1985) reported the development of mediated (focused) attention as a result of learning activity. Yet another product of learning activity is the development of an intrinsic motivation to learn. When they are engaged in carefully crafted activity, learning at great speed and being aware of their increasing accumulation of skills and knowledge, children start learning and develop intrinsic motivation for it.

The learning activity approach has been implemented successfully in teaching reading, writing, and mathematics in primary school (Davydov, 1986, 1988b; Davydov, Lompscher, & Markova, 1982). It appears that the approach results in the enhanced ability of students to solve problems that are nontrivial in nature and require the transfer of skills to a new domain or the restructuring of data. The ultimate goal of this deliberate and systematic educational approach is metacognition.

CONCLUSION

The purpose of this chapter was to demonstrate the applicability of Vygotsky's theory of the tools of the mind to classroom settings. This theory has been an inspiration and a challenge to many educators for years. Although he established the general theory, Vygotsky neither developed it in detail nor elaborated on the particulars of its implementation in schools. It is not fair to say now that his theory has been proven or disproven in educational settings. Many of the elements of his theory have influenced educational practices all over the world and made it into many experts' "bags of tricks."

Moreover, educators keep returning to Vygotsky's theory for new pedagogical ideas and inspirations, and I certainly share this attraction.

From my point of view, three aspects of Vygotsky's theory and the subsequent theoretical developments that emerged on the basis of this theory, are of special importance for educators.

First, by introducing the concept of the zone of proximal development, Vygotsky located the child in the course of his or her development and placed the process of acquiring and mastering the tools of the mind in social context. According to Vygotsky, development is not a solitary endeavor that can be observed at a distance. Development is a dynamic, interactive process, and, to a large degree, caregivers and teachers determine its results. The particular child—teacher dynamic interaction is most highly charged with developmental potential for a given child and a given skill, and the hottest spot of development is located in the ZPD.

Second, further developments of the concept of the zone of proximal development have added to our understanding of the shared reality of the ZPD. Now we know how the ZPD is organized, what assisted performance is all about, what the purposes of the ZPD are, and what the outcomes of the shared learning activity are. Moreover, years of research has resulted in widespread acceptance of some of the concepts introduced by Vygotsky. For example, Rogoff's (1990) work on apprenticeship in different cultures demonstrated the applicability of Vygotsky's concept of socially shared interactions. Rogoff (1990) suggested viewing the process of appropriation of shared activity as the natural mode of human existence, as important to us as the exchange of air and water is important to our cells.

Finally, the last key aspect of the ZPD and, correspondingly, of the process of the development of the mental tools, is the creative nature of everything happening in the ZPD. For interactions and developments in the ZPD, there are no recipes, only principles. Every interaction in the ZPD is unique due to the individuality of the partners and the specificity of the object (e.g., mental tool) that is the center of the interaction. The shared nature of the ZPD requires creative understanding, interaction, and management.

According to Vygotsky (1993), people prove the truth of their thoughts only by application. Certainly, the broad and ongoing application of Vygotsky's ideas to educational practice over almost 50 years seems proof enough of the validity of his ideas.

REFERENCES

Bodrova, E., & Leong, D. (1996). *Tools of the mind (The Vygotskian approach to early childhood education)*. Columbus, OH: Merrill.

Bredecamp. S. (Ed.). (1992). *Developmentally appropriate practice in early childhood programs serving children from birth to age 8* (Rev. ed.). Washington, DC: National Association for the Education of Young Children.

Bruner J. S. (1983). Education as social invention. *Journal of Social Issues, 39,* 129–141.

Das, J. P. (1995). Some thoughts on two aspects of Vygotsky's work. *Educational Psychologist, 30,* 93–98.

Davydov, V. V. (1982) *Vidy obobschenia v obuchenii* [The types of generalization in learning]. Moscow: Pedagogika.

Davydov, V. V. (1986). *Problemy razvivaiushchego obuchenia.* [Issues in developing learning]. Moscow: Pedagogika.

Davydov, V. V. (1988a). The concept of theoretical generalization. *Studies in Soviet Thought, 36,* 169–202.

Davydov, V. V. (1988b). Problems of developmental teaching (Part I–III). *Soviet Education, 30,* 8–10.

Davydov, V. V., Lompscher, J., Markova, A. (Eds.). (1982). *Ausbildung der lerntatigkeit schulern* [Development of learning activity in schoolchildren]. Berlin: Volk & Wissen.

Davydov, V. V., & Markova, A. (1983). A concept of educational activity for schoolchildren. *Soviet Psychology, 21,* 50–76.

Donald, M. (1993). Précis of "Origins of the mind: Three stages in the evolution of culture and cognition." *Behavioral and Brain Sciences, 16,* 737–791.

El'konin, D. B. (1960). Opyt psikhologicheskogo issledovaniia v eksperimental'nom klasse [A sample of psychological research in an intervention class]. *Voprosy Psikhologii, 5,* 30–40.

El'konin, D. B. (1966). Intellectual'nye vozmozhnosti mladshikh shkol'nikov i soderzhanie obuchenia [Intellectual potentials of elementary school students and the content of learning]. In D. B. El'konin & V. V. Davydov (Eds.), *Vozrasnye vozmozhnosti usvoenia znanii* (pp. 13–53). Moscow: Prosveschenie.

El'konin, D. (1971). Toward the problem of stages in the mental development of the child. *Soviet Psychology, 10,* 225–251.

El'konin, D. B. (1989). *Izbrannye psikhologicheskie trudy* [selected psychological works]. Moscow: Pedagogika.

Gal'perin, P. Ya. (1957). Umstvennoe destvie kak osnova formirovania mysli i obraza [Mental act as the basis for formation of thought and image]. *Voprosy Psikhologii, 6,* 25–32.

Gal'perin, P. Ya. (1966a). K issledovaniu intellectual'nogo razvitia rebenka [on the study of the child's intellectual development]. *Voprosy Psikhologii, 1,* 15–25.

Gal'perin, P. Ya. (1966b). K ucheniu ob interiorizatsii [On the concept of internalization]. *Voprosy Psikhologii, 6,* 25–32.

Gal'perin, P. Ya. (1966c). Stages in the development of mental acts. In M. Cole & I. Maltzman (Eds.), *A handbook on contemporary Soviet psychology* (pp. 34–61). New York: Basic Books.

Gal'perin, P. Ya. (1985). *Metody obuchenia i umstvennoe razvitie rebenka* [Methods of instruction and the child's mental development]. Moscow: Izdatel'stvo MGU.

Gal'perin, P. Ya., & Talyzina, N. F. (1961). Formation of elementary geometrical concepts and their dependence on directed participation by the pupils. In N. O'Connor (Ed.), *Recent Soviet Psychology* (pp. 247–272). New York: Leviright.

Gal'perin, P. Ya., Zaporozhets, A. V., & El'konin, D. B. (1963). Problemy formirovania znanii i umenii u schol'nikov i novye method obuchenia v shkole [The problem of formation of knowledge and skills in schoolchildren and the new methods of instruction at school]. *Voprosy Psikhologii, 5,* 61–72.

Haenen, J. (1996). *Piotr Gal'perin: psychologist in Vygotsky's footsteps.* Commack, NY: Nova Science Publishers.

Karpov, Y. V., & Bransford, J. D. (1995). L. S. Vygotsky and the doctrine of empirical and theoretical learning. *Educational Psychologist, 30,* 61–66.

Kozulin, A. (1986). The concept of activity in Soviet psychology. *American Psychologist, 41,* 264–274.

Kozulin, A. (1990a). Mediation: Psychological activity and psychological tools. *International Journal of Cognitive Education and Mediated Learning, 1,* 151–159.

Kozulin, A. (1990b). *Vygotsky's psychology: A biography of ideas.* Cambridge, MA: Harvard University Press.

Kozulin, A., & Presseisen, B. (1995). Mediated learning experience and psychological tools: Vygotsky's and Feuerstein's perspective in a study of student learning. *Educational Psychologist, 30,* 67–76.

Luria, A. R. (1976). *Cognitive development.* Cambridge, MA: Harvard University Press.

Michaels, S., & Cazden, C. B. (1986). Teacher/child collaboration as oral preparation for literacy. In B. B. Schieffelin & P. Gilmore (Eds.), *The acquisition of literacy: Ethnographic perspectives.* Norwood, NJ: Ablex.

Newman, D., Griffin, P., & Cole, M. (Eds.) (1989). *The construction zone. Working for cognitive change in school.* New York, NY: Cambridge University Press.

Newman, F., & Holzman, L. (1993). *Lev Vygotsky: Revolutionary scientist.* London: Routledge.

Obukhova, L. F. (1972). Etapy razvitia detskogo myshlenia [Stages of the development of children's thinking]. Moscow: MGU.

Paris, S. C., & Winograd, P. (1990). How metacognition can promote academic learning and instruction. In B. F. Jones & L. Idol (Eds.), *Dimensions of thinking and cognitive instruction* (pp. 15–51). Hillsdale, NJ: Lawrence Erlbaum Associates.

Rogoff, B. (1990). *Apprenticeship in thinking. Cognitive development in social context.* New York: Oxford University Press.

Salmina, N., & Kolmogorova, L. S. (1980). Usvoenie nachal'nykh matematicheskikh poniatii pri raznykh vidakh materializatsii ob'ektov i orudii deistvia [The acquisition of elementary math concepts through different types of representation of objects and tools]. *Voprosy Psikhologii, 1,* 47–56.

Talyzina, N. F. (1981). *The psychology of learning.* Moscow: Progress.

Talyzina, N. F. (Ed.). (1995). *Formirovanie priemov matematicheskogo myshlenia* [The formation of mathematical thinking skills]. Moscow: Ventana-Graf.

Tomasello, M., Conti-Ramsden, G., & Ewert, B. (1990). Young children's conversations with their mothers and fathers: Differences in breakdown and repair. *Journal of Child Language, 17,* 115–130.

Vygotsky, L. S. (1978). *Mind in society.* Cambridge, MA: Harvard University Press.

Vygotsky, L. S. (1981). The genesis of higher mental functions. In J. V. Wertsch (Ed.), *The concept of activity in Soviet psychology* (pp. 144–188). Armonk, NY: Sharpe.

Vygotsky, L. S. (1983). *Izbrannye psikhologicheskie trudy* [Selected works] (Vol. 1–6). Moscow: Pedagogika.

Vygotsky, L. S. (1986). *Thought and language.* Cambridge, MA: Harvard University Press.

Vygotsky, L. S. (1987). *Problems of general psychology.* New York: Plenum.

Vygotsky, L. S. (1993). *Pedagogicheskaia psikhologia* [Pedagogical Psychology]. Moscow: Pedagogika.

Wertsch, J. (1985). *L. S. Vygotsky and the social formation of mind.* Cambridge, MA: Harvard University Press.

Wood, D., Bruner, J. S., & Ross, G. (1976). The role of tutoring in problem solving. *Journal of Child Psychology and Psychiatry, and Allied Disciplines, 17*, 89–100.

Zaporozhets, A. (1986). *Izbrannye psikhologicheskie trudy* [Selected works]. Moscow: Pedagogika.

Zaporozhets, A. V., & El'konin, D. B. (Eds.). (1971). *The psychology of preschool children.* Cambridge, MA: MIT Press.

Author Index

A

Adey, P., 185, 193, *196*
Allen, R., 136, 144, *147*
Alliger, G. M., 115, *128*
Almeida, C., 36, *41*
Amsel, E., 193, *198*
Ankney, C. D., 119, *130*
Armbruster, B., 78, *91*
Armor, D., 140, *147*
Asch, D. A., 136, *147*
Astington, J., 21, *39*
Atkinson, R. C., 124, *128*

B

Baddeley, A., 166, *196*
Badgio, P., 139, *146*
Baltes, P. B., 119, *128*
Bandura, A., 96, *110*, 193, *196*
Barell, J., 87, *92*
Baron, J., 67, 73, 81, *91*, 135, 136, 137, 138, 139, *146, 147*
Baron, J. B., 30, 33, *39*, 73, *91*
Beck, A. T., 137, *146*
Bell, B., 55, *65*
Bereiter, C., 72, 78, 86, *91, 93, 94*
Berliner, D. C., 168, *196*
Bernicot, J., 157, *196*
Bernstein, M., 71, *94*, 163, *199*
Bhattacharyya, M., 121, *129*
Bidell, T. R., 98, *110*
Bill, V., 175, *199*
Binet, A., 70, *91*
Birren, J. E., 119, *128*
Bleiker, C., 160, *196*

Bloom, B. S., 192, *196*
Blythe, T., 25, 35, 36, *39, 41, 42*
Bobocel, D. R., 145, *147*
Bodrova, E., 209, 210, 212, 213, 224, 225, 227, 228
Bonoti, P., 151, 186, *196*
Boring, E. G., 139, *146*
Bouchard, T. J., Jr., 118, *130*
Bransford, J. D., 86, *91*, 222, *230*
Bredecamp. S., 212, *229*
Briars, D., 33, *41*
Brody, N., 71, 72, *91*
Bronfenbrenner, U., 21, *39*
Brown, A. L., 21, *39*, 69, 74, 78, *91, 92, 93*
Brown, J. S., 73, *92*
Bruner, J. S., 213, 214, *229, 231*
Bushey, B., 81, *93*
Butterworth, G., 152, *196*

C

Campbell, B., 22, *39*
Campbell, F. A., 72, *92*, 120, *128*
Capdevielle, B., 81, *93*
Capie, W., 193, *199*
Cardon, L. R., 118, *128*
Carpendale, J. I., 178, *196*
Carroll, J. B., 19, *39*, 114, 115, *128*, 192, *196*
Caryl, P. G., 119, *128*
Case, R., 160, 166, 180, *196*
Cattell, R. B., 19, *40*, 119, *128*
Cazden, C. B., 220, *230*
Ceci, S. J., 19, 21, *39*, 72, *92*
Chandler, M. J., 178, *196*
Changeux, J. P., *197*
Chapman, P. D., 123, *128*

Chard, S., 26–27, *40*
Charness, N., 74, *92*
Chen, J., 24, *39*
Cheng, P., 185, *197*
Cherney, S. S., 118, *128*
Chipman, S. F., 67, 73, *92, 94*
Chonco, S., 81, *93*
Cilliers, C., 81, *93*
Clarke, A. D. B., 120, *128*
Clarke, M. A., 120, *128*
Cleary, C., 51, 61, *65*
Cleveland, H. H., 120, *130*
Clinkenbeard, P., 3, *15*
Cohen, D., 31, *39*
Cole, M., 215, 216, 217, 218, *230*
Collins, A., 21, 33, *39*, 73, *92*
Comer, J., 24, *39*
Connes, A., *197*
Conti-Ramsden, G., 221, *230*
Conway, B. E., 70, *94*, 163, *199*
Cronbach, L. J., 115, *128*
Csikszentmihalyi, M., 22, *39*

D

Damasio, A., 21, *39*
Das, J. P., 209, *229*
Davydov, V. V., 222, 224, 225, 226, 227, *229*
Deary, I. J., 119, *128*
De Corte, E., *197*
Demetriou, A., 150, 151, 154, 155, 156, 157, 158, 160, 161, 162, 163, 164, 165, 166, 167, 169, 178, 179, 180, 181, 182, 186, 191, 193, 194, 195, *197, 198, 199*
Detterman, D. K., 86, *92*, 118, *131*
Dillon, E., 141, *146*
Donald, M., 208, *229*
Dooley, S., 55, *65*
Duguid, P., 21, *39*, 73, *92*
Dunn, K., 22, *39*
Dunn, R., 22, *39*

E

Echols, C., 78, *91*
Economou, A., 151, 156, *197*
Efklides, A., 150, 151, 155, 156, 158, 160, 161, 162, 163, 164, 165, 166, 169, 178, 179, 181, 191, 195, *197, 198*
El'konin, D. B., 204, 221, 222, 224, 225, *229*, *231*
Ennis, R. H., 81, *92*
Ericsson, K. A., 72, 74, *92*
Ewert, B., 221, *230*
Eysenck, H., 19, *39*

F

Fabricius, W. V., 163, 178, *198*
Fano, A., 55, *65*
Farady, M., 81, *93*
Farrar, M. J., 97, *110*
Ferrari, M., 3, *15*
Feuerstein, R., 21, *39*
Fischer, K. W., 96, 97, 98, *110*
Fischhoff, B., 138, *147*
Flannery, D. J., 120, *130*
Flavell, E. R., 178, *198*
Flavell, J. H., 69, 78, *92*, 178, *198*
Flower, L. A., 78, *92*
Fogarty, R., 87, *92*
Franks, J. J., 86, *91*
Frederiksen, J. R., 33, *39*
Fulker, D. W., 118, *128*

G

Gagne, R. M., *198*
Gallistel, C. R., 155, 175, *198*
Gal'perin, P. Ya., 221, 222, 227, *229*
Gardner, H., 19–22, 23, 25, 26, 27, 30–31, 33, *39, 40, 41, 42*, 71, 72, 73, *92*, 118, *128, 129*
Gardner, M. K., 117, *131*
Gaskins, I. W., 139, *146*
Gedye, C. A., 115, *129*
Gelman, R., 175, 184, *198*
Gilovich, T., 138, *146*
Gitta, M. Z., 145, *147*
Glaser, R., 67, 73, *92, 94*
Goodrich, H., 68, 76, 81, 82, 84, *92, 93*
Gordon, E. W., 121, *129*
Gordon, R. A., 116, *129*
Gottfredson, L. S., 116, *129*
Gould, S. J., 70, *92*
Granott, N., 97, 98, 109, *110*
Greeley, K., 27, 28, *40*
Green, F. L., 178, *198*
Greer, B., *197*
Gregorc, T., 22, *40*
Griffin, P., 215, 216, 217, 218, *230*
Griffin, S., 160, *196*
Grigorenko, E. L., 3, 13, *15*
Guilford, J. P., 19, *40*, 71, *92*
Gustafsson, J. E., 160, 161, 195, *197, 198*

H

Haenen, J., 223, *230*
Hafner, J., 136, 144, *147*
Hagen, E., 117, *131*

Haier, R. J., 129
Halford, G., 166, 198
Harter, S., 179, 180, 193, 198
Hartnett, P., 184, 198
Hatch, T., 22, 40, 84, 92
Hayes, J. R., 78, 92
Hecker, L., 22, 26, 40
Heine, S. J., 137, 146
Henderson, B., 160, 196
Herek, G. M., 138, 147
Herman, J., 57, 65
Herrnstein, R. J., 19, 21, 40, 71, 92, 121, 123, 129
Hershey, J. C., 136, 147
Hirsch, E. D., Jr., 59, 64
Holyoak, K., 185, 197
Holzman, W., 215
Horn, J., 19, 40
Hunter, B., 84, 93
Hunter, J. E., 72, 93
Huth, P., 138, 147

I

Iacono, W. G., 118, 130
Inhelder, B., 176, 198

J

Janis, I. L., 138, 147
Jay, E., 81, 90, 93, 94
Jensen, A. R., 19, 40, 71, 93, 115, 116, 117, 118, 119, 120, 121, 122, 129
Jona, M., 55, 57, 65
Jones, B. F., 84, 93
Joseph, D. M., 57, 65

K

Kail, R., 166, 198
Kamin, L., 19, 39
Karmiloff-Smith, A., 176, 198
Karpov, Y. V., 222, 230
Kass, A., 55, 65
Katz, L., 26–27, 40
Kaufman, A., 117
Kazi, S., 150, 151, 155, 158, 163, 164, 165, 166, 167, 179, 180, 182, 191, 193, 197, 198
Keeney, R. L., 134, 147
Ketron, J. L., 70, 94, 163, 199
Kiosseoglou, G., 151, 163, 164, 165, 166, 167, 169, 179, 180, 182, 191, 193, 197, 199
Kirby, E., 41
Klein, K., 26, 40
Kliegl, R., 119, 128
Knight, C. C., 97, 110

Kolmogorova, L. S., 224, 230
Korcuska, M., 57, 65
Koriat, A., 138, 147
Kornhaber, M. L., 22, 23, 27, 40, 118, 129
Kozulin, A., 203, 204, 225, 230
Krechevsky, M., 24, 25, 27, 40
Kuhn, D., 136, 147, 193, 198
Kunreuther, H., 136, 147
Ky, X. N., 21, 41

L

Langer, E. J., 81, 93
Lave, J., 21, 40, 41
Lehman, D. R., 137, 146
Leong, D., 209, 210, 212, 213, 224, 225, 227, 228
Lesgold, S., 33, 41, 175, 199
Levine, J. M., 21, 41
Li, J., 25, 42
Lichtenstein, S., 138, 147
Lohman, O., 116, 119
Loizos, L., 151, 158, 198
Lompscher, J., 227, 229
Lubart, T. I., 12, 15
Luksa, F., 55, 65
Luria, A. R., 207, 230
Lykken, D. T., 118, 130
Lyman, F. T., 84, 93

M

MacIver, D., 179, 199
Makris, N., 164, 198
Mann, C., 22, 40
Markman, E., 157, 199
Markova, A., 224, 227, 229
Matarazzo, J. D., 117, 129
McCarthy, B., 22, 40
McClearn, G. E., 118, 130
McGue, M., 118, 130
McKeough, A., 160, 196
McTighe, J., 84, 93
Meszaros, J. R., 136, 147
Metallidou, Y., 150, 155, 158, 198
Michaels, S., 220, 230
Mirman Owen, J., 76, 93
Morley, J. E., 141, 147
Murray, C., 19, 21, 40, 71, 92, 121, 123, 129
Myers, I. B., 22, 41

N

Newman, D., 215, 216, 217, 218, 230
Nicholls, J. G., 179, 198
Nickerson, R. S., 67, 73, 93, 137, 147

Nisbet, R. E., 185, *197*

O

Oagaki, L., *40*
Obukhova, L. F., 224, *230*
Ogbu, J. U., 121, *130*
Okamoto, Y., 160, *196*
Olff, N., *41*
Oliver, L. M., 185, *197*
O'Loughlin, M., 193, *198*
Olson, J. M., 145, *147*
Osherson, D. N., 157, *199*

P

Pachaury, A., 150, 155, 158, *198*
Palincsar, A. S., 74, 78, *92, 93*
Papadaki, M., 151, 156, 158, *197*
Papantoniou, A., 151, 156, *197*
Paris, S. C., 203, *230*
Parks, S., 84, *94*
Parziale, J., 97, 98, *110*
Pascual-Leone, J., 166, *199*
Pea, R., 21, *41*
Pedersen, N. L., 118, *130*
Perkins, D. N., 21, *41*, 67, 71, 72, 73, 76, 81, 84, 86, 87, 90, *92, 93, 94*, 136, 144, *147*
Peterson, R. S., 140, *147*
Phillips, D. A., 179, *199*
Piaget, J., 96, *110*
Pierce, J., 84, *93*
Pinkard, N., 56, *65*
Pipp, S. L., 97, *110*
Platsidou, M., 150, 151, 155, 156, 158, 160, 161, 163, 164, 165, 166, 167, 169, 178, 179, 180, 181, 182, 191, 193, 195, *197, 198, 199*
Plomin, R., 118, *131*
Powell, K., *41*
Presseisen, B., 203, 204, 225, *230*
Prevez, M., 151, 154, 157, *199*

R

Ramey, C. T., 72, *92*, 120, *128, 130*
Rauscher, F., 21, *41*
Remer, A., 80, *93*
Resnick, L. B., 21, 33, *41*, 175, *199*
Rogoff, B., 21, *41*, 219, 228, *230*
Ross, G., 213, *231*
Rowe, D. C., 118, 120, *130*
Rushton, J. P., 119, 121, *130*

S

Salmina, N., 224, *230*
Salomon, G., 21, *41*, 82, 86, *93*
Sattler, J., 117, *131*
Scardamalia, M., 72, 78, 86, *91, 93, 94*
Schank, R. C., 44, 46, 47, 51, 55, 61, *65*
Schoenfeld, A. H., 74, 78, *94*
Schwanenflugel, P. J., 163, 178, *198*
Schwartz-Buzaglo, J., 136, *147*
Scripp, L., *41*
Segal, J. W., 67, 73, *92, 94*
Seidel, S., 33, 35, 36, *39, 41*
Shaw, G. L., 21, *41*
Shayer, M., 151, 154, 155, 157, 158, 185, 193, 196, *198, 199*
Sherwood, R. D., 86, *91*
Shurkin, J. N., 121, *130*
Sibisi, S., 81, *93*
Siegler, R., 187, *199*
Silvern, L., 97, *110*
Simon, T., 70, *91*
Singer, P., 143, *147*
Sirmali, K., 151, 163, 164, 165, 166, 167, 169, 179, 180, 182, 191, 193, *197, 199*
Sizer, T., 24, *41*
Skinner, B. F., 96, *110*
Smith, E., 67, 73, *93*
Smith, J., 72, *92*
Snow, R. E., 116, 119, *128, 130*
Sorrentino, R. M., 145, *147*
Sowell, T., 121, *130*
Spanoudis, G., 166, 169, 191, *199*
Spearman, C., 19, 21, *41, 94*, 115, *130*
Spear-Swerling, L., 3, *15*
Spitz, H. H., 120, *130*
Stanovich, K. E., 136, 137, *147*
Steinbach, R., 78, *94*
Steinberg, A., 27, *41*
Stephenson, K. M., 160, *196*
Stern, V., 31, *39*
Sternberg, R. J., 2, 3, 12, 13, *15*, 19, 25, *40, 41, 42*, 67, 70, 71, 72, 73, 86, *91, 92, 94*, 117, 118, *130, 131*, 163, *199*
Sternberg, S., 165, *199*
Stipek, D., 179, *199*
Stroop, J. R., 165, 166, *199*
Swartz, R. J., 84, *94*

T

Talyzina, N. F., 222, 224, 229, *230*
Teasley, S. D., 21, *41*
Tetlock, P. E., 140, 144, *147*
Thompson, L. A., 118, *131*

Thorndike, R. L., 117, *131*
Thurstone, L. L., 19, *41*
Tishman, S., 76, 80, 81, 90, *93, 94*
Tobin, K., 193, *199*
Tolchinsky-Landsmann, L., 186, *199*
Tomasello, M., 221, *230*
Torff, B., 13, *15*
Towle, B. T., 56, *65*

U

Unger, C., 84, *92*

V

Valanides, N., 185, 193, *199*
van Heusden, M., 81, *93*
Vazsonyi, A. T., 120, *130*
Veenema, S., 36, *41*
Vernon, P. E., 19, *41*
Verschaffel, L., *197*
Viljoen, R., 81, *93*
Vye, N. J., 86, *91*
Vygotsky, L. S., 21, *41*, 96, *110*, 201, 202, 208, 209, 210, 228, *230*

W

Wagner, R. K., 118, *131*
Wake, W. K., 118, *129*
Walters, J., 33, 34, *41*
Walters, R. H., 96, *110*
Weinert, F. E., 78, *94*
Weinstein, C., 78, *94*
Wellman, H. M., 163, *199*
Wertsch, J., 203, *230*
West, R. F., 136, 137, *147*
White, N., 25, *42*
Wiatrowski, G., 84, *92*
Wiggins, G., 30, 33, *42*
Williams, W. M., 13, *15*, 25, *42*
Winner, E., 34, *42*
Winograd, P., 203, *230*
Wolf, D. P., 30, *42*
Wood, D., 213, *231*

Y

Yalow, E., 116, 119, *130*

Z

Zaporozhets, A. V., 212, 221, 229, 231
Zimmerman, M., 179, *199*

Subject Index

A

Abececedarian Study, 120
Ability, *see also* Learning abilities
  defined, 112
  vs. intelligence, 179
Academic inquiry, 139
Acculturation, 137
Action, and interaction, 209
Actively open-minded thinking
  counterarguments of, 144–146
  definition of, 137
  essay assignments for, 139–140
  examples of, 141–143
  and grading, 140, 143–145
Activity, and shared activity, 209
Advise the President, 56–57
Algebraic reasoning, 176, 183
Amplification, 212
Analytical abilities, 3, *see also* Triarchic teaching
Apprenticeship, Rogoff's work on, 219–221, 228
Aptitude, 192
Architecture of mind, *see* Mental architecture
Art
  -infused curriculum, 27–28
  triarchic teaching in, 6–7
Arts Propel, 33–34
Assessment, *see also* Grading; Tests
  of change mechanisms, 193–194
  in computer-assisted education model, 127
  and dispositions, 82
  of environment-oriented thought, 192–193
  of hypercognition, 193
  in intelligent schooling, 63–64
  MI theory implications, 29–35
  of processing thought system, 191–192
  in skill theory, 106–110
  in triarchic teaching, 10–12
Assisted performance, 211–212
Attention span, 209–210

B

Behaviorists theories of learning, 96
Beliefs, and thinking, 134, 152–154
Biases, in thinking, 136–138, 141–143
Binet, Alfred, 69–70
Bodily-kinesthetic intelligence, 20
Brain
  physical correlation to IQ, 119
  study of, 111
Bridging mechanism, 183, 184, 190
Broadcast News, 55

C

CAI, 124, 126–128
Categorical thought, 154
Causal thought, 155–156, 176–178, 183
Change mechanisms, in mental architecture
  assessment of, 193–194
  bottom-up, 181–183
  and development, 187
  horizontal, 182, 183–185
  top-down, 182, 185–186
Classification, 207
Coalition of Essential Schools, 24
Cognition, in long-term hypercognition, 162–163
Cognitive change, and ZPD, 218–219

Cognitive development
  as branch of study, 112
  and changes in mental architecture, 187, 195
    bottom-up, 181–183
    horizontal, 182, 183–185
    top-down, 182, 185–186
  in environment-oriented thought, 169–178
  in hypercognition, 171–173, 178–180
  and learning, 202–204
  in processing thought system, 169
  psychology of, 149–150
  Rogoff's investigation of, 219–221
  in skill theory
    levels of, 97–101
    linked to classroom learning, 100–101,
      105–108
    uneven, 107–108
Cognitive science, and curricula analysis,
  195–196
Cognitive self-image, 163–167, 179–180, 182
Cognitive stretch, 220–221
Collaborative learning, 84
Combinatorial thought, 177
Common factors, 113–114
Computer-assisted instruction (CAI), 124,
  126–128
Confidence, and thinking, 137–138
Construction zone, 215–217
Constructivism, 96
Contextualization
  of assessments, 30
  of mathematics, 62
  vs. memorization, 60–61
Control function, 165–166
CORE categories, 74–75, 87, see also specific
    categories
Core processes, in environmental thought,
  152–154
Creative abilities, 3, see also Triarchic teaching
Cultural contexts, and HMF, 207
Cultural development, general law of (Vygot-
    sky's), 209
Culture of thinking, creating, 87–91
Curiosity, see Surprise
Curricula
  analysis of, 195–196
  art-infused, 27–28
  and mental architecture, 195
  passion, 57–59

D

Descriptive model of thinking, 135–136
Developmental science, and curricula analysis,
  195–196

Differential psychology, 112
Differentiation mechanism, 184, 188
Dispositions, 75, 81–82
Distributed cognition, 75, 82–86
Diversity
  in the classroom, 18–19
  in theories of intelligence, 71
Documentation, as MI assessment tool, 32
Domain-general learning, 188–191
Domain-specific learning, 188–191

E

Elimination mechanism, 185, 188
Empirical learning, 222
Encoding function, 165, 181
English, see Language arts
Environment
  and intelligence, 138–139
  and learning, 96–97
Environment-oriented thought
  assessment of, 192–193
  change mechanisms in, 183–187
  development of, 169–178, 194
  educational relevance of, 160–161
  interdependence of, 166–167, 181
  and learning and instruction, 188–191,
    195
  systems and processes in, 151–158, 194
  validation of, 158–160
Errorless learning, 223–224
Evaluation, see Assessment
Expectations
  in goal-based scenarios, 55, 57
  in intelligent instruction, 50–52
  in learning process, 45–47
Experiential intelligence, 72–73
Experimentation
  and bridging mechanism, 183
  in causal thought, 156, 177
  in hypercognition development, 179
Expert-novice interactions, 215–216,
  219–220
Explanations
  in goal-based scenarios, 56, 59
  in intelligent instruction, 53

F

Fact-centered education, 59–61
Factor analysis, 113–114
Fire Commander, 56
Frames of Mind (Gardner), 19, 31
Frameworks, developmental, 96

Fusion mechanism, 183–184, 187, 188, 190

G

General mental ability, *see* g factor
Genetics
  behavioral, 112–114
  and g factor, 118–119
  and intelligence, 138–139
g factor
  development of, 70, 115
  in mental abilities tests, 114–116
  and scholastic achievement, 114–122
Goal-based scenarios (GBSs), 54–59
Goals
  in goal-based scenarios, 55, 57
  in intelligent instruction, 49–50
  in learning process, 45
Grading, *see also* Assessment
  and actively open-minded thinking, 140,
    143–145
  on improvement, 64
Graphic organizers, 84
Group differences, and g factor, 120–121
Group factors, defined, 114
Guided participation, 219–220

H

Hand over principle (Bruner), 214
Hecker, L., 26
Heritability, of IQ, 118–119
Higher mental functions (HMF), 206–209, 227
HL, 188–191
Hypercognition, 151, 153
  assessment of, 193
  change mechanisms in, 185–186
  development of, 171–173, 178–180, 194–195
  educational relevance of, 164–165
  interdependence of, 166–167, 181
  and learning and instruction, 188–191, 195
  processes in, 161–163, 194
  validation of, 163–164
Hyperlearning (HL), 188–191
Hypothesis formation, 156, 177

I

ILS, 44, 54
"Improved" intelligence, 120, 139
Individual differences
  and actively open-minded thinking, 144
  and educational practice, 112, 124–128
  in g factor

  biological roots of, 118–119
  compared to group differences,
    120–121
  and learning rates, 119
  and scholastic variance, 116–118
  in intrinsic motivation, 124
  and psychology of cognitive develop-
    ment, 150
Individualized education
  in goal-based scenarios, 59
  as MI theory implication, 24–25
Inferences, in thinking, 134
Institute for Learning Sciences (ILS), 44, 54
Instruction
  and domain-specific vs. domain-general
    learning, 189–191
  errorless learning strategy, 223–224
  and learning and development, 203
  MI theory implications for, 23–29
  principles for intelligent
    described, 48–54
    in goal-based scenarios, 54–59
  suited to assessment methods, 10
  suited to learning abilities, 2–3
Instructional science, and curricula
  analysis, 195–196
Instructional time, 168
Instruction (applied psychology), 112
Intelligence, *see also* specific types
  diversity in theories of, 71
  informal conception of, 70–71
  in long-term hypercognition, 163
  science of, 69–70
  vs. ability, 179
Intelligent schooling
  instruction principles in, 48–54
  learning environments for, 54–59
  learning process defined in, 44–48
  in traditional classroom, 59–63
Interaction
  and action, 209
  in zone of proximal development,
    211–212, 215–216, 219–221
Internalization, 96, 217, 222
Interpersonal intelligence, 20
Interweaving mechanism, 183, 184, 187, 188
Intrapersonal intelligence, 20
Intrinsic motivation, 124, 227
IQ
  heritability of, 118–119
  and neural viewpoint, 71–72
  and occupational achievement, 121
  physical correlates of, 119
IQ tests, 116–117, 120, 139

K

Kaufman Assessment Battery for Children, 117
Keys to Thinking (Perkins et al.), 81
Klein, K., 26
Knowledge, and thinking, 152–154

L

Labeling, 29
Language arts
    in intelligent instruction, 62
    triarchic teaching in, 4–5
Language of thinking, 84, 86
Learnable intelligence, 67–69
Learning abilities, and teaching methods, 2–3
Learning activity, 203–204, 224–227
Learning by doing, 55–56, 58, 62
Learning objectives, in intelligent instruction,
    50–52
Learning process
    assessment in, 30–31
    behaviorists theories of, 96
    and cognitive development, 202–204
    developmental frameworks of, 96
    domain-specific vs. domain-general,
        188–191, 195
    empirical vs. theoretical, 222
    instruction based on, 48–54
    mental components of, 44–48, *see also spe-
        cific components*
    project-based, 26–27
Learning rates, and *g* factor, 119
Learning styles, 22–23
Linguistic intelligence, 20
LMF, 206–207
Logical-mathematical intelligence, 20
Logical reasoning, 188
Long-term hypercognition, 162–163
Lower mental functions (LMF), 206–207

M

Mathematics
    and environment-oriented thought,
        154–155, 160–161, 175–176
    and hypercognitive development, 179
    in intelligent instruction, 62
    triarchic teaching in, 5
Mechanical reasoning tests, 114
Mediators, 214
Memorization
    case study in, 1–2
    integrating with triarchic teaching, 3–8

vs. contextualization, 60–61
Memory, working, 168, 170
Memory tests, 114
Mental ability, 112–114
Mental architecture
    and curriculum, 195
    environment-oriented level, 151–161,
        166–167, 169–178, 181,
        183–189, 192–195
    hypercognitive (self-oriented) level, 151,
        153, 161–167, 171–173,
        178–181, 185–186, 188–191,
        193–195
    interdependence of levels in, 166, 181
    processing level, 151, 153, 165–170, 181,
        191–192, 194
Mental Management strategy, 87, 88
Mental maps, 162, 187
Mental tools (Vygotsky's)
    acquisition of, 202–203, 209
    described, 202
    mastering and internalizing, 205–208,
        210–215, 221–222
    purposes of, 205–210
Metacognition, 68–69, 75, 78–81, 185, 227
Metarepresentation, 185, 187, 188, 190, 191,
    194
MI, *see* Multiple intelligences
Mind
    theory of, 163
    tools of, *see* Mental tools (Vygotsky's)
Mindful abstraction, 86
ML, 188–191
Model construction, 156, 177, 183, 184
Modular learning (ML), 188–191
Multiple intelligences
    assessment implications of, 29–35
    classroom implications of, 23–29
    development of, 19
    evolution of, 21–22
    list of, 20
    misconceptions about, 22–23
    misuses of, 28–29
    professional development implications
        of, 35–37
    vs. traditional theory, 19–21
Music, triarchic teaching in, 6–7
Musical intelligence, 20
Myside bias, 136–138, 141–143

N

Naturalist intelligence, 20, 21
Neural intelligence, 71–73
The New Standards Project, 33

Normative model of thinking, 135–136
Numerical reasoning tests, 114

O

Observation
    learning through, 96
    as MI assessment tool, 31–32
Occupational achievement
    and g factor, 116
    and IQ, 121
Oceanside School Project, 215–219
Open-mindedness, see Actively open-minded
    thinking

P

Passion curricula, 57–59
Performance ranges, and skill theory, 108–109
Performance tasks, as MI assessment tool,
    32–33
Physical education, triarchic teaching in, 8
PIFS, 24–25
Portfolios, as MI assessment tool, 33–34
Practical abilities, 3, see also Triarchic teaching
Practical Intelligence for School (PIFS) Pro-
    ject, 24–25
Practice
    deliberate, 74, 86
    developmentally appropriate, 212–213
Prescriptive model of thinking, 135–137
Problem-solving, 8–10, 76, 84–86
Processing thought system, 151, 153, 170
    assessment of, 191–192
    and change mechanisms, 181
    development of, 169, 194
    educational relevance of, 167–168
    interdependence of, 166–167, 181
    structure and functions of, 165–167, 194
Professional development, 35–37
Project-based learning, 26–27
Project Spectrum, 24
Project Zero, 22, 30–31, 75
Project Zero/Massachusetts Schools Network,
    35–37
Proportional reasoning, 175–176, 183, 184
Propositional thought, 157–158
Protoquantitative schemes, 175
Psychometric g, see g factor
Psychometrics, defined, 112
Psychometric tests, 114–116
Public education
    and individual differences, 112, 124
    suggestions for, 124–128
    traditional, 122–123
PZ/MSN, 35–37

Q

Quantitative thought, 154–155, 175–176,
    183, 184

R

Racial differences, in g factor, 120–121
Refinement mechanism, 185
Reflection
    in goal-based scenarios, 56–57
    and learning process, 54
    in MI assessment, 30–31, 34–35
Reflective intelligence, 73, 81
Regression, adaptive, 109
Reorganization, cognitive, 48, 54, 74–75, see
    also CORE categories
Representation, 169–175
Rules, and thinking, 134, 138, 152–154

S

Say Say Oh Playmate, 56
Scaffolding, 213–215
Scholastic achievement, and g factor,
    114–122
Science
    in intelligent instruction, 62–63
    triarchic teaching in, 7
Science of Education and the Psychology of
    the Child (Piaget), 96
Scoring rubrics, 79–80, 82, 83
Search, in thinking, 134
Self-assessment
    and learning, 191
    and metacognition, 68–69, 78–80
    in MI assessment, 30–31, 34–35
Self-image, cognitive, 163–167, 179–180, 182
Self-oriented thought, see Hypercognition
Skills
    as expectations, 51
    processing, 152–154
    in propositional thought, 157–158
    in skill theory
        defined, 98
        diagraming, 103–105
        progression of, 98–103
Skill theory
    assessment in, 106–110
    balance of child and environment in,
        96–97
    creating task sequence in, 103–104
    defined, 97
    and mental development, 100–101,
        105–108

predictions of, 97, 109
progression of learning in, 98–103
Smart Thinking, 84–86, 87
Social class, and *g* factor, 120–121
Social settings
    and cognitive tasks, 217–219
    and HMF, 207
Social studies
    in intelligent schooling, 63
    triarchic teaching in, 5–6
Spatial intelligence, 20
Spatial thought, 156–157, 179, 183
Spatial visualization tests, 114
Spearman, Charles, 70, 115
Special education, 207
Stage structures, 96
Stanford-Binet Intelligence Scale, 116–117
Storage function, 166, 181
Stories, mental
    in goal-based scenarios, 55–56, 58
    in intelligent instruction, 53–54
    in learning process, 46–48
    and memorization, 60–61
Strategies, classroom, 74, 76–78
Strengths and weaknesses, 3, 28
Stroop phenomenon, 166
Subsidization, 155, 175
Superfactor. *See g* factor
Surprise
    in goal-based scenarios, 56, 58
    in intelligent instruction, 52–53
    in learning process, 45–46
Symbolic individuation, 186, 187, 188
Systematic formation, 222–224

T

Tasks, guiding in goal-based scenarios, 58
Teachers
    as obstacles to triarchic teaching, 14
    personal influence of, 126
Tests, standardized, 63, *see also* Assessment;
    specific tests or types of tests
Theoretical learning, 222
Theoretical reasoning, 227
Thinking, *see also* Cognitive development;
    Mental architecture
    actively open-minded, 137, 139–146
    and beliefs, 134, 152–154
    biases in, 136–138, 141–143
    culture of, creating, 87–91
    description of, 134–135
    descriptive model of, 135–136
    and knowledge, 152–154
    normative model of, 135–136
    prescriptive model of, 135–137

private vs. public expression, 144–145
and rules, 134, 138, 152–154
and values, 134
wishful, 137
The Thinking Classroom (Tishman et al.), 90
Thinking Connections (Perkins et al.), 78,
    86–87
Thinking structures, *see* Skills; Skill theory
*The Thinking Teacher's Guide to the Visual
    Arts* (Remer, Tishman), 80–81
Thought, *see* Thinking
Tools of the mind, *see* Mental tools (Vygot-
    sky's)
Transfer of learning, 75, 86–87, 89–90, 188,
    218
Triarchic intelligence, defined, 2–3
Triarchic teaching
assessment in, 10–12
benefits of, 14
integrating with memorization, 3–8
obstacles to, 12–14

U

Understanding Through Design (Perkins et
    al.), 76–78, 82
The Unschooled Mind (Gardner), 26

V

Values, and thinking, 134
Variance, defined, 113
Verbal tests, defined, 114
Video Project, 57–59
Vygotsky theory, *see also* Higher mental
    functions (HMF); Lower mental
    functions (LMF); Mental tools (Vy-
    gotsky's); Zone of proximal develop-
    ment (ZPD)
in American schools, 215–221
in Russian schools, 221–227

W

Weaknesses, *see* Strengths and weaknesses
Wechsler Intelligence scales, 117
Wishful thinking, 137
Working hypercognition, 161–162, 165

Z

Zone of proximal development (ZPD)
    about, 96, 210–213
    in Oceanside School Project, 215–219
    Rogoff's investigation of, 219–221
    significance to educators, 228

List of Contributors

Jonathan Baron
Department of Psychology
University of Pennsylvania
Philadelphia, PA 19104

Andreas Demetriou
Department of Educational Sciences
University of Cyprus
Nicosia, Cyprus

Kurt Fischer
Harvard Graduate School of Education
Cambridge, MA 02138

Heidi L. Goodrich Andrade
Project Zero
Harvard Graduate School of Education
Cambridge, MA 02138

Elena Grigorenko
Department of Psychology and Child Study Center
Yale University
New Haven, CT 06520-8205
and
Department of Psychology
Moscow State University
Moscow, Russia

Arthur R. Jensen
School of Education
University of California
Berkeley, CA 94720-1670

Diana M. Joseph
The Institute for the Learning Sciences
Northwestern University
Evanston, IL 60208

Mara Krechevsky
Project Zero
Harvard Graduate School of Education
Cambridge, MA 02138

Jim Parziale
Harvard Graduate School of Education
Cambridge, MA 02138

David N. Perkins
Project Zero
Harvard Graduate School of Education
Cambridge, MA 02138

Robert C. Schank
Institute for the Learning Sciences
Northwestern University
Evanston, IL 60208

Steve Seidel
Project Zero
Harvard Graduate School of Education
Cambridge, MA 02138

Robert J. Sternberg
Department of Psychology
Yale University
New Haven, CT 06520-8205

Nicos Valanides
Department of Educational Sciences
University of Cyprus
Nicosia, Cypru